America after Empire

After the end of America's longest (20-year) war in Afghanistan and Iraq that cost more than $6 trillion and nearly half a million lives, what does the future hold for America and the American people in the 21st century? In this timely and important book, Berch Berberoglu provides an eye-opening account of the history of the American Empire from its inception to the present, with prospects for its future. Examining the worldwide expansion of the American Empire over the course of its turbulent history in great detail, Berberoglu assesses America's imperial legacy in a sober way, highlighting its failure to come to terms with the enormous cost of this adventure in imperial overreach. But Berberoglu sees light at the end of the long, dark tunnel, when the American people will awaken and lead the way to a new America after empire in the coming decades of the 21st century.

Berch Berberoglu is Foundation Professor of Sociology, Emeritus, at the University of Nevada, Reno. He received his PhD in sociology from the University of Oregon in 1977. He has been teaching and conducting research at the University of Nevada, Reno, for the past 45 years. Dr. Berberoglu has written and edited 33 books and many articles. His latest books include *Globalization in the 21st Century*; *Beyond the Global Capitalist Crisis: The World Economy in Transition*; *The Global Capitalist Crisis and Its Aftermath*; *The Palgrave Handbook of Social Movements, Revolution, and Social Transformation*; and *The Global Rise of Authoritarianism in the 21st Century: Crisis of Neoliberal Globalization and the Nationalist Response.*

"Empire is oft the child of imperialism, and as imperialist practices multiplied, so too did empires grow. Yet, as sociologist William Graham Sumner warned his fellow Americans in 1924, '[t]he thrust of imperialist glory is an epidemic which robs a people of their judgment, seduces their vanity, cheats them of their interests, and corrupts their consciences.' It does all this and more, including the breeding of reaction against the harsh treatment of oppressed populations, including its own. In his thirty-fourth book, working-class intellectual and acclaimed scholar Berch Berberoglu notes that all empires either fail or shrivel. He offers a detailed description and analysis of how the American empire arose and developed in the first place and why its demise is now at hand. Of equal interest is Professor Berberoglu's treatment of what America could be after the end of imperialism and the collapse of empire. *America after Empire* is indeed a must read!"

Larry T. Reynolds, *Professor of Sociology, Emeritus, Central Michigan University*

"This is an incredibly illuminating and important study of the rise of the American Empire in the 20th century and the 'awakening of the American people from the shackles of a false dream', opening up the United States to the possibilities of a 'new beginning'. There is a voluminous literature and many recent studies and explorations of the dynamics of U.S. imperialism, but none as informative as provided by this book. It both deserves and needs to be read not only by scholars and students of the history and current predicament of the United States and its leading, albeit deeply flawed, role as a global superpower, but by everyone concerned with rescuing the United States from itself."

Henry Veltmeyer, *Research Professor of Development Studies, Universidad Autónoma de Zacatecas, Mexico and Professor of Development Studies, Emeritus, Saint Mary's University, Halifax, Nova Scotia, Canada*

"*America after Empire* makes a valuable contribution towards understanding the past, present, and possibilities for the future of U.S. society. It examines the origins and development of U.S. imperialism and effectively shows its impact on the U.S. and the world today. It does this in a thorough way without compromising on academic rigor, while making it highly accessible to students and the general public. Highly recommended!"

Alan J. Spector, *Professor of Sociology, Emeritus, Purdue University Northwest*

"Berch Berberoglu is a veteran analyst of imperialism. Both those new to the topic and those who have been following the course of Washington's endless wars and interventions throughout the world for a long time will find new information and insights here. Above all, this book addresses one of the critical issues of our time: the conditions governing the Decline and Fall of the U.S. Empire."

John Bellamy Foster, *editor of* Monthly Review; *author of* Naked Imperialism

America after Empire

The Vision for a New America in the 21st Century

Berch Berberoglu

Routledge
Taylor & Francis Group
NEW YORK AND LONDON

Cover image: Planet Earth in space, with very little clouds covering the land masses, by Chris J Mitchell (Shutterstock)

First published 2023
by Routledge
605 Third Avenue, New York, NY 10158

and by Routledge
4 Park Square, Milton Park, Abingdon, Oxon, OX14 4RN

Routledge is an imprint of the Taylor & Francis Group, an informa business

ISBN: 9781032252131 (hbk)
ISBN: 9781032222837 (pbk)
ISBN: 9781003282105 (ebk)

DOI: 10.4324/9781003282105

Typeset in Bembo
by codeMantra

Contents

Preface and Acknowledgments

I began writing this book more than a decade ago at the height of the "Great Recession" of 2008–2009, when the U.S. economy had come crashing down in a big way in the deepest and worst recession since the Great Depression of the 1930s. With similar such economic slumps in the postwar period—in the mid-1970s, early 1980s, early 1990s, and early 2000s—many analysts had come to declare the end of "the American Century" that barely lasted more than a few decades. But after its tragic defeat in Vietnam, followed by similar misadventures in Iraq and Afghanistan, the "Great Recession" of a decade ago was the first salvo of things to come that would seal the coffin of U.S. imperialism, when American supremacy in superpower rivalry during the Cold War was thought to have assured the victory of the American Empire that supposedly brought in its wake "the end of history," i.e., the triumph of capitalism over socialism in the late 20th and early 21st century.

Ironically, not only the "Great Recession" of 2008–2009 proved this to be wrong, but an unexpected health crisis in the form of the Coronavirus Pandemic (COVID-19), compounded by another (social) virus of rampant systemic and institutional racism and police brutality against people of color—that led to the murder of an unarmed African American man, George Floyd, triggering an outrage by millions of people who poured into the streets of more than 350 cities across the United States and major cities across the world, protesting the racist crimes of the Empire—were exacerbated by the sharp downturn of the U.S. economy due to the COVID-19 lockdown that led to the stock market crash of March 2020 and the loss of 42 million jobs, as well as the humiliating defeat of the United States in Afghanistan in 2021, all of which together accelerated the decline and fall of the American Empire that brought it to a screeching halt.

What happens next, when working people of America speak up in "the land of the free and the home of the brave" will determine the nature and extent of the change that is necessary to transition to a new and promising America that will fulfill a vision that is needed to set the nation on a new and prosperous course that meets the needs and aspirations of its people in the 21st century.

Over the past two and a half centuries of America's turbulent history, many have contributed their labor to make America a great country and had hoped it would live up to its promise as a society that fulfills the needs of its people who have been struggling day in and day out to make a living through their arduous work. From the days of slavery and human bondage at the margins of civilization to the days of wage-labor under the yoke of capital, working people and their movements have struggled to gain their freedom and build the basis of a civilized society that respects their rights and meets their needs and aspirations. As the backbone of this country, working people deserve to have their voices heard through their collective will to advance their interests as workers. Thus, it is to all working people in America that this book is dedicated, for they represent the future of this great nation.

Under capitalism, workers everywhere are the natural agents of social change. So, too, in America workers will become the leading force in the transformation of the Empire into a democratic republic to make America a worker's paradise with all the wealth and resources at its disposal *owned* collectively and *distributed* collectively to *all* the people, not just the top 1 percent and a few of their cronies, as is the case today. To this end, it is the working people who deserve to control and decide what is theirs and what shall belong to them, as they alone are the rightful owners and rulers of this great nation that they have inherited through their blood, sweat, and tears over the centuries. Long live America and long live the working people of America—*after Empire!*

I would like to thank, first and foremost, the working people of America and of all lands across the globe for giving me the strength, inspiration, and pride in fighting for their rights all of my adult life. And in this effort, many others—comrades, friends, allies, and supporters—have also played a crucial role in influencing and shaping my thinking in favor of the oppressed, exploited, and enslaved peoples of the world. While my thinking along these lines were in their formative stages during my studies at Central Michigan University, where I learned much from my mentors Larry T. Reynolds and Blaine Stevenson, and at the State University of New York at Binghamton from my mentor James Petras, my ideas about class, exploitation, oppression, class struggle, and revolution based on the power of wage-labor (the working class) became crystallized during my graduate studies at the University of Oregon, where I worked toward my doctoral degree under the supervision of Albert J. Szymanski. Thus, I owe much to Al for his keen understanding of the centrality of labor and working-class politics, as well as the necessity for organization and independent leadership of labor through a disciplined political party of the working class to confront capitalist tyranny and to wage struggle against it in order to transform capitalist society to establish a new one in its place that is based on the leadership of working people and other oppressed peoples of America.

Many others have also made a contribution to the formation of my thinking about these and related issues of epochal significance that are both historical and contemporary in terms of their importance. Here, I would like to thank Walda Katz-Fishman, Marty Orr, Alan Spector, Michael Parenti, Howard Sherman, Henry Veltmeyer, Patrick Bond, David L. Harvey, Karl Kreplin, Johnson W. Makoba, and others. My special thanks go to Dean Birkenkamp, my editor at Routledge, who has given me much encouragement and freedom to pursue this project, which promises to make an important contribution to the future of America and the American people in a prosperous life *after* Empire. My wife Suzan and my sons Stephen and Michael have always stood by me and provided the support that I needed in maintaining the moral high ground in championing the cause of those who have been wronged and deserve better—the rightful fruits of their labor—which they are denied today. May tomorrow be their day, and may a bright and prosperous future belong to them, so working people everywhere create a heaven here on earth, especially here in the United States of America, *after Empire.*

Figures

Tables

1 Introduction

The Fate of the American Empire

The American Empire has been declining for the past several decades and its fate is uncertain; it may soon dissolve and come to a screeching halt. The question is: what will come after the Empire? Further decline and collapse, or rejuvenation and renewal, i.e., the rise of a new nation free of its global entanglements that caused its people and others across the world so much harm and pain? As its predecessors in centuries past that set the world on a dark path, threatening humanity with slavery, death, and extinction, the American Empire—no less than the Spanish, Portuguese, French, Dutch, British, and other lesser colonial powers that came and went in the aftermath of the rise and fall of the Roman Empire and its subsequent off-springs, such as the Byzantine Empire, that met the same fate—faces a similar destiny if it continues on its torturous path of global dominance and destruction that it has caused for more than a century.[1]

In the end, all Empires have disappeared or are today a fraction of their former glorious past that rested on their plunder and devastation that they wrought on humanity so much pain—all in the name of wealth, power, and glory that enriched only the masters of an enslaved world that brought joy to the few at the cost of so much misery and torment for the many that degraded their toil and expropriated the fruits of their labor for private gain. But such plunder, such callous and indeed scandalous crimes against humanity by a handful of slave-masters, landlords, and capitalists against those working people who through their labor have created all wealth but enjoyed very little of it in a world based on exploitation and oppression that have brought nothing but misery to the many in a system of class rule under the tyranny of expropriated property in the means of production in flesh, land, and resources transformed into capital in its commercial, industrial, and financial forms that has established the dynasty of the rich few draining the blood of the many to sustain a system, has brought us and our planet to the darkest hour of humanity.[2]

But no more! The game is over! The masses have awakened and are on the march in every corner of the world, crying in one voice: enough is enough! We're not going to take this anymore! Chanting: "¡el pueblo unido jamás será vencido!" ("the people united will never be defeated!"). The working class to the rescue! Only the working class and the labor movement, organized

DOI: 10.4324/9781003282105-1

into a powerful political force, under the leadership of a committed political organization of ordinary working people with a working-class ideology that respects and rewards labor in all its shades and kinds (black, brown, and white, male and female, gay and straight, young and old, local and global, able and disabled, in short, all) is the only hope for America and the rest of the world, if we have the chance in this final hour of our existence to save humanity and the world from the final apocalypse that may be upon us.

The Legacy of the American Empire

More than three decades ago, on the eve of the October 1987 stock market crash, I published a book titled *The Internationalization of Capital: Imperialism and Capitalist Development on a World Scale* in which I outlined the rise of postwar U.S. imperialism and its dynamics and contradictions.[3] After examining the origins and development of the American Empire in the 20th century and its impending crises at century's end, I wrote:

> As the 20th century closes out its penultimate decade, world capitalism is in deep and profound crisis. The signs of decline and decay are everywhere throughout the advanced and less developed regions of the world capitalist system, where despite some short-term reversals in some countries yielding a limited recovery, the long-term direction of the downward spiral is unquestionably permanent and irreversible, affecting a majority of the countries bound up in it – above all, the current center of world capitalism, the United States.[4]

Clearly, the crisis of the U.S. and global economy in the late 1980s was a manifestation of the crisis of global capitalism on a world scale. And this was amply demonstrated by those who have been fierce critics of global capitalism and who have exposed the fault lines of the system in great detail.[5] Focusing on the crisis of the late 1980s, I went on to explain that "The crisis manifests itself in high unemployment and inflation, decline in purchasing power of workers, overproduction and underconsumption, recessions and depressions, heightened social and class struggles, and repression and revolution in an increasing number of countries around the world,"[6] pointing out, in no uncertain terms, that:

> These are the outcomes of the development of capitalism on the world scene during the past 100 years, from the local to the national to the international levels. As the internationalization of capital has spread capitalism and capitalist relations, with it their deep-seated contradictions, throughout the world, the crisis of world capitalism has come to manifest itself as the crisis of world imperialism. It is for this reason that imperialism represents the highest, but also the decaying, stage of capitalism, when millions under its sway come to recognize the urgency of the struggle against it.[7]

In a follow-up book that I published a few years later in 1992 titled *The Legacy of Empire: Economic Decline and Class Polarization in the United States*,[8] I went on to examine the pitfalls of empire and its legacy for working people in America and urged a thorough investigation of the plunder and havoc that the empire has wrought upon the world, warning that this arrogance of power, this plunder, and this human catastrophe will cause much suffering and loss to those who have become its victims, unless they respond—and respond soon—to salvage what little still remains for future generations.[9]

Many others, writing on these disturbing misdeeds of the American Empire, have drawn our attention to the dangers of the arrogance of global power projected on the nations and peoples of the world by the sole superpower imposing its rule through the "New World Order" in the aftermath of the Cold War, when the U.S. imperialist presence across the globe became the order of the day, with the invasion of Kuwait and Iraq that culminated in the First Gulf War in 1991, the invasion of Afghanistan in 2001 and of Iraq in 2003, as well as more recent threats to intervene in Syria, Iran, and Venezuela. Some three decades have passed since these warnings were issued in these books—and more so subsequently in nearly a dozen other books that I published over the intervening period—which, not surprisingly, have fallen on deaf ears, while America and the world continues to suffer from the effects of the empire at home and abroad.

Writing in the early 1990s, in my book *The Legacy of Empire*, I stated in clear and concise terms that the problems faced by the prevailing capitalist-imperialist system will not go away on their own, and I stressed the fact that:

> Never before in the recent history of the United States has the future of the U.S. economy been at center stage of discussion and debate as it is today. The internationalization of U.S. capital, which has been taking place ever since the end of the Second World War, has immensely accelerated during the past two decades, and as a result the U.S. domestic economy has begun a process of decline and decay that is now irreversible. . . Such decline, which has been in effect since the early 1970s, is now threatening to become a permanent feature of life in the United States and thus has immense political implications.[10]

In attempting to understand the depth and breadth of this unfolding crisis of unprecedented proportions, I went on to point out that this crisis had been developing in a contradictory way, such that:

> the super profits obtained from corporate takeovers and acquisitions resulting from the bull market and the mega-mergers of the 1980s have been accompanied by record business bankruptcies, bank failures, the savings and loan crisis, huge trade and budget deficits, declining real wages, and a widening gap between the wealthy and the working class[11]

and that:

> the October 1987 stock market crash, the 1989–91 $500 billion savings and loan disaster, and subsequently the collapse of the Trump Empire have shown the limits of capital accumulation through frenzied speculative financial activity and empire-building on the backs of the working people.[12]

Thus, I concluded:

> The contradictions of this process of worldwide expansion and accumulation have brought to the fore new realities of capitalist economics, now characterized by industrial decline and class polarization, accompanied by renewed assault on the living standards of millions of working people in the United States, while a small minority of the corporate rich continues to accumulate great wealth and fortunes from the ever-growing expansion of capitalism on a world scale.[13]

Examining the deteriorating economic position of workers in the United States, I emphasized the "growing indebtedness, the crisis in housing and health care, and increasing impoverishment of working people," and pointed out that:

> a general decline in the living standard of the U.S. working class, affecting the material existence of workers on an everyday level, would in turn have a profound negative impact on the structure of the economy itself, thus exacerbating the developing economic crisis.[14]

That this crisis and this decline is a central legacy of the American Empire is hardly disputed by serious observers of the U.S. political economy over the past several decades.[15] But so far, no one has done anything to avert an impending catastrophe that has been in the making for some time now—a catastrophe that sunk the U.S. economy in 2008–2009 into the depths of the greatest recession (depression?) since the Great Depression of the 1930s.

Writing in the aftermath of the first Gulf War that took the United States to full-scale military intervention in the Middle East, I argued in my book *The Legacy of Empire* published in 1992 that the massive U.S. invasion of Iraq in 1991, which critics warned would turn into another Vietnam, would drag the United States into yet another costly war and bankrupt the American Empire. "Such military misadventures," I argued, "are the signs of a superpower in decline—one that is desperate to convey an image of global strength that is no longer real."[16] It turns out that this was a turning point in America's global role as the sole superpower in the post-Cold War era—one that would hasten its decline and fall as a global empire.[17] While this was the beginning of a series of interventions yet to come a decade later, the military intervention of the United States into the Middle East in the early 1990s through the First Gulf War and its massive invasion of Afghanistan and Iraq in 2001 and 2003, respectively, following the attacks on the twin towers in New York City, effectively sealed America's fate as a declining empire, which had a devastating effect that led to total economic collapse a few years later with the financial meltdown of 2008–2009, discussed at great length in Chapter 6 of this book.

The Crisis Unfolds

The "Great Recession" that followed over the next several years had originated in Wall Street and was associated with the sub-prime mortgage debacle and speculative activities of banks and other financial institutions that engaged in questionable derivatives and exotic debt-driven financial instruments.[18] These were the culprits that led to the bankruptcy and collapse of major players in high finance, such as Lehman Brothers, Bear Stearns, and others that suffered from the aftershocks of the 2008–2009 meltdown, including the Citigroup, General Motors, Chrysler, Fannie Mae, Freddie Mac, and a dozen other bastions of high finance, insurance, and corporate capital—the heartbeat of U.S. capitalism and the economic nucleus of the American Empire—that triggered the "Great Recession" and led to its spread across the world.[19]

In my book *Beyond the Global Capitalist Crisis* published in 2012 and subsequently in a follow-up book *The Global Capitalist Crisis and Its Aftermath* published in 2014, I examined in great detail the major fault-lines of contemporary global capitalism by focusing on its fundamental, inherent contradictions that have paralyzed the global capitalist system to its core.[20] I pointed out that this level of contradictions and crises that the system has faced spells the end of the American Empire and its global domination that had been established in the second half of the 20th century. But no one could have predicted that a mere decade after the "Great Recession" of 2008–2009, a virus that spread across the world in late 2019, causing a global pandemic, would bring the U.S. economy to its knees through the COVID-19 lockdown that effectively triggered a second Great Depression of the 21st century—one that would nail the coffin of the American Empire that several trillions of dollars printed by the U.S. Treasury and disbursed to big business to bail out the economy could not salvage the once mighty icon of global capitalism from its ruins in the early 21st century.

Now, as we enter the third decade of the 21st century, the relationship between excessive military spending, economic crisis, and decline of the American Empire, resulting in its inevitable collapse, has become increasingly evident. This process is not simply the result of military interventions and wars exacerbated by the economic meltdown that followed, nor the trillions of dollars that were spent on these wars for more than two decades and trillions more to bail out failed private banks and corporations that robbed the public purse twice in the first two decades of the 21st century. The decline and fall of the American Empire, in fact, began in its infancy, merely a quarter of a century after its rise in the postwar period from 1945 to the early to mid-1970s, when the "great slump" of the postwar period (in 1974–1975) sounded the alarm bells of the deeper crises yet to come.[21] But the band was still playing, as it did on the deck of the Titanic, and the ruling class was still dancing to the tune of Empire, while the big ship was sinking and millions of the dispossessed were drowning in unemployment, poverty, and despair!

The dot.com crisis and crash of 2000–2001, which followed the rise in the Nasdaq index by five-fold between 1995 and 2000, only to tumble from a peak of 5,048 on March 10, 2000, to 1,139 on October 4, 2002 (a 76.8 percent fall), were the precursors to things to come in the new millennium several years later when the "Great Recession" of 2008–2009 sank the entire U.S. and global economy into a full-blown depression—a crisis of great proportions discussed at length in Chapter 6 of this book.

As all past empires have done so before their eventual collapse, dominant powers that experience economic crises and decline resort to war and repression under the cloak of pseudo-nationalism that is both militaristic and racist. In their last ditch effort to maintain law and order and military supremacy in a world that has turned against them, imperialist states unleash their brute force to regain their eroded supremacy by wars abroad and repression at home under right-wing authoritarian/fascist regimes that resort to outright dictatorship. This becomes all the more imperative during economic crises of vast proportions that characterize the nature of capitalist states plagued by recessions and depressions. While this is not always evident to ordinary citizens who must bear the burden of decline and fall of empire in their home base, the frantic efforts of the dominant class in its last ditch struggle to maintain order prompts the right wing of this class to make a sharp turn to the right by unleashing a "fascist solution" to the empire's problems to keep them in power.

We witnessed such resurgence of naked right-wing response to the decline of U.S. global supremacy through the imperialist crusade of Reaganism (and its counterpart in the U.K., Thatcherism) that launched in the early 1980s an all-out ideological war on its arch enemy, Soviet communism. The postwar U.S. hostility toward the Soviet Union—largely an outcome of an unrelenting super-power military rivalry through the Cold War—gave the right wing in the United States an opportunity as early as the 1970s and the 1980s to launch a massive global assault—economically through capitalist globalization and militarily through global expansion of the Empire's war machine, particularly its decade-long war in Vietnam.[22] It is with this resurgence of the American Empire through its economic force and military might in re-entering the global scene threatening all its enemies with an imperial project that the initial implementation of a fascist plan unfolded under the guise of "neoliberalism," as in Chile in 1973 and Argentina in 1976 and throughout the rest of Latin America in the 1980s. The economic doctrine of neoliberalism was thus used to launch a political-military assault on all those who attempted to prevent the American Empire from the plunder and pillage of global wealth and resources to dominate and enslave the peoples of the world to the dictates of U.S. imperialism.

In *The Legacy of Empire*, I warned that this arrogant and aggressive posture of the American Empire that gained the resentment of peoples around the world against the United States would soon translate into economic decline and class polarization that could lead to rebellions and revolutions across the world, including the United States. And it did. Thus, the subtitle of *The Legacy of Empire*, "Economic Decline and Class Polarization in the United States," came to pass.[23] It is through such decline and polarization of a dominant superpower, such as the United States, that one could see the signals of the impending crises and conflicts of empire yet to come, challenging its unbridled rule on a global scale.[24]

Rebellions and Revolutions—Against the Empire!

The rebellions and revolutions around the world that unfolded following the Cuban Revolution in 1959 turned into anti-imperialist national liberation struggles across the globe starting in the 1960s, when such movements in many countries around the world took up arms to struggle against U.S. imperialism. The U.S. war in Vietnam and racist repression of African Americans in the United States in the 1960s, in the aftermath of the struggles of the Civil Rights Movement during this period, triggered mass protests across America that culminated in the anti-war, peace, student, youth, Black Power, and women's movements in the United States in the 1960s and early 1970s, and set the stage for things to come in subsequent decades.

After the U.S. defeat in Vietnam in the mid-1970s, movements for national liberation spread to every corner of the world, challenging the American Empire at its foundations. The overthrow of U.S.-backed dictatorships in many countries around the world in the 1970s and 1980s—in Asia, Africa, and Latin America—opened the way to revolutionary movements to rise up against the American Empire throughout the world. Following fierce resistance against U.S. imperialism in the U.S.-led Contra War in Nicaragua and against fascist death squads in support of counter-revolutionary forces in military dictatorships across Central America during the 1980s, the United States became deeply involved in the suppression of rebellions and revolutions in this region, including in El Salvador, Guatemala, and Honduras, but to no avail, when revolutionary forces in these countries fought to stop U.S. imperialism in its tracks.

Less than a decade later, in the immediate aftermath of the signing of the North American Free Trade Agreement (NAFTA) in 1994, a rebellious army of revolutionaries, the Zapatista Army of National Liberation (EZLN) rose up in Chiapas, Mexico in response to the imperialist schemes of NAFTA designed to further expand the interests of North American transnational corporations in their control and domination of the entire region, with all the devastating consequences for the indigenous peoples in Mexico (peasants, workers, and the poor in general) under the yoke of the American Empire and its collaborating compliant states. During this period at century's end, the people's movements around the world went into action to protest against neoliberal capitalist globalization—from Seattle to Prague, Quebec City, Genoa, Barcelona, Washington, D.C., and other cities around the globe—to counter capitalist domination of the world under the auspices of the transnational corporations, the World Trade Organization (WTO), the World Bank (WB), the International Monetary Fund (IMF), and other supportive institutions of the advanced capitalist states—first and foremost the United States.[25] These protests, which were quite successful in disrupting the WTO meetings and derailing corporate efforts to impose their draconian policies on the people, reached new heights when over 15 million people across the globe protested against the planned U.S. invasion of Iraq.

While the attacks on September 11, 2001, became a reminder of problems the empire has faced in its entanglements across the world, the reaction of the American Empire to this through its invasion of Afghanistan in October 2001 and of Iraq in March 2003 which together resulted in what turned out to be a two-decade-long imperialist war (in effect, "another Vietnam") that ultimately cost the lives of over half a million people who died in these two wars at a financial cost of over $6 trillion to the U.S. taxpayers through 2019,[26] and more so by the time the United States was forced out of Afghanistan by the Taliban at the end of August 2021.[27] Whereas wars such as these have historically projected U.S. imperial power onto countries and regions of the world to maintain the supremacy of the American Empire, people around the world have risen up in rebellions and revolutions against both local tyrants and their foreign imperialist backers, first and foremost the United States.

As the U.S. wars in the Middle East and Asia have meant greater oppression and domination of the peoples of these regions, the spontaneous uprising of peoples across the Middle East and North Africa in what became known as "the Arab Spring" in 2010–2011 was a turning point in toppling entrenched dictatorships backed by the American Empire. Thus, the decade-long U.S. wars in and occupation of these regions gave rise to the popular resistance, rebellions, and revolutions that called into question not only the legitimacy of a string of neocolonial despotic puppet regimes from Tunisia to Egypt and beyond that were overthrown in a short period of time, but also the presence and machinations of the American Empire throughout the region.[28] Thus, the Arab Spring of 2011 across the Middle East ushered in a period of mass rebellions and revolutions that will have major political repercussions for the American Empire across many regions of the world in the coming years.

In North America, the anti-corporate-globalization demonstrations in Seattle in 1999 and Toronto in 2010 that targeted the WTO became the training grounds for the Occupy Wall Street Movement of 2011, which mobilized millions of people across the United States and the world.[29] The biggest and most vocal protest movement of recent times, the Occupy Wall Street Movement was no doubt inspired by the Arab Spring and the people's struggles across the globe and became a symbol of the struggle against the big banks, corporations, and the capitalist class (the top 1 percent of the population) who raked in billions of dollars in profits, while a large segment of the 99 percent struggled to survive in the midst of a capitalist crisis that devastated the lives of millions of people around the globe. Clearly, the millionaires and billionaires have seen their wealth and income grow and expand during these crisis-ridden times, while millions of working people have lost their jobs, have been evicted from their homes, are without health care, and are in desperate conditions. It is this tragic situation that has finally forced people to the streets to reclaim their communities, their government, and their country, despite the corrosive machinations of the American Empire at home and abroad.

As rebellions and revolutions continue to erupt across the world and as the material conditions of life under capitalism deteriorate and the crimes of the powers that be become unbearable, more and more people are bound to come together to express their frustration against the prevailing global capitalist system led by the American Empire. Therein one faces both the problem and the solution to the crisis of advanced capitalist/imperialist society in general and of the American Empire in particular. The capitalist crisis that has affected millions of working people in the United States and its satellites across the globe cannot be resolved without a thorough transformation of the American Empire and its client states throughout the world.

The cost of U.S. imperialist misadventures in policing the world has severely affected the home front with the incurring of enormous public debt resulting from the Empire's endless wars that has contributed to dragging the U.S. economy into a series of severe crises. The political response that such crises have generated, leading to the mobilization of social movements opposing the system and rebelling against it, have inspired millions of people in the United States and throughout the world against neoliberalism, imperialism, and corporate rule—in effect, leading to rebellions and revolutions against the American Empire across the globe.[30]

As the American Empire has been in dire straits in all its entanglements around the world, its right-wing shock troops at home attempted to stage a fascist coup billed as a second "tea party" through a pseudo-nationalist political drama to "Make America Great Again" that turned out to be a delusionary cheap entertainment for many, but was in fact "the big lie" of the new century! Thus, in a last ditch effort to save a moribund empire on the verge of collapse, the American Empire became in the end the laughing stock of the entire world as its pseudo-protagonists found their (white) supremacy in repressing a segment of their own people in their racist attempts to blame others for the utter failures and misdeeds of the American Empire. The misdeeds of the self-proclaimed "shock-troops" of an emergent neo-fascist force to regain the empire its lost power to turn things around actually resulted in divisions and discord among its own people along racial and political lines in the aftermath of the brutal murder of George Floyd by a police officer that led to the hot summer of 2020 when it reached a boiling point, erupting in the raged protests of millions of people across the nation with the impassioned chant "Black Lives Matter!"[31]

Rescuing the Empire? Or a New America *after Empire*

Who shall rescue the American Empire and its "subjects" who have suffered so much since the days of slavery and global pillage and plunder? On the eve of the "Great Recession" of 2008–2009 and in the ruins of another cycle of economic collapse that America suffered at the end of the first decade of the 21st century, we ushered in a new emperor to enter the scene in the image of a savior to take his place among a host of previous leaders who came to rescue the empire through the Imperial Presidency—enter President Barak Obama! Serving two terms to steer the big ship toward an unknown future, the commander-in-chief (i.e., the chief executive officer) of the "public corporation"—the U.S. state—controlled by private interests that was at the edge of a "fiscal cliff" (on the verge of bankruptcy), pondered over new pathways to transform a colossal empire into a respectable neighbor in a community of nations poised to launch the true ideals of its people for "equality and justice for all"—through "a government of the people, by the people, and for the people"—*working people!* But the "promise" was never fulfilled. Notwithstanding a mild recovery following the "Great Recession," the Obama Administration failed to deliver and ultimately set the stage for a right-wing, fascist response to the decline and fall of the American Empire and its rescue by a new emperor: enter President Donald J. Trump!

Beating the drums of pseudo-ultra-nationalism, racism, and xenophobia and in a last ditch effort to save the empire for him and his corrupt global capitalist cronies, Trump went all out with a right-wing Wall Street agenda to prop up a big business regime while paying lip-service to "Making America Great Again" with a con job to fool a segment of the U.S. working class to get his grand scheme through to enrich himself, his family, and his class while America and the American people, including those who foolishly voted for him, continued to suffer from his authoritarian, racist, and pro-capitalist fascist rule that exacerbated the decline and fall of the American Empire. While ultimately he lost the 2020 elections and the "insurrection" that he fomented on January 6, 2021, failed to reverse the outcome of the elections to keep him in the White House, the arrival of Joe Biden in taking back the presidency and in setting the course of America's future trajectory in a new direction through the same failed policies of the Obama Administration has not been effective in reversing the decline and fall of the American Empire. As a result, the same capitalist forces in control of the U.S. state will inevitably drag the Empire to its final collapse, despite its last ditch effort to survive the onset of the forces of change that will ultimately win and dismantle the Empire.

Today, capitalism is thoroughly global, and the globalization of capital through the process of imperialist expansion has brought us to the latest, highest, and most dangerous stage of capitalist imperialism that is threatening the future of our planet. The question that is now before us is: how will we be able to get out of this desperate situation, and who will lead us to a new and vibrant America that is responsive to the needs of its people? It is for attempting to answer this central, pivotal question that this book project was undertaken—a project that is so important for the future of America that I decided to take it up for an in-depth analysis that will help us address the crucial issues that affect us and to find solutions to them that we so urgently need.

America can become a shining light of equality and justice for all, and, given its enormous wealth and resources, is equipped to do so for generations to come. Unfortunately, this is not the vision of the corporate elite, the corrupt pro-capitalist politicians, and the wealthy capitalist class who are solely interested in serving their own class and personal interests of expanding their wealth. Thus, systemic change can only come from those who are oppressed and exploited by the forces that are maintaining the existing social, economic, and political order. And, therefore, the agents of change are those who are most affected by it in a profound way. The *working class and other oppressed classes and groups* that are the direct victims of this predicament are clearly the leading agents of social change and transformation and are the ones to build the foundations of a new America that we can all be proud of in the 21st century—an America devoid of empire and imperialism and devoid of capital and capitalism, with a vision to fulfill the dreams, desires, and hopes of all of its people in re-casting and re-constructing a new and just society for all.

In order to understand the logic of this process in a concrete way, we shall examine in the chapters that follow the development and transformation of American society in greater detail over the course of its turbulent history.[32] Through such analysis, we can come to a better understanding of the nature and dynamics of the social transformations in American society that are rooted in class relations, class conflict, and class struggles compounded by racial, ethnic, gender, and other forms of oppression and inequality for more than two centuries. It is only through a clear and honest examination of our past that we will be able to come to terms with our history and understand who we are as a people and where we are going as we face the challenges that we confront in America in the 21st century.

In envisioning a new America for the 21st century, a number of steps must be taken to live up to the vision of a prosperous egalitarian society. These include, first and foremost, the abolition of corporate capitalist ownership of the means of production, equitable distribution of wealth and income, full employment, comprehensive universal healthcare, free public university education, increasing living standards of working people, democratic governance, racial and gender equity, peaceful relations with other countries and the resolution of conflicts without resorting to war, and global cooperation on the environment and the ecosystem to safeguard our planet for future generations of Americans and all other people who inhabit the earth.

These are modest changes that must be implemented now. But they are of such magnitude and go against the interests of those who hold power that they will be resisted by the wealthy who will refuse to comply with the demands of the people for systemic, structural, and institutional change. If this becomes the case, such change will of necessity come directly from the people through organized collective political action by mass movements poised to transform the current social, economic, and political order. If major systemic reforms are not carried out in an urgent way, it would not be surprising to see working people wage a protracted struggle to achieve their demands through a collective, revolutionary process that challenges the very foundations of the capitalist state and the capitalist system on which it is built and replace it with a socially responsive system based on the collective will and power of working people in building a new, egalitarian society from which all (not just the few) would benefit. And the day is fast approaching when we will all take part in this process of re-constructing a new and a "more perfect" union of working people in America and the world.

Notes

1 This painful reality was explored by Victor Perlo in his book *American Imperialism* as early as 1951, who discussed in great detail the misdeeds of U.S. imperialism in the early 20th century as it was becoming a world power in the aftermath of World War II. See Victor Perlo, *American Imperialism* (New York: International Publishers, 1951).

2 Pierre Jalée, in his book *The Pillage of the Third World* published in the late 1960s, went to great lengths in chronicling the crimes of empire that plundered nations and peoples across the world in this immediate postcolonial period which became much more intensified later under conditions of globalization to the present, when countries across the third world continued to serve as permanent targets of exploitation and oppression of their peoples

and resources under advanced capitalist imperialism when local ruling classes served as willing collaborators of neocolonial domination that facilitated this continuing pillage and plunder. See Pierre Jalée, *The Pillage of the Third World* (New York: Monthly Review Press, 1968).

3 Berch Berberoglu, *The Internationalization of Capital: Imperialism and Capitalist Development on a World Scale* (New York: Praeger, 1987).

4 Berberoglu, *The Internationalization of Capital*, p. xiii.

5 See Paul M. Sweezy and Harry Magdoff, "The Stock Market Crash and Its Aftermath" *Monthly Review* 39, no. 10 (March 1988), pp. 1–13.

6 Berberoglu, *The Internationalization of Capital*, p. xiii.

7 Berberoglu, *The Internationalization of Capital*, p. xiii.

8 Berch Berberoglu, *The Legacy of Empire: Economic Decline and Class Polarization in the United States* (New York: Praeger, 1992).

9 There were many other voices during the 1970s and 1980s that sounded the alarm bells of imperialist plunder across the world, among them Harry Magdoff, Felix Greene, Douglas Dowd, James Petras, Albert Szymanski, Michael Parenti, and others, who exposed the machinations of U.S. imperialism during these Cold War years. See Harry Magdoff, *The Age of Imperialism* (New York: Monthly Review Press, 1969) and *Imperialism: From the Colonial Age to the Present* (New York: Monthly Review Press, 1978); Felix Greene, *The Enemy: What Every American Should Know about Imperialism* (New York: Random House, 1971); Douglas F. Dowd, *The Twisted Dream: Capitalist Development in the United States Since 1776* (Cambridge, MA: Winthrop, 1974); James Petras, *Critical Perspectives on Imperialism and Social Class in the Third World* (New York: Monthly Review Press, 1978); and Albert J. Szymanski, *The Logic of Imperialism* (Westport, CT: Praeger, 1981).

10 Berberoglu, *The Legacy of Empire*, p. xi.

11 Berberoglu, *The Legacy of Empire*, p. 49. See also Victor Perlo, *Super Profits and Crises: Modern U.S. Capitalism* (New York: International Publishers, 1988).

12 Berberoglu, *The Legacy of Empire*, p. 49. See also Sweezy and Magdoff, "The Stock Market Crash and Its Aftermath."

13 Berberoglu, *The Legacy of Empire*, pp. 49–50.

14 Berberoglu, *The Legacy of Empire*, p. 71.

15 This theme of the relationship of global imperialism led by the American Empire to the recurrent crises of global capitalism and its impact on the future of the entire capitalist system was taken up by Ernesto Screpanti some two decades later in the aftermath of the "Great Recession" which he refers to as "The Great Crisis." See Ernesto Screpanti, *Global Imperialism and the Great Crisis: The Uncertain Future of Capitalism* (New York: Monthly Review, 2014). See also David S. Mason, *The End of the American Century* (Lanham, MD: Rowman and Littlefield, 2009).

16 Berberoglu, *The Legacy of Empire*, p. 2.

17 Michael Parenti was an important voice waging a determined struggle against the American Empire in this period of post-Cold War aggressive posture of the United States as the sole superpower in the 1990s. See Michael Parenti, *Against Empire* (San Francisco, CA: City Lights, 1995).

18 See Richard D. Wolff, *Capitalism Hits the Fan: The Global Economic Meltdown and What to Do about It* (Northampton, MA: Interlink Pub Group, 2013) and Richard D. Wolff, *Capitalism's Crisis Deepens: Essays on the Global Economic Meltdown* (Chicago, IL: Haymarket Books, 2016).

19 Michel Chossudovsky and Andrew Gavin Marshall (eds.), *The Global Economic Crisis: The Great Depression of XXI Century* (Montreal, Quebec: Global Research Publishers, 2010).

20 See Berch Berberoglu, *Beyond the Global Capitalist Crisis: The World Economy in Transition* (Burlington, VT: Ashgate, 2012) and Berch Berberoglu, *The Global Capitalist Crisis and Its Aftermath: The Causes and Consequences of the Great Recession of 2008-2009* (Burlington, VT: Ashgate, 2014).

21 Ernest Mandel, *The Second Slump: A Marxist Analysis of Recession in the Seventies*, Revised and Enlarged Edition (London: Verso, 1978).

22 While the American Empire was finally defeated and forced out of Vietnam by 1975, U.S. military action during the 1980s included the invasion of Grenada that overthrew the leftist government of Maurice Bishop in this Caribbean island and the Contra War against the Sandinista Revolution that overthrew the Samosa dictatorship installed by the United States decades earlier as part of the U.S.'s anti-communist crusade against Cuba and the Soviet Union during the 1980s.

23 Berberoglu, *The Legacy of Empire.*

24 For a conservative perspective on the American Empire, see Niall Ferguson, *Colossus: The Rise and Fall of the American Empire* (New York: Penguin Books, 2005). For an earlier liberal perspective on the fate of empires, see Paul Kennedy, *The Rise and Fall of the Great Powers* (New York: Random House, 1987).

25 Martin Orr, "The Struggle against Capitalist Globalization: The Worldwide Protests against the WTO" in Berch Berberoglu (ed.), *Globalization and Change: The Transformation of Global Capitalism* (Lanham, MD: Lexington Books, 2005). See also Jackie Smith, "Globalizing Resistance: The Battle of Seattle and the Future of Social Movements," in Jackie Smith and H. Johnston (eds.), *Globalizing Resistance: Transnational Dimensions of Social Movements* (Lanham, MD: Rowman and Littlefield, 2002).

26 Neta C. Crawford, "Human Cost of the Post-9/11 Wars: Lethality and the Need for Transparency," Costs of War Project, Watson Institute for International and Public Affairs, Brown University, Providence, Rhode Island (November 2018). https://watson.brown.edu/costsofwar/files/cow/imce/papers/2018/Human%20Costs%2C%20Nov%208%202018%20CoW.pdf (accessed August 28, 2021). See also Neta C. Crawford, "United States Budgetary Costs and Obligations of Post-9/11 Wars through FY2020: $6.4 Trillion," *20 Years of War: A Costs of War Research Series*, Watson Institute for International and Public Affairs, Brown University, Providence, RI and The Frederick S. Pardee Center for the Study of the Longer-Range Future, Boston University, Boston, MA (November 13, 2019). https://watson.brown.edu/costsofwar/files/cow/imce/papers/2019/US%20Budgetary%20Costs%20of%20Wars%20November%202019.pdf?utm_source=Daily%20on%20Defense%20(2019%20TEMPLATE)_11/15/2019&utm_medium=email&utm_campaign=WEX_Daily%20on%20Defense&rid=84648 (accessed August 28, 2021). See also Amanda Macias, "America Has Spent $6.4 Trillion on Wars in the Middle East and Asia Since 2001, A New Study Says" (November 20, 2019). https://www.cnbc.com/2019/11/20/us-spent-6point4-trillion-on-middle-east-wars-since-2001-study.html (accessed August 28, 2021).

27 In all, U.S. post-9/11 wars in Iraq, Afghanistan, Pakistan, Syria, Yemen, and elsewhere have cost an estimated $8 trillion in FY2001–FY2022 and 929,000 lives. See Brown University, Watson Institute for International and Public Affairs, "Costs of War" Project https://watson.brown.edu/costsofwar/figures/2021/BudgetaryCosts (accessed September 11, 2021) and https://watson.brown.edu/costsofwar/figures/2021/WarDeathToll (accessed September 11, 2021).

28 James Petras and Henry Veltmeyer, *Beyond Neoliberalism: A World to Win* (Farnham, UK: Ashgate, 2011), pp. 175–197.

29 See Todd Gitlin, *Occupy Nation: The Roots, the Spirit, and the Promise of Occupy Wall Street* (New York: It Books, Harper Collins Publishers, 2012).

30 See the series of important essays on various social movements in the United States and around the world that have brought about revolutionary transformations across the globe in Berch Berberoglu (ed.), *The Palgrave Handbook of Social Movements, Revolution, and Social Transformation* (New York: Palgrave Macmillan, 2019).

31 For a background to the origins and development of the Black Lives Matter Movement, see Keeanga-Yamahtta Taylor, *From #BlackLivesMatter to Black Liberation*, Expanded 2nd ed. (Chicago, IL: Haymarket Books, 2021).

32 To explore aspects of various developments related to the expansion of the American Empire in the 20th and early 21st centuries in greater detail, sections of Chapters 4 and 7 of this book include material from my earlier study *Globalization of Capital and the Nation State: Imperialism, Class Struggle, and the State in the Age of Global Capitalism* published by Rowman and Littlefield, and sections of Chapters 5 and 6 include material from two of my articles in *International Review of Modern Sociology*, Vol. 43 (2) and Vol. 37 (2), respectively, which are included here with permission of the publishers.

2 The Empire Revisited

A Close Look at Our Past

Our future is based on our present, and our present is informed by our past. That much is clear. A close look at our past is therefore necessary to understand the shape of things today and what our future holds for us tomorrow. Thus, it is imperative that we take a close look at our history and learn from our mistakes while celebrating what is good and honorable in our legacy as a people. There is much that is good in what "We, the people of the United States of America" have built and are proud inheritors of the fruits of our labor as are millions of other working people who have come before us to make this nation a great place to live in—upholding the promise of "one nation indivisible" and "liberty and justice for all!"

What has been the true history of our nation and what is its legacy that we have come to inherit? What milestones have we achieved and what tragedies have we endured? What historic turning points have come to define us as Americans and what ugly chapters that we wish were never written in our name?

From a Colonial Outpost to a New Global Empire

Once upon a time in the not too distant past, there was no United States, let alone an American Empire. The conglomeration of people of European stock had come to these shores simply as an extension of their own now-defunct colonial empires. The Spanish, the Dutch, the French, and the British Empires were the dominant colonial and imperial powers that had expanded to and enslaved the indigenous peoples of distant lands. The imposition of home rule over local societies resulted in the greatest crimes against humanity through torture, massacre, and genocide of native indigenous populations. The Mayans of Mexico, the Incas of Peru, and the Native peoples of North America were slaughtered by the millions over several centuries of foreign domination and colonial rule.[1]

The arrival of the Pilgrims at Plymouth Rock (an event that most Americans celebrate with thanks each year) was thus the opening chapter of the long and arduous history of the United States inherited from our British masters who together with their junior partners committed these atrocities against the rightful inhabitants of these lands who had been

DOI: 10.4324/9781003282105-2

there for thousands of years. The British, no less the Dutch, the French, and the Spanish, were keen on acquiring land, resources, and local labor to build their colonial and imperial outposts in distant lands. They were the frenzied foot-soldiers of slavery, feudalism, and capitalism that took hold of the Americas, North and South, as conquered territories ripe for plunder to enrich slave-owners, landlords, and capitalists alike, as they spread their rule over vast stretches of land.

The Spanish conquest of the Western part of North America and much of South America, and the French conquest of Quebec and other parts of North America and the Caribbean, as well as the Dutch colonization of New York and a few other coastal cities aside, the British Empire was the chief imperial power that took over much of North America. The wealthy people of British descent were the dominant immigrant population that claimed ownership and control of this territory through the force of arms against natives of inferior military power who were no match to the vicious onslaught they faced from their soon to be masters.

The master-slave relationship, first imposed on the natives and later on those brought in from other distant colonies through the Transatlantic slave trade, was gradually established in much of southern North America as an appendage of the expanding capitalist system that was intent on transforming the newly acquired territories into capitalist societies. This was done to incorporate these regions into the global network of colonies and semi-colonies that defined the outer boundaries of the British Empire. Thus, capitalism in the North and slavery in the South became the dominant modes of production that defined the basis of early American society that was founded on the dual oppression and exploitation of "free" wage-labor (wage slaves) and slaves in chains, just the same. The continuation of the slave system in the South for decades after Independence until the Civil War was certainly a black mark on the new nation that only highlighted the dark side of the new American experience for a significant segment of the laboring population in the United States, so much so that the practice of human bondage imposed on some of its inhabitants (the slaves) outraged friend and foe alike as a crime against humanity.[2]

Even an ardent admirer of America as Alexis de Tocqueville, who in his *Democracy in America* glorified the new nation that he considered to be a political paradise in a new world, recognized its unforgiveable crimes from the very start. Writing in Maria Weston Chapman's *Liberty Bell: Testimony against Slavery*, Tocqueville stated:

> I am pained and astonished by the fact that the freest people in the world is, at the present time, almost the only one among civilized and Christian nations which yet maintains personal servitude; and this while serfdom itself is about disappearing, where it has not already disappeared, from the most degraded nations of Europe. An old and sincere friend of America, I am uneasy at seeing Slavery retard her

> progress, tarnish her glory, furnish arms to her detractors, compromise the future career of the Union which is the guaranty of her safety and greatness, and point out beforehand to her, to all her enemies, the spot where they are to strike. As a man, too, I am moved at the spectacle of man's degradation by man, and I hope to see the day when the law will grant equal civil liberty to all the inhabitants of the same empire, as God accords the freedom of the will, without distinction, to the dwellers upon earth.[3]

Slavery was but *one* dark chapter in the predicament of the Empire in the making in the years that followed its controversial beginnings. The entire affair rested, to be sure, in its structure and composition during its formation. Notwithstanding Tocqueville's understanding of its democratic origins, the land that he described as "free" was not only "half slave and half free," as Abraham Lincoln later recognized and criticized, but the democracy that Tocqueville boasted about was in fact a "democracy for the few," as Michael Parenti has reminded us more recently.[4] "The deck was stacked," as they say, against the laboring people from the very start—serving the interests of not "We, the people" but "We, the merchants, the manufacturers, the bankers, and the slave-owners" who actually wrote the Constitution to define the parameters of life in a class-divided society in which the wealthy plutocracy legitimized itself as the rulers of the land. How did all this happen and how did the common laboring people allow this to happen? This takes us to the beginning of our story—a story that explains the origins and development of the United States as an emerging capitalist nation.

The transformation of the United States from a colonial outpost of the British Empire to an independent capitalist state with jurisdiction over the entire national territory did not occur until the late 19th century. The War of Independence did, to be sure, change the political relations between Britain and its former American colony, but this change was not accompanied by a social transformation transferring power from one class to another. In this sense, the American Revolution was not a social revolution; rather, it was a transfer of power from Britain to its ex-colony without effecting a change in internal class power and class relations.[5] What we in America inherited, therefore, was a British culture and a British heritage imposed on native and slave labor that made the acquisition and accumulation of capital by a small minority of wealthy individuals into a dominant class possible.

The Early Years, 1776–1800

The early U.S. state, evolving from a colony to an independent nation-state, was based on this premise of elite rule—as an extension of capitalist class domination from the home front (in Europe) to the colonies (in North America). This helped establish the basis of the emergence of a new, local capitalist class of British ancestry that now defined itself as "American" and went on to declare war against its colonial master. "Down with King George" of London and "Long Live King George Washington" were the outcries of the American "revolutionaries" who were the supporters of a new monarchy copied from their British masters. They were ready to draft a constitution that would guarantee the power of wealth and privilege bestowed upon the wealthy elite of slave-owners, financiers, manufacturers, and merchants of a new republic that would develop as a new class-divided society imposed on the indigenous peoples that they confronted in the "New World."

Dispossessed first by the foreign conquerors and now by the established local elites that wanted to maintain their place on top of the social, political, and economic pyramid to dictate their rule over the masses—Black, White, and Native—the laboring people were able to put up a protracted struggle to resist the exploitation and oppression forced upon them.[6] Fortunately, some level-headed leaders among the elite prevailed to reject the imposition of a monarchy over the people, fearing a revolt and revolution that would transform class relations and put an end to the rule of the wealthy. Thus, despite the initial efforts of numerous delegates who attended the Constitutional Convention and voted for a monarchy, a majority of the delegates were able to defeat this authoritarian project that was to impose a dictatorship by choosing instead a system of "checks and balances" that *appeared* to be democratic but was, in fact, *designed to prevent a popular government from coming to power that would limit the power and interests of the new propertied ruling class.*

The balance of class forces in the state apparatus from the post-independence period to the Civil War was maintained by the Constitution drawn up by the two rival propertied classes in 1787. Intent on replacing the Articles of Confederation (the law of the land at the time) with a Constitution that would give power to a central state, the delegates to the Constitutional Convention in Philadelphia pushed through a document designed to protect their class interests and prevent popular democratic control of the U.S. state. Precisely, 53 of the 55 delegates to the Convention were or represented the economic interests of the propertied classes of slave-owners, merchants, creditors, and manufacturers.[7] Forty of the delegates held the paper money issued by the Continental Congress to finance the Revolutionary War, 14 held vast tracts of land, 24 were creditors and mortgage holders, 11 were merchants or manufacturers, and 15 were slave-owners.[8] They included James Madison, plantation owner and lawyer; Edmund Randolph of Virginia, owner of 5,000 acres and 200 slaves; Robert Morris, the Philadelphia banker; and Gouverneur Morris, land speculator of New York and Philadelphia.[9] Aware of widespread opposition among the people to the new Constitution, the delegates passed a resolution at the beginning of the convention to keep what they were doing completely secret; they even passed a subsequent resolution that no one was to take notes.[10] This was done to prevent the public from finding out the true nature of the document being written and the motives of those responsible for it. Despite the fact that the delegates were instructed both by the Congress and their own states to consider only a revision of the Articles of Confederation and to submit their recommendations to the Congress and the states for approval,[11] they ignored these instructions and came up with a new document to replace the Articles:

> They did not amend the Articles of Confederation; they cast that instrument aside and drafted a fresh plan of government. Nor did they merely send the new document to Congress and then to the state legislatures for approval; on the contrary they appealed over the heads of these authorities to the voters of the states for a ratification of their revolutionary work. Finally, declining to obey the clause of the Articles which required unanimous approval for every amendment, they frankly proposed that the new system of government should go into effect when sanctioned by nine of the thirteen states, leaving the others out in the cold under the wreck of the existing legal order, in case they refused to ratify.[12]

Despite these maneuvers, the convention was unable to meet even its own requirements and secure the nine states necessary for ratification; the people of New York, New Hampshire, Massachusetts, Rhode Island, and North Carolina voted against ratification. Keenly aware of the need to reverse the situation by securing the votes, the pro-Constitution forces persuaded some of the delegates to the state conventions who had been elected to vote against the Constitution to vote for it instead. This maneuver reversed the results in three crucial states—New York, New Hampshire, and Massachusetts:

> In New Hampshire, New York, and Massachusetts, where the election returned avowed majorities opposed to the Constitution, a great deal of clever engineering induced several delegates to depart from their apparent instructions and cast their ballots for ratification. But to the very end, two states, North Carolina and Rhode Island, refused to give their consent. . . . From the fragmentary figures that are available, it appears that no more than one-fourth of the adult white males in the country voted one way or the other in the elections at which delegates to the state ratifying conventions were chosen. According to a cautious reckoning, probably one-sixth of them—namely, one hundred thousand—favored the ratification of the new form of government.[13]

After the Constitution was finally ratified and became the basis of government, both the intent of the framers and the content of the document became increasingly clear to people, especially small farmers, who constituted the majority of the population:

> The people as a whole were opposed to the document. Particularly hostile were the small farmers of the country. . . . They were quick to point out the essentially undemocratic character of the new frame of government. . . . They resented the fact that the proposed instrument was more concerned with the protection of property rights than in the maintenance of human rights. They did not fail to note that what the constitution was trying to do was to establish the same centralized system of political, judicial, and economic controls that the British ruling classes had attempted to foist upon them in the days of Grenville, Townshend, and North.[14]

Under pressure from the small farmers and other democratic forces in society, the newly emerging U.S. state, controlled by the wealthy, had no choice but to come forward with a Bill of Rights—the first ten amendments to the Constitution, which were added to the document in 1791.[15]

That the framers of the Constitution wanted to establish a state guided by laws and principles reflecting the interests of the propertied classes is no secret even to a casual observer of the events of the time. Their antidemocratic pronouncements were in line with their class interests and against those of the slaves, the workers, the artisans, and the farmers as well as the Native American people—in effect, the vast majority of the population.[16] The critical linkage between class and state in postcolonial America, then, was established precisely by the class nature and role of the U.S. Constitution, which provided the basis of the rule of property over labor and gave the state its subsequent class character.[17] For this reason, the Constitution can be seen both as a product and an instrument of the class forces that came to dominate the U.S. state until the Civil War.

Nevertheless, it soon became clear that the state apparatus that came under the control of the ruling classes could not function properly unless some mechanisms of mediation of conflict were instituted to resolve differences between rival forces within the ruling-class coalition. Thus:

> In order to regulate the conflict of interests between capitalists and landowners, a series of checks and balances between judiciary, congressional, and executive powers were introduced, as well as different methods of representation for the Senate and the House of Representatives.[18]

This was also recognized and articulated in no uncertain terms by the framers of the Constitution who established the foundations of the modern U.S. state, as the following passage from James Madison's *Federalist Papers* indicates:

> But the most common and durable source of factions has been the various and unequal distribution of property. Those who hold and those who are without property have ever formed distinct interests in

> society. . . . A landed interest, a manufacturing interest, a mercantile interest, a moneyed interest, with many lesser interests, grow up of necessity in civilized nations, and divide them into different classes, actuated by different sentiments and views. The regulation of these various and interfering interests forms the principal task of modern legislation, and involves the spirit of party and faction in the necessary and ordinary operations of the government.[19]

The state in the United States thus became an arbiter of competing ruling class interests that controlled it to advance their own particular class agenda as against that of other rival forces in American society.

Consolidation of the Emerging Empire on the Home Front, 1800–1861

The development and expansion of the United States as a newly independent state following the War of Independence that resulted in the American Revolution against its colonial master, Britain, was just the beginning of American power to spread from its origins in the Eastern flank of North America to the West, where other colonial powers (France and Spain) had their foothold that held back the further expansion of a future American Empire now divided into several territories across the land.

The grand prize in the consolidation of U.S. power in territorial expansion came with the Louisiana Purchase in 1803, when a vast territory that today covers some or all of the land area of 15 states was purchased from France for $15 million (or about $18 per square mile). The purchase of this territory doubled the land mass of the United States at that time (see Figure 2.1). It also opened the path to the subsequent purchase of Florida from Spain in 1821 and to Westward expansion of the nation in the decades that followed.

The Westward expansion of the United States through these acquisitions culminated some four decades later in the Mexican-American War of 1846–1848, when the expanding American Empire confronted Mexico across another vast territory that would take the United States all the way to California—to the Pacific Ocean! The U.S. war against Mexico, which lasted nearly two years, resulted in the forced annexation of territory held by the Republic of Mexico, including California, Nevada, Utah, much of Arizona, and the western part of New Mexico and Colorado (see Figure 2.2).

The conquest of Mexican territory by the United States through the force of arms that culminated in the signing of the Treaty of Guadalupe Hidalgo, transferring this land to its new owners, effectively gave the emerging American Empire another boost to its newly won position as a future superpower on the global scene.

The Westward expansion of the United States during the 1800s continued through the Civil War and the subsequent period when the Alaska Purchase from Russia in 1867 for $7.2 million opened the way to United States' transcontinental hegemony in North America.

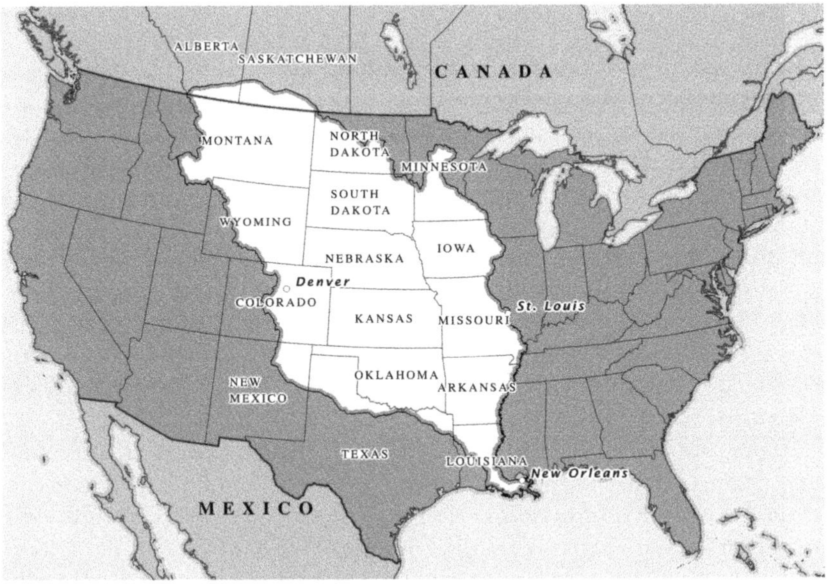

Figure 2.1 The Louisiana Purchase of 1803 from France.
Source: https://en.wikipedia.org/wiki/Louisiana_Purchase#/media/File:Louisiana_Purchase.jpg.

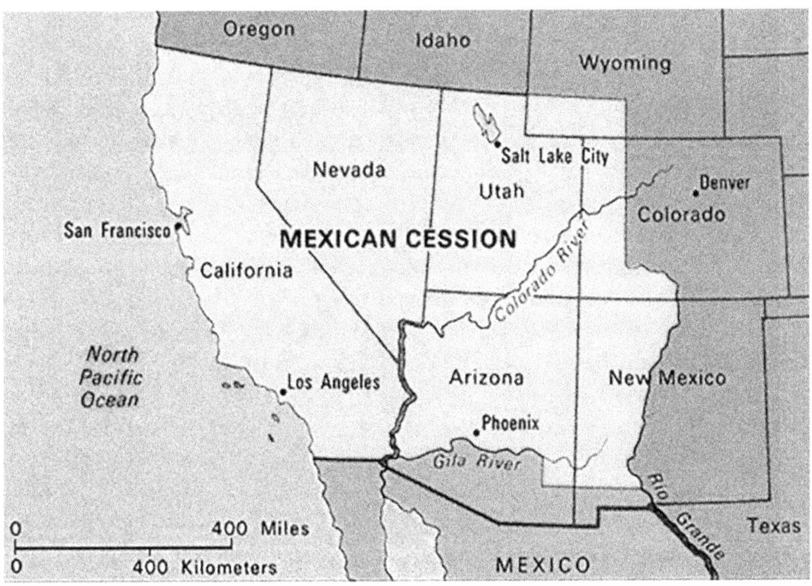

Figure 2.2 Loss of Mexican Territory to the United States after the Mexican-American War, 1846–1848.
Source: World Book 1999.

The Settling of Internal Conflicts: The Civil War and Its Aftermath, 1861–1900

Whereas the War of Independence established a new nation-state on North American soil subsequent to its turbulent colonial past, the Civil War marked a new era in America through what became a major social revolution that ushered in a social transformation of vast proportions. Given its social character and subsequent transformation, it is clear that the U.S. Civil War was, in effect, a class war that led to the supremacy and domination of one class over another, i.e., the victorious northern capitalist class over the defeated southern plantation slave-owning master class. Thus, the Civil War was, in effect, America's *bourgeois* (capitalist) revolution that firmly secured the hegemony of the capitalist class over the new (reconstituted) state that was established following northern victory in the war.

To provide a brief background to the Civil War and its aftermath in *class terms*, from 1776 to the end of the Civil War in 1865, the United States developed within the framework of a "neocolonial" relationship with Britain, when the state represented the interests of both the emerging capitalist class in the North and the slave-owning planter class in the South, with the latter dominating the government which was tied to and dependent on the British-controlled world economy. This political configuration of class forces continued until the Civil War.

Specializing in agro-industrial raw material production (cotton) geared to the needs of the textile industry in England, the slave-owning planter class in the South came to articulate the interests of its ex-colonial master poised against northern capital, from which it carved out for itself a substantial territory and a significant portion of the profits guaranteed by the imperial crown (Britain). The contradictory class relationship between the two rival ruling classes in postcolonial America continued to evolve and develop within the framework of a truce that permitted the coexistence of two distinct social-economic systems (capitalism and plantation slavery). This allowed the simultaneous exploitation of wage-labor by capital and of slave labor by the southern slavocracy through the sharing of state power tipped in favor of the latter that maintained the legality of slavery, which lasted nearly a century—until the end of the Civil War.

During the first half of the 19th century, slave-owners were the dominant force within the ruling-class alliance. This is evidenced by the fact that key positions within the federal government were controlled by slave-owners, assisted by their financial and mercantile allies in the North. The executive and legislative branches of the state were pro-slave-owner, and the Supreme Court's decisions often upheld slavery, as in the fugitive slave laws. However, the inherent contradictions between a growing industrial capitalism based on wage-labor in the North and a plantation system based on slave labor in the South was coming to a head:

> Slave and wage-labor capitalism had complemented each other during the early decades of the nineteenth century. Slaves toiled in southern fields to produce cotton that was spun and woven into textiles in British and northern factories. Northern and southern elites had joined together to wrest independence from the British.[20]

By the middle of the 19th century, however, capitalist development had reached new heights throughout the North, requiring new markets, access to raw materials, cheap and abundant labor, and further capital accumulation. The slave-owning class in the South held on to its source of wealth through the exploitation of slave labor and safeguarded its "neocolonial" role in the world economy through continued alliance with and reliance on British imperialism. "By the 1850s," writes James Russell, "the interests of the two elites were diverging":

> The North was expanding the infrastructure for the marketing of its products and wanted to use the federal government to finance construction of a railroad to the west coast. It wanted preferential access to southern raw materials and tariffs to protect its resulting products from foreign, especially British, competition. The South had little interest in financing a railroad to California since its raw materials went mostly east to be shipped to Britain and secondarily northward. The South with no industries to protect did not favor tariffs, which would only make its imports more costly. The South seceded when it lost control over the direction of federal policy. Because the North saw the southern territory as being an integral part of the country's economic destiny, loss of it would severely weaken its own developmental prospects.[21]

The contradictions that had been developing between the two systems since the formation of the Union could no longer be contained within the existing state. Thus, the two dominant classes finally clashed to solve, once and for all, the question of state power:

> The Nation's most-costly war in lives broke out in 1861. The northern victory settled the issue, and the United States embarked upon its most ambitious period of industrialization with the active support of the federal government. The Civil War removed the final obstacle, the slavocracy, in the path of the full industrial development of the United States.[22]

The level of development reached by the two divergent and competing systems at the onset of independence was such that it took nearly a century for the underlying contradictions and conflicts to surface and burst open, leading to civil war that would finally decide the answer to the decisive question: which class alone shall rule the state? The northern capitalist victory against the slave-owning South resulted in the forced transfer of state power to the capitalist class and thereby ushered in the rule of the capitalist state.[23] In this sense, the northern victory in the Civil War marked a turning point in the social transformation of postcolonial America, as it not only prevented the spread of slavery to the West and the North but assured that capitalism would become the dominant mode of production and the capitalist state the dominant political authority in the land.[24]

"It had taken two nineteenth-century acts of force parallel to the expropriation of Indian land," writes Russell, "to prepare the terrain for the emergence of the United States as a world industrial power—one directed against Mexico and the other against the southern slavocracy."[25] Thus:

> the acquisitions through conquest of Indian and Mexican lands removed two key spatial obstacles to the development of the U.S. economy, and the northern victory in the Civil War removed the agrarian slave system that had been an organizational obstacle to corporate-led industrialization.[26]

New Frontiers: Capitalism Triumphant, 1900–1945

As capitalism came to dominate the national economy and the state during the period following the Civil War, the capitalist class turned the state into its instrument, with the state subsidizing industry by establishing protective tariffs, granting land for railway construction, and other benefits to capital for Westward expansion, while preventing labor from organizing into unions to improve their lot through higher wages and better working conditions. Thus, the capitalist state did everything it could to facilitate the rapid growth and development of industrial capital in the United States, hence the establishment on firm grounds of the emerging capitalist system across the nation.[27]

As a result, a tremendous expansion of capital took place in the United States during this period through the exploitation of wage-labor on a grand scale, leading to the concentration and centralization of wealth in the hands of the capitalists. As industry grew, production expanded and capitalism spread across America, the ex-slaves (now paid wage-labor), together with the established industrial working class of the northern cities, generated ever-higher rates of profit for the capitalists, fueling the fortunes of the superrich who accumulated immense financial wealth that led to the formation of the first capitalist monopolies, cartels, and trusts. Through this process of expansion, capital—now in its monopoly stage—came to completely dominate the U.S. economy and the state by the late 19th and early 20th centuries. And this was the outcome of the northern victory that transformed the United States from a backward semi-capitalist/semi-slave agrarian postcolonial society to an advanced capitalist state and society that evolved into one of the most powerful capitalist nations in the world.

Throughout this period, the state's role in regulating the economy on behalf of capital began to increase, as did its role in repressing an increasingly militant working class, while expanding its presence around the world through military intervention in the Americas, the Pacific, and other regions. Chronicling this aggressive posture, Richard O. Boyer and Herbert M. Morais in their book *Labor's Untold Story* provide a piercing account of the crimes of the rising American Empire at home and abroad:

> The fierce conflicts of Chicago and Colorado, the strikes of steel workers, metal miners, and railroad men, the jailing of literally thousands of labor's rank and file . . . were cruel and bloody years that stretched between 1890 and 1900. . . .
>
> It was the time in which American finance underwent a qualitative change, beginning to export its money and Marines into the Caribbean and the Pacific, grabbing Puerto Rico and the Philippines by force of arms, controlling Cuba as a protectorate, and annexing Hawaii outright.[28]

Such military adventures on behalf of American finance capital were revealed in no uncertain terms by Major General Smedley D. Butler, at the time of his death the most decorated Marine in U.S. history, who stated in his book *War is a Racket*:

> I spent 33 years and four months in active military service and during that period I spent most of my time as a high class muscle man for Big Business, for Wall Street and the bankers. In short, I was a racketeer, a gangster for capitalism. I helped make Mexico and especially Tampico safe for American oil interests in 1914. I helped make Haiti and Cuba a decent place for the National City Bank boys to collect revenues in. I helped in the raping of half a dozen Central American republics for the benefit of Wall Street. I helped purify Nicaragua for the International Banking House of Brown Brothers in 1902–1912. I brought light to the Dominican Republic for the American sugar interests in 1916. I helped make Honduras right for the American fruit companies in 1903. In China in 1927 I helped see to it that Standard Oil went on its way unmolested. Looking back on it, I might have given Al Capone a few hints. The best he could do was to operate his racket in three districts. I operated on three continents.[29]

But this economic and military expansion of the American Empire to establish the supremacy of capital over labor across the world did not go unanswered, as:

> it was the decade which saw one more gallant effort by the common people, the workers and farmers, to wrest the country from the control

> of Wall Street through independent political action. It was the time of labor's tall Gene Debs and the miners' Big Bill Haywood, of Sockless Jerry Simpson and Mary Elizabeth Lease, who advised the nation's farmers to "raise less corn and more hell." It was a decade in which monopoly, steadily growing since the Civil War, pyramided into new heights of power . . . while the Knights of Labor . . . called for the abolition of the wage system and the establishment of an order whose factories, mines, mills, railroads, and utilities were owned and operated by the people.[30]

Despite these political struggles, however:

> monopoly steadily grew . . . ever increasing their grip on every aspect of American life. . . . And the great age of financial concentration, of the narrowing control of the few who reaped fabulous profits from the work of the many, had just begun.[31]

Beginning in the first two decades of the 20th century and continuing through the Great Depression and World War II, the U.S. state played a key role in safeguarding and promoting the capitalist economy. With the U.S. entry into World War II, the United States embarked on the road to full recovery, and thereby became a powerful force on the world scene, its economy rivaling that of Britain, France, Germany, and other mature capitalist states. In fact, with the devastation of Europe during World War II and the *de facto* defeat of the major European states at the conclusion of the war, the United States emerged as the leading imperial state among the rival powers dominating the world economy. The growth and expansion of U.S. transnational corporations during this period thus corresponds to the global rise to power and prominence of the United States in the postwar period.

The Postwar Expansion of the American Empire on a Global Scale, 1945–

The transfer of political and economic control from Britain to the United States in the British spheres of influence (Latin America, Asia, Africa, and the Middle East) in the aftermath of World War II gave the United States access to oil and other raw materials and investment outlets in manufacturing to tap sources of cheap and abundant labor. With the postwar expansion of U.S. capital on a global scale came the political expansion of the U.S. state; together, they came to articulate and advance the interests of U.S. capitalism throughout the world.

The turning point for the rise to world prominence of the United States was at the conclusion of World War II. While Europe was devastated and in ruins, the United States emerged as the leading center of the capitalist world, practically unaffected by the war. In fact, the collapse of the infrastructure of the major European economies by war's end worked to the advantage of U.S. capital and permitted its penetration into Western Europe through the Marshall Plan. From 1945 to the early 1970s, U.S. capital maintained its dominance of the global economy, supported by the might of the U.S. state. The role of the state in overseas political and military ventures during this period in support of the expansion of global investments of large U.S. transnational corporations throughout the world led to the projection of U.S. imperial power on a global scale.

The ascendancy of the United States in the global economy thus dates mainly from the end of World War II, when weakened European economies coincided with a tremendous growth and expansion of U.S. transnationals on the world scene. As a result, the globalization of U.S. capital began to take root on a world scale under the auspices of U.S. transnational corporations in the postwar period, a development we will explore in greater depth in Chapter 4.

Notes

1 Ward Churchill, *A Little Matter of Genocide: Holocaust and Denial in the Americas 1492 to the Present* (San Francisco, CA: City Lights Publishers, 2001). See also Ward Churchill, *Struggle for the Land: Native North American Resistance to Genocide, Ecocide, and Colonization* (San Francisco, CA: City Lights Publishers, 2002).

2 Howard J. Sherman, "Slavery in the United States, 1776-1865" Ch. 6 in Howard J. Sherman (ed.), *How Society Makes Itself: The Evolution of Political and Economic Institutions* (Armonk, NY: M.E. Sharpe, 2006), pp. 81–92. See also, Eugene Genovese, *Roll Jordan Roll: The World the Slaves Made* (New York: Vintage, 1976) and Eugene Genovese, *The Political Economy of Slavery: Studies in the Economy and Society of the Slave South*, 2nd ed. (Middletown, CT: Wesleyan University Press, 1988).

3 Alexis de Tocqueville, cited in Gallimard, *Ouevres Completes,* VII: 1663–1664.

4 Michael Parenti, *Democracy for the Few*, 9th ed. (Boston, MA: Wadsworth, 2011).

5 Berch Berberoglu, *Political Sociology in a Global Era* (Boulder, CO: Paradigm Publishers, 2013), pp. 75–76.

6 Howard Zinn, *A People's History of the United States*, Reissue ed. (New York: Harper Perennial Modern Classics, 2015).

7 Parenti, *Democracy for the Few.* The only exceptions were Benjamin Franklin (Pennsylvania) and Luther Martin (Maryland). Martin refused to sign the Constitution, and both Martin and Franklin campaigned against the ratification of the Constitution in their respective states.

8 Charles Beard, *An Economic Interpretation of the Constitution of the United States* (New York: Macmillan, 1962). They included James Madison, plantation owner and lawyer; Edmund Randolph of Virginia, owner of 5,000 acres and 200 slaves; Robert Morris, the Philadelphia banker; and Gouverneur Morris, land speculator of New York and Philadelphia. Kenneth Neill Cameron, *Humanity and Society: A World History* (New York: Monthly Review Press, 1977), p. 421.

9 Cameron, *Humanity and Society*, p. 421.
10 One of the delegates, James Madison, did not abide by the group's decision, and his notes were later published, which contain revealing statements by some of the delegates during the convention. See also the essays by James Madison and others in *The Federalist Papers,* especially No. 10.
11 Herbert M. Morais, *The Struggle for American Freedom* (New York: International Publishers, 1944).
12 Charles Beard and Mary Beard, *The Rise of American Civilization* (New York: Macmillan, 1930), pp. 313–314.
13 Beard and Beard, *The Rise of American Civilization*, p. 332. Of course, women, who constituted half the adult population; slaves, who made up one-fourth of the population; Native Americans; and poor, propertyless whites were not allowed to vote. This, many have argued, is another testimony to the racist, sexist, elitist, and class-based nature of the early U.S. state and the Constitution, both of which reflected the class interests of the forces that came to dominate the state after independence (wealthy white men).
14 Morais, *The Struggle for American Freedom*, pp. 253–254.
15 Colonel Mason recommended at the Constitutional Convention that a committee be formed to draft "a Bill of Rights," but his motion was voted down unanimously.
16 Herbert Aptheker, *The American Revolution, 1763-1783* (New York: International Publishers, 1976).
17 Aptheker, *The American Revolution, 1763-1783.*
18 Cameron, *Humanity and Society*, p. 421.
19 James Madison, *Federalist Papers* No. 10 in Hamilton, Madison, and Jay [1787] 1961.
20 James W. Russell, *Class and Race Formation in North America* (Toronto: University of Toronto Press, 2009), p. 41.
21 Russell, *Class and Race Formation in North America*, p. 41.
22 Russell, *Class and Race Formation in North America*, p. 41.
23 Sherman, *How Society Makes Itself*, pp. 93–98.
24 Sherman, *How Society Makes Itself*, pp. 93–98.
25 Russell, *Class and Race Formation in North America*, p. 41.
26 Russell, *Class and Race Formation in North America*, p. 41.
27 Albert J. Szymanski, *The Capitalist State and the Politics of Class* (Cambridge, MA: Winthrop, 1978), p. 160.
28 Richard O. Boyer and Herbert M. Morais, *Labor's Untold Story*, 3rd ed. (New York: United Electrical, Radio, and Machine Workers of America, 1984), pp. 105–106.
29 Smedley D. Butler, *War Is a Racket* (New York: Round Table Press, 1935). See also Jonathan M. Katz, *Gangsters of Capitalism: Smedley Butler, the Marines, and the Making and Breaking of America's Empire* (New York: St. Martin's Press, 2022).
30 Boyer and Morais, *Labor's Untold Story*, p. 106.
31 Boyer and Morais, *Labor's Untold Story*, p. 107.

3 Who We Are as Americans

One Nation Indivisible or a Divided Empire?

All through our lives—from primary school through adulthood and beyond—we have been told that we are "the chosen people" and are "one nation, indivisible, under God" selected to be the custodians of the world, bringing to earth "liberty and justice for all." These highly charged emotional words have much propaganda value to ignite patriotic passions that governments, like ours, would like to cultivate to secure and maintain loyalty and devotion to the nation throughout the tumultuous history of our Republic. But upon a closer look at our history, we have discovered in the previous chapter a completely different picture of our past as to who we are as Americans and how others see us among the community of nations across the globe.

There is, to be sure, much to be proud of one's self, family, neighbors, community, and nation, especially when working Americans have contributed so much to the development of this unique society of immigrants from across the world. The hard work of ordinary laboring people in building a society far away from their original homeland in Europe and elsewhere is a legend in the annals of humanity—one that has made America a great nation and gained the respect of people throughout the world. But much has been done in our name by social forces beyond our reach and control—by political and economic elites—who have damaged our reputation as a peace-loving people who cherish the basic principles of "life, liberty, and the pursuit of happiness" by *all*.

In looking at our history, we have observed horrendous crimes that have been committed in our name. Wars, genocide, slavery, racism, patriarchy, political repression, exploitation of labor, colonialism, imperialism, and other crimes have been an integral part of the American experience, but were committed by those whose primary interests were money, wealth, and power. They were the "founding fathers" of this Republic who drew the roadmap of their riches and glory that were yet to come by drafting a document—the U.S. Constitution—to serve their own narrow class interests—those of not the American people as a whole, but of the wealthy propertied classes that came to rule this country from the very beginning.[1] Thus, the slave masters, merchants, manufacturers, bankers, and other privileged segments of society came to impose their rule over the

DOI: 10.4324/9781003282105-3

American people to establish and dictate their unbridled power based on private wealth generated through the exploitation of labor—the labor of American working people, half slave and half "free."

America has always been a racially and ethnically divided society from its very beginning. The genocide committed against the rightful owners of these lands (the Native Americans) and the enslavement, torture, and lynching of African Americans subsequent to their forced transport to the "New World" as slaves through the Transatlantic slave trade were the first acts of violence. The mistreatment of waves of poor immigrants who have endured the sweatshops and mines of the rising industrial and financial interests that came to rule over this land after the victory of the North in the Civil War set the course of history across the nation over the subsequent century and a half that followed.[2] Built on racial and ethnic oppression over much of the entire stretch of American history, the United States came to epitomize a racially divided (in effect, a segregated racist) society—one that continues to manifest itself in all aspects of racial and ethnic relations—from the internment of Japanese-Americans during World War II to racist immigration policy and police brutality that is both cruel and inhumane.

As our history and present predicament amply illustrate, we are not one people, one nation, indivisible, under one God that defines us as Americans. We are an Empire, divided along multiple identities—racial, gender, class, religious, cultural, linguistic, and more—with histories and narratives that nevertheless bind us together as a people (mainly working people). We have been dominated, exploited, oppressed, and repressed by those who own the wealth of this great nation and wield power through the government that they control, the wealth that working people have created for them through their blood, sweat, and tears and are subordinated to a government of, by, and for the wealthy, and not the people—working people.

A "Middle Class" Society?

We have been told in school, by the media, by our government, and our major institutions that we Americans are all part of a giant "middle class"—a vast conglomeration of people whose income ranges from just above poverty to the upper rungs of the income structure that would differentiate us by being a part of the "upper" or the "lower" middle class, but "middle class" just the same. Where that middle lies between the wealthy capitalists who have fortunes of billions of dollars to their names and the homeless poor "will work for food," no one knows. But while calling oneself "rich" might be a bit of a stretch and "working poor" from paycheck to paycheck a bit embarrassing and humiliating, "the middle" certainly sounds close to our comfort zone for emotional and psychological gratification, even if we have just been fired from our job, lost our health insurance, foreclosed and evicted from our mortgaged and bank-owned homes, and have nowhere to go; still, we are at least "middle class"—in the middle of nowhere in the twilight zone!

So, what does America look like if we take a close look at ourselves and assess our predicament in this wealthiest and most advanced society in the world in the early 21st century? We would most certainly discover that we are, indeed, a class-divided society. The class structure of the United States consists of not just one class (the "middle class"), but at least two (and perhaps three) classes—the employers (the owners of capital or the capitalists), the employees (the workers or wage-labor), and the independent self-employed ("mom-and-pop" small-business owners—the "old middle class") operating on their own account, positioned in the middle between the capitalists and wage-laborers. Additionally, there exists a similarly positioned group of professionals (doctors, lawyers, engineers, professors, middle-level corporate managers, etc.), often referred to as "the new middle class." And a sizeable group of people who are permanently unemployed remain outside of the labor force or outside of the "economically active population." Thus, sifting through these various groups, *the two main classes* that emerge in American society are *wage-labor (workers) and capital (capitalists).*

The class origins of the United States go back to the early years of the Republic when the dominant classes of slave-owners in the South and capitalists in the North enjoyed their reign over the people who owned no more than their labor power, which effectively placed them within the laboring class. But a large mass of independent family farmers exceeded three-quarters of the U.S. population as of the mid-1800s. The development of capitalism and corporate agriculture in the United States over the course of the 19th and later the 20th centuries, however, forced most of these small family farmers off the land. As more and more farms went bankrupt and became absorbed into corporate agribusiness, they were effectively transformed into farm workers or industrial wage-labor (i.e., the proletarianization of the U.S. labor force). This led to the transformation of the U.S. class structure and set the stage for further expansion of capitalist relations of production in the United States in the 20th century.

The Class Structure of the United States

We have been divided into classes throughout our history, just like others who have been living in class-divided societies elsewhere for centuries. Under slavery, we had slave-owners and slaves; under capitalism we had (and continue to have) capitalists and wage-laborers—the modern-day owners of capital whose profits derive from the exploitation of wage-labor and those whose "free" lives are not much better than their predecessors in chains and who are, in effect, *wage-slaves*. While wage-labor has created the wealth of this nation for more than a century and a half during our brief but turbulent history, this wealth has been expropriated by a handful of modern-day masters that form a ruling class made up of rich capitalists who have amassed vast fortunes on the backs of working people of this great nation—a people who have paid a heavy price for their exploitation under contemporary U.S. capitalism.[3]

Let us take a brief look at the class structure of the United States today by focusing on the various classes, their size, composition, and level of class consciousness as well as the balance of class forces and the nature of class conflict that periodically erupt into class struggles. The contemporary class structure of the United States is characterized by the two main contending classes in the production process—labor and capital—that have been engaged in struggle since the emergence of capitalism in the United States in the 18th century. While numerous other classes and strata have existed within the social-economic boundaries of American society since its inception, the capitalist class and the working class are the two major antagonistic classes that define the main parameters of class relations and class conflict in modern American society.[4]

Looking at the U.S. class structure more closely, we find four distinct classes and groups in the United States. These include (1) the capitalist class, which is made up of two sectors—the monopoly sector and the non-monopoly sector—together constituting about 1 percent of the population; (2) the working class, which is made up of several sectors—industrial, agricultural, clerical, service, and highly technical as well as retired and/or temporarily unemployed workers—which together constitute upwards of 85 percent of the labor force; (3) the self-employed (small business), which is made up of three sectors—shopkeepers, family farmers, and professionals/managers—totaling about 15 percent of the labor force; and (4) the permanently unemployed, which is made up of several sectors—permanently unemployed poor on welfare, homeless/street people, the disabled, and others—all of which remain outside of the labor force and constitute part of an "underclass" (see Table 3.1).[5]

The defining characteristic of the rival classes in contemporary American society is the relationship that these classes have to the ownership and control of the means of production. The capitalist class owns and controls the means of production and accumulates capital through the exploitation of labor. Surplus value—the value produced by the workers over and above the wages they receive—is extracted by the capitalists in the form of profits for purposes of accumulation of wealth and capital.[6] The working class, however, does not own means of production and labors for the capitalist for wages in order to live. This relationship in the production sphere, which has a social-economic character, becomes a political one as soon as the social forces in question struggle to advance their own class interests.[7]

Figure 3.1 illustrates relations between various classes in the United States and the central role of the capitalist state controlled and dominated by the capitalist class.

While relations between the capitalist class and the working class constitute the main relations of production for the accumulation of capital in

Table 3.1 The Contemporary Class Structure of the United States

I	**Capitalist Class** (owners) (~ 1% of the population)
	a monopoly (big business) sector
	b non-monopoly (competitive) sector
II	**Working Class** (wage-labor) (~ 85% of the labor force)
	a industrial workers
	b farm workers
	c clerical workers
	d service workers
	e highly technical workers
	f retired and/or temporarily unemployed
III	**Self-employed** (own account) (~15% of the labor force)
	a shopkeepers
	b family farmers
	c professionals and managers
IV	**Unemployed** (underclass) welfare/poor (~ 8–10% of the population)
	a permanently unemployed
	b the homeless
	c disabled/unemployed
	d dropouts

Source: Constructed by the author.
Note: The capitalist class and the unemployed are not part of the labor force or the economically active population; figures given for these groups are for percentage of the population.

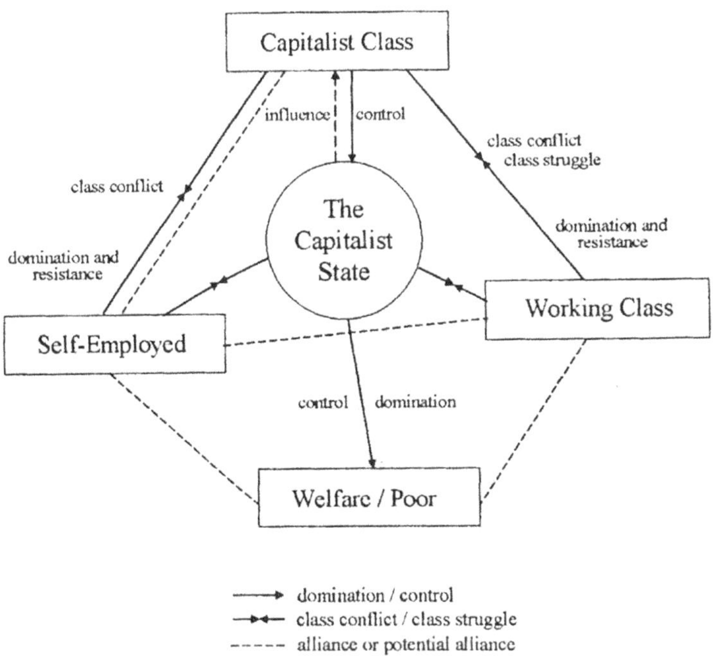

Figure 3.1 Class Relations, the State, and Political Power in the United States.
Source: Constructed by the author.

the United States, relations between the self-employed and the capitalists as well as that between all other classes and the permanently unemployed poor constitute the totality of class relations that span across various strata in American society. As control of the state by the capitalist class shapes relations between the state and all other classes in the United States, thus leading to class conflict, the class struggle between labor and capital takes on its political character, such that while this becomes a political struggle for gains in the social-economic sphere, it ultimately leads to a larger struggle for control of the state. Thus, the control of the state by the capitalist class in the United States has turned the U.S. state into a capitalist state.[8] The following poster, designed and distributed by the radical anarcho-syndicalist/socialist industrial labor union, Industrial Workers of the World (IWW), depicts the essence of the capitalist control of the state and the hierarchic structure of capitalist society based on the power of capital and the exploitation of labor (see Figure 3.2).

Beginning in the first two decades of the 20th century and continuing throughout the Great Depression and World War II, the U.S. state played a key role in safeguarding and further promoting the capitalist economy. With the entry of the United States into World War II, the American economy embarked on the road to full recovery, and thus soon became a powerful force on the world scene. Within a short period of time at the war's end, the American Empire emerged as the leading imperial power and became the dominant economic, political, and military force in the world. The postwar expansion of U.S. capital on a world scale thus resulted in the global expansion of the U.S. state; together, these developments came to express in the latter half of the 20th century the widening interests of U.S. capital and the state throughout the world.

Changes in the U.S. Class Structure in the Postwar Period

The unprecedented expansion of the U.S. economy in the postwar period prompted a similar process of growth and expansion in the U.S. labor force. The manufacturing sector grew as the size of the industrial working class grew during this period. This expansion on the domestic front continued until the early 1970s. During the decade of the 1970s, a number of factors (e.g., increasing global rivalry with other capitalist powers such as Japan and Germany) brought a major shift in production from the domestic front to the global sphere through a shift in the location of production from the United States to the rest of the world, especially the less-developed countries. The accelerated transfer of U.S. capital from the United States to the low-wage areas of the global economy began to have an enormous impact on the composition of the labor force structure, such that a process of decline in size of the manufacturing workforce in direct proportion to the decline in the manufacturing sector resulting from the

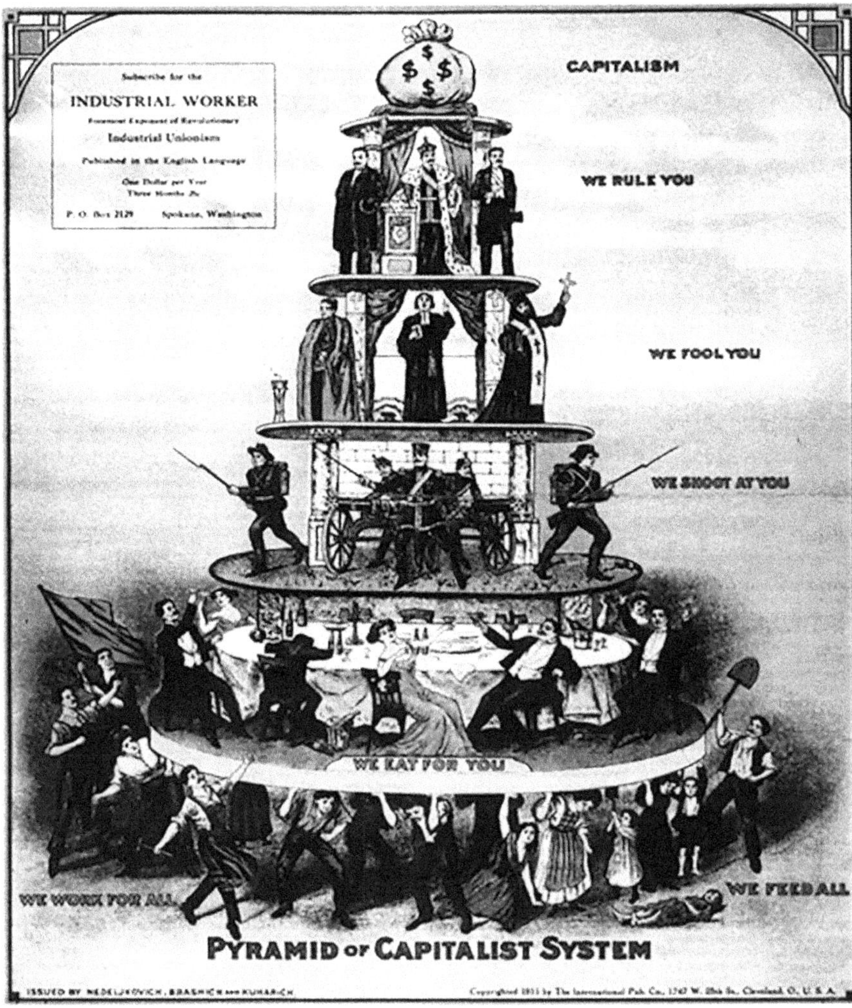

Figure 3.2 Pyramid of Capitalist System.
Source: Industrial Workers of the World (IWW), *The Industrial Worker* (Cleveland, OH: The International Pub. Co., 1911).

relocation of plants to overseas territories began to take place starting in the early 1970s. The consequences of this process of de-industrialization[9] of the United States are numerous, but the central dynamic of this has been the dislocation of the traditional manufacturing workforce, which has resulted in greater unemployment and underemployment together with a shift from manufacturing employment to service and other tertiary sectors of the economy that pay much lower wages than in manufacturing, hence bringing about a consequent drop in the standard of living of workers in the United States over the course of this period to the present.[10]

During the 50-year period from 1970 to 2020, the proportion of workers in manufacturing industry declined from 25.0 percent in 1970 to 20.7 percent in 1980, to 16.2 percent in 1990, to 13.1 percent in 2000, to 8.3 percent in 2009, to 7.9 percent in 2019, with projections to 7.3 percent in 2029.[11] However, a segment of the unemployed manufacturing workforce that was able to obtain employment in the private service sector accelerated the growth of this sector, such that the proportion of workers in this sector, relative to the total private labor force, increased from 67.3 percent in 1980 to 74.0 percent in 1990, to 77.8 percent in 2000, to 83.5 percent in 2010, and 83.6 percent in 2019.[12]

The shift in employment from the manufacturing to the service sector over the past five decades has resulted in continued decline in real wages of U.S. workers over this period, and this has greatly affected the living standards of workers in the United States and forced them to live on lower real incomes for the past several decades.[13]

Looking at data on earnings in private nonagricultural industries for the past several decades (1975–2019), we find that the average real weekly earnings of production and nonsupervisory workers have mostly declined during this period, especially during the recessions of 1974–1975, 1980, 1990, 2001, and 2008 (see Table 3.2).

The massive layoffs and dislocations prompted by the COVID-19 pandemic in 2020 exacerbated the decline in earnings of workers across many

Table 3.2 Earnings of Production and Nonsupervisory Employees, 1975–2019 (in Current and 1982–84 Dollars)[a]

	Average Weekly Earnings		
	Level		*Percent Change From Year Earlier*
Year	*Current Dollars*	*1982–84 Dollars*	*1982–84 Dollars*
1975	170.45	315.06	−3.4
1980	240.83	290.51	−5.8
1985	304.37	284.72	−1.3
1990	349.63	271.03	−1.8
1995	399.93	266.98	−0.6
2001	493.53	284.46	−0.1
2005	543.94	284.79	−0.6
2008	607.10	287.65	−1.0
2010	636.02	297.25	1.2
2015	708.70	305.72	2.4
2019	790.67	317.26	1.4

Source: Council of Economic Advisers, *Economic Report of the President 2021*, Table B-30, p. 494.

a In private nonagricultural industries.

industries and sent millions of workers into unemployment and poverty. Declining real wages, rising unemployment, growing indebtedness, inability to obtain affordable housing and health care, and a general decline in living standards of workers in the United States during the past several decades have led to increasing impoverishment of the working class, both in relative and absolute terms. This became especially critical during the COVID-19 pandemic in 2020, which threatened the very survival of millions of workers in providing their families adequate food and shelter to sustain life at the subsistence level. In a matter of few months from mid-March to July 2020, more than 56 million Americans filed for jobless claims due to the lockdown stemming from the Coronavirus outbreak, raising the national unemployment rate to 15 percent.[14] This dire situation facing working people in the United States in 2020–2021 especially hit hard racial and ethnic minorities, households headed by women, and the working poor in general, who suffered great losses due to income insecurity and inequality, in addition to the growing number of COVID-19 deaths among these vulnerable populations.

The Racial and Gender Divide in Income in the United States

The unequal distribution of income in the United States over the past century, especially the past several decades, has had a devastating effect on working-class households among racial and ethnic minorities and those headed by women. This is clearly evident in the racial/ethnic and gender wage ratio in earnings in the United States over the past several decades.

The Racial Wage Ratio in Earnings

Looking at the racial wage ratio in household income in the United States between 1982 and 2000, Edward N. Wolff reports that:

> while the average real income of non-Hispanic White households increased by 37 percent and the median by 13 percent, the former rose by only 23 percent for non-Hispanic Black households and the latter by 15 percent. As a result, the ratio of mean income slipped from 0.54 in 1982 to 0.48 in 2000, while the ratio of median income rose slightly, from 0.56 to 0.57.[15]

Moving forward, in looking at the period 1990 to 2020, we find that very little has changed in the share of Black and Hispanic income as percentage of White households during this period. While the earnings ratio for Black households was 58 percent that of Whites and for Hispanic households a bit higher at 63.5 percent that of Whites in 1990, the racial wage gap has remained between 58 percent and 65 percent for Blacks and 63 percent and 68 percent for Hispanics throughout the three decades from 1990 to 2020, with a small increase in the position of both groups vis-à-vis Whites by 2020 (see Table 3.3).

In 2007, the year prior to the "Great Recession" of 2008–2009, the median annual household income for Whites was $56,200, whereas for Blacks it was $33,700 and for Hispanics $39,300 (in 2013 U.S. dollars). By 2013, the median annual household income had dropped to $54,000 for Whites, to $30,000 for Blacks, and to $32,000 for Hispanics. This drop in household income was largely the result of the "Great Recession" and its devastating impact on working people, but the gap between White and non-White household income continued to persist during the post-recession period (see Figure 3.3).

Table 3.3 Money Income of Families: Median Annual Income by Race and Hispanic Origin, 1990 to 2020, Selected Years (in Current Dollars)

Year	*White*	*Black*	*Black as % of White*	*Hispanic*	*Hispanic as % of White*
1990	36,915	21,423	(58.0)	23,431	(63.5)
2000	53,029	33,676	(63.5)	34,442	(64.9)
2010	62,914	38,594	(61.3)	39,300	(62.5)
2020	88,123	57,476	(65.2)	59,976	(68.1)

Source: U.S. Census Bureau, *Historical Income Tables: Families*, Table F-7, https://www.census.gov/data/tables/time-series/demo/income-poverty/historical-income-families.html (accessed November 8, 2021).

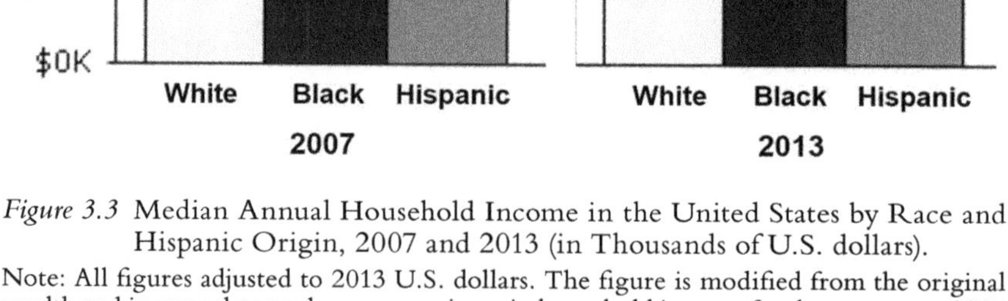

Figure 3.3 Median Annual Household Income in the United States by Race and Hispanic Origin, 2007 and 2013 (in Thousands of U.S. dollars).

Note: All figures adjusted to 2013 U.S. dollars. The figure is modified from the original wealth and income data to show comparisons in household income for the two years, 2007 and 2013. For a similar comparison of data on wealth distribution for the same years, see Figure 5.8 in Chapter 5 of this book.

Source: Edward N. Wolff, *A Century of Wealth in America* (Cambridge, MA: Harvard University Press, 2017) reported by G. William Domhoff in url: http://www2.ucsc.edu/whorulesamerica/power/wealth.html.

The Gender Wage Ratio in Earnings

When looking at the gender wage ratio and real earnings of full-time workers with median annual earnings between 1960 and 2018, the ratio between male and female workers was around 60 percent during the 1960s and 1970s and remained around 60 percent until 1980; it went up slightly to 65 percent in the mid-1980s and then to around 70 percent during the 1990s, climbing to 80 percent by 2015. The gender wage ratio of median full-time weekly workers was slightly higher during each of the comparable periods between 1980 and 2018, reaching 81.1 percent in 2018 (see Table 3.4).

While clearly women in general earn less than White men in the United States, it is also the case that women of all major racial/ethnic groups earn less than men of the same group, so that White women earn less than White men, Black women earn less than Black men, and Hispanic women earn less than Hispanic men, in addition to Black and Hispanic women earning less than White men. Given this, although White women continue to earn less than White men, Black and Hispanic women earn *much less* than White men and also less than men of their own racial/ethnic group. Data on median weekly earnings and gender earnings ratio for

Table 3.4 The Gender Wage Ratio and Real Earnings, Full-Time Workers, Median Annual and Weekly Earnings, 1955–2018 (in 2018 Dollars)

	Median Annual Earnings (2018 Dollars)			*Median Usual Weekly Earnings (2018 Dollars)*		
	Full-time, Year-Round Workers			*Full-time Weekly Workers*[a]		
Year	*Women*	*Men*	*Female-to-Male Earnings Ratio (%)*	*Women*	*Men*	*Female-to-Male Earnings Ratio (%)*
1955	n/a	n/a	63.9	n/a	n/a	n/a
1960	$24,235	$39,943	60.7	n/a	n/a	n/a
1965	$26,761	$44,658	59.9	n/a	n/a	n/a
1970	$30,807	$51,890	59.4	n/a	n/a	n/a
1975	$31,934	$54,293	58.8	n/a	n/a	n/a
1980	$32,580	$54,154	60.2	$585	$911	64.2
1985	$34,870	$53,999	64.6	$618	$909	68.0
1990	$37,041	$51,722	71.6	$646	$899	71.9
1995	$36,927	$51,699	71.4	$667	$883	75.5
2000	$40,157	$54,474	73.7	$720	$936	76.9
2005	$41,065	$53,347	77.0	$754	$930	81.1
2010	$42,577	$55,347	76.9	$771	$951	81.1
2015	$43,185	$54,282	79.6	$770	$950	81.1
2018	n/a	n/a	n/a	$789	$973	81.1

Source: Adopted from the Institute for Women's Policy Research, *Fact Sheet* #C478 (March 2019).

a Median weekly earnings data for full-time workers were not collected until 1979. Thus, no data is available for the years 1955 through 1975.

Table 3.5 Median Weekly Earnings and Gender Earnings Ratio for Full-Time Workers, 16 Years and Older by Race/Ethnic Background, 2018

	2018			
Racial/Ethnic Background	*Women*	*Men*	*Female Earnings as % of Male Earnings of Same Group*	*Female Earnings as % of White Male Earnings*
All Races/ Ethnicities	$789	$973	81.1	N/A
White	$817	$1,002	81.5	81.5
Black	$654	$735	89.0	65.3
Hispanic	$617	$720	85.7	61.6

Source: Institute for Women's Policy Research, *Fact Sheet* #C478 (March 2019).
Notes: Hispanic workers may be of any race. White and Black workers include Hispanics. Annual averages of median weekly earnings.

full-time workers by race/ethnic background for the latest year available (2018) show that while White women earned 81.5 percent of the earnings of White men, Black women earned only 65.3 percent of the earnings of White men and Hispanic women earned only 61.6 percent of the earnings of White men (see Table 3.4). However, to highlight the decisive impact of race on income, it should also be pointed out that Black and Hispanic women earn less than White women. Thus, in 2018 the median weekly earnings of full-time Black women workers ($654) was 80 percent of that of White women workers ($817) and the median weekly earnings of full-time Hispanic women workers ($617) was 75.5 percent of that of White women workers ($817) (see Table 3.5).

The women's movement in the 1980s and 1990s played an important role in the struggle to reduce the gender wage gap, such that steady progress was made during this period that elevated the position of full-time working women to reach 75 percent of the wages of men by century's end and to 81 percent by 2018.[16] However, when considering the gender earnings ratio for *all* workers, we find that the gap in earnings is much larger. This is because there are more women who are employed as part-time contingent workers and whose wages are much lower. Thus, in looking at the wages of *all* workers over a 15-year period (2001–2015), Stephen J. Rose and Heidi I. Hartmann at the Institute for Women's Policy Research in Washington, D.C., have found that "women workers' earnings were just 49 percent—less than half—of men's earnings, a wage gap of 51 percent in 2001–2015."[17] And many of these part-time workers were racial and ethnic minority women workers.

Despite the fact that there has been progress in narrowing the gender wage gap for full-time workers in the United States over the past several decades, when looking at percentage changes over the past four decades from 1979 to 2018, we see a steady decline in the rate of change,

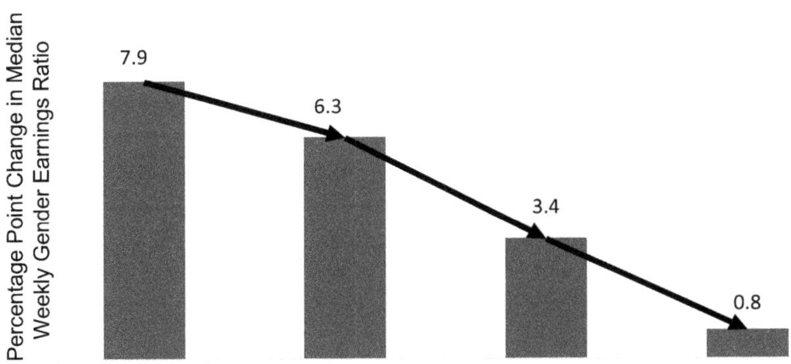

Figure 3.4 Declining Progress in Raising the Median Weekly Gender Earnings Ratio, 1979–2018 (Decade by Decade Percentage Point Change in the Gender Earnings Ratio for Full-Time Workers).
Source: Institute for Women's Policy Research, *Fact Sheet* #C478 (March 2019), p 2.

decade by decade, from 7.9 percent during the decade of 1979–1988 to 6.3 percent during the decade of 1989–1998, to 3.4 percent during the decade of 1999–2008, to 0.8 percent during the decade of 2009–2018 (see Figure 3.4).

Given the declining progress in closing the gender earnings gap based on median weekly and annual earnings in raising the gender earnings ratio for full-time workers, researchers at the Institute for Women's Policy Research project state that:

> If the pace of change in the annual earnings ratio were to continue at the same rate as it has since 1984, it would take until 2059 for women and men to reach earnings parity, and substantially longer for women of color. Black women's median annual earnings would reach parity with White men's in 2119, and Hispanic women's in 2224![18]

Decline in the Standard of Living of the Working Class and Poverty in the United States

A key factor in the decline in purchasing power and living standard for workers in the United States has been a rise in the rate of surplus value (or value-added by workers) and a consequent drop in labor's share in production over the years.[19] Thus, while both production and productivity per labor hour increased continuously during the postwar period, labor's share drastically fell from 40 percent in 1950 to 25 percent in 1984, to 18 percent in 2000, to 14.7 percent in 2011. At the same time, the rate of surplus value in U.S. manufacturing industry quadrupled since 1950, from 150 percent in 1950 to 302 percent in 1984, to 453 percent in 2000, to 580 percent in 2011.[20] By 2020, it had surpassed 650 percent! This, together with favorable government tax policies toward large corporations, has resulted in record corporate profits.

Looking at the past five decades, from 1970 to 2020, we find that total corporate profits rose from $80 billion in 1970 to $290 billion in 1985, to $730 billion in 2000, to $2.2 trillion in 2015, reaching $2.3 trillion in 2020 (see Table 4.3 in Chapter 4).[21] Even taking inflation into account, net corporate profits have surged during this period to unprecedented levels.

The immense wealth that has been accumulating in the coffers of the owners of capital on the one hand and the continued drop in workers' real wages and living standard on the other has accelerated the polarization of the main classes in American society—labor and capital—and crystallized the growing gap in the distribution of wealth and income in the United States.[22]

As the concentration and centralization of wealth and income moved ahead full speed during this period, the continuing class polarization has widened the gap between labor and capital still further and placed the workers into a desperate situation, living paycheck-to-paycheck if they are lucky enough to have a job, facing permanent unemployment and underemployment, indebtedness, economic uncertainty, and fear in securing the basic necessities of life such as food, housing, and health care for themselves and their families.

Finding themselves at such dire straits, a growing number of workers have been forced to join the ranks of the poverty population which has become a permanent fixture of contemporary American society. Persons below the poverty level increased in number from 29 million in 1980 to 33.6 million in 1990 dropping to 31.6 million in 2000 and then surging to 46.3 million in 2010 at the height of the "Great Recession" (accounting for 15 percent of the total population in 2010), and dropping to 34 million nearly a decade later in 2019, accounting for 10.5 percent of the total population. Considering people living below 125 percent of the poverty level, we find that in 1980 there were 40.7 million people in this category, while in 1990 it had climbed to 44.8 million, in 2000 dropped slightly to 43.6 million, and in 2010 it surged to 60.7 million during the "Great Recession" (accounting for nearly 20 percent of the total population), then dropping to 46.5 million (or 14 percent of the total population) in 2019 (see Table 3.6).[23]

Looking at the gravity of the impact of the "Great Recession" on racial and ethnic minorities, of the 46.3 million people below the poverty level in 2010, 31.1 million were Whites, 10.7 million were African Americans, and 13.5 million were Hispanic Americans. In proportionate terms, however, only 13 percent of Whites were below the poverty level, while for African Americans and Hispanic Americans the rate was 27.4 percent and 26.5 percent, respectively, i.e., more than double the rate for Whites. The pattern remained practically the same nearly a decade later in 2019, as the poverty

Table 3.6 People below Poverty Level by Race and Hispanic Origin, and below 125 Percent of Poverty Level, 1990–2019 (in Numbers and Percent)

	Number of Persons below Poverty Level (1,000)				*Percent of Persons below Poverty Level*				*Below 125 Percent of Poverty Level*	
Year	*All Races*	*White*	*Black*	*Hispanic*	*All Races*	*White*	*Black*	*Hispanic*	*Number (1,000)*	*% of Total Population*
1990	33,585	22,326	9,837	6,006	13.5	10.7	31.9	28.1	44,837	18.0
1995	36,425	24,423	9,872	8,574	13.8	11.2	29.3	30.3	48,761	18.5
2000	31,581	21,645	7,982	7,747	11.3	9.5	22.5	21.5	43,612	15.6
2005	36,950	24,872	9,168	9,368	12.6	10.6	24.9	21.8	49,327	16.8
2010	46,343	31,083	10,746	13,522	15.1	13.0	27.4	26.5	60,669	19.8
2015	43,123	28,566	10,020	12,133	13.5	11.6	24.1	21.4	56,912	17.9
2019	33,984	22,512	8,073	9,545	10.5	9.1	18.8	15.7	46,538	14.3

Source: ProQuest Statistical Abstract of the United States 2022 Edition, Table 753.

rate for Whites was 9.1 percent, while it was 18.8 percent for African Americans and 15.7 percent for Hispanic Americans—again, at or near double the rates for racial and ethnic minorities as that of Whites (see Table 3.6).[24]

Clearly, a large segment of the working class is seriously affected by poverty, and the effects of racism have compounded the deteriorating situation of working people of color who have come to suffer disproportionately from the increasing impoverishment of the working class as a whole in the United States in recent decades. The Coronavirus Pandemic in 2020 has made the situation worse for most working-class Americans, as high levels of unemployment due to the lockdown during much of 2020 and 2021 increased poverty levels, leading to some 50 million Americans (including more than 15 million children) suffering from food insecurity and facing hunger, as millions have desperately waited in car lines across the nation for more than five hours at a time for a box of food from Food Banks to feed their families!

Class Conflict and Class Struggles in the United States

Responding to their deteriorating living conditions and to economic uncertainty threatening their jobs and their very existence, workers in America have resorted to various forms of resistance and struggle. In many industries across the nation, workers have engaged in strikes, walkouts, protests, and other forms of defiance to show that they can no longer be taken for granted as subservient tools of capital and capitalist profit.

The limited but real victories achieved in rank-and-file struggles of the past several decades are a beginning for longer-lasting, protracted struggles that require a much more resilient nationwide effort to unleash labor militancy on an unprecedented scale, so that the early decades of the 21st century would once again become a period of militant labor struggles at the grassroots level.

Throughout the 20th century, workers in many industries across the United States engaged in a large number of strikes, walkouts, and other forms of protest. Many of the rank-and-file struggles were in fact for the very right to strike—an inalienable right of workers' collective might. This period saw intensified labor struggles in confronting the power of capital at the point of production. Increasingly conscious of their interests, more and more workers began to take the initiative on the rungs below to exert their collective strength and fight back to protect their hard-won rights.[25]

While the development of class-consciousness among the working class is not an automatic process, it *is* nonetheless a direct outcome of the conditions of work and life experienced by millions of workers under capitalism. This process, once fully developed, draws workers into the class struggle—a struggle which is *political* in nature and is waged against the ruling capitalist class and the entire institutional structure of the capitalist system, including the capitalist state.[26]

Historically, the central facilitators of the development of class consciousness and class struggle, beyond the narrow economic battles waged through the instrumentality of trade unions at the point of production, have always been workers' political organizations and parties, that is, organizations of workers that have articulated and advanced the class interests of the working class in a broader political context, with the aim of taking state power away from the capitalists so that the state would come to represent the needs and aspirations of working people throughout the land.

The longer history of capitalist development in Europe led at an earlier period to the development of radical workers' organizations of different political persuasions—from anarcho-syndicalist to socialist to communist as well as traditional reformist—as manifested in the Paris Commune, the First International, and later the Bolshevik Revolution, among others. Various radical anarcho-syndicalist, socialist, communist, and other labor organization and parties thus have their origins in these and other struggles of the working class against capitalism in Europe from the late 18th to the early 20th centuries.[27]

In the United States, the later development of capitalism delayed by a century the emergence of a labor movement to struggle against capitalism, but did result in the formation of similar, parallel organizations informed by the collective historic experiences of labor in Europe and elsewhere that span over two centuries. By the mid-19th century, the U.S. working class had all the signs of developing into a mature labor movement ready to take on the capitalist system that controlled and exploited them.[28] Playing a critical role in the Civil War and in the victory over the slave system that blocked further development of labor's interests in the fight against capitalism in the North, the U.S. working class scored many victories in protracted struggles against their bosses. These struggles resulted in the formation and development of important labor organizations in the late 19th and early 20th centuries; the Knights of Labor, the IWW, the Socialist and Communist Parties, and numerous other politically oriented radical unions and parties were all the outcome of this unfolding process of maturing working-class consciousness and class struggles that labor began to wage during this period of turmoil and unrest in the United States.[29]

Similar struggles during the Great Depression, led by communists within the organized labor movement, scored important victories in organizing efforts through unions and political action. The Congress of Industrial Organizations (CIO), for example, worked to improve the condition of labor, while at the same time helped to advance working-class consciousness among a growing number of workers in the midst of a great economic catastrophe of rarely seen proportions.[30] "What made the difference in the thirties," writes Gil Green, a veteran labor organizer:

> was not only the greater depth of economic and social crisis, but the preparatory work before the conditions of upsurge had fully matured

> in order to bring them to fruition. The Communists and other left-wing militants slowly and methodically began to organize. . . . By their example they proved that organization was possible, and by their policies they helped bring about the necessary unity.[31]

The postwar repression of labor, which through the McCarthyist witch-hunts and expulsions of leftists from the major unions such as the CIO and the UAW, effectively set back the labor movement by many years and had a devastating impact on labor's political power. It successfully neutralized the influence of organized leftist groups on the labor movement and altered its direction in the conservative 1950s—a predicament from which U.S. labor was never able to fully recover to this day.

The class-collaborationist leadership and policies of the sanitized postwar AFL-CIO officialdom which, in the absence of a strong socialist or communist presence in the union, came to define the nature of "business unionism" wedded to reformist capitalist party-politics rallied behind the Democratic Party are what distinguishes the current state of the U.S. labor movement from its counterparts in Europe and elsewhere in the advanced capitalist world. The decisive current presence and role of communist, socialist, labor, and other workers' political parties in Europe (and their absence or extreme weakness in the United States) is the chief factor that explains the differential position and prospects of labor in Europe and the United States in recent decades. The existence and strength of an independent workers' political party is, therefore, of crucial importance to labor and the labor movement in its political (class) struggle against capitalism and the capitalist state.

Things are beginning to change on this front, however. There are renewed calls to establish a new independent workers' party, while other existing older parties and organizations on the left are beginning to mobilize their forces and energies with increasing vigor. As the transformation of the world economy continues and as the globalization of U.S. capital further weakens the U.S. domestic economy and plunges it into another economic crisis in the coming years, hence forcing workers to experience a further decline in their standard of living, there will be increasing pressure from below to mobilize and fight back. The critical factor in this regard will increasingly become the central role of an independent workers' party which will have to take up the task of leading U.S. labor in the class struggle that will surely intensify and spread in the years ahead.

Notes

1 Charles Beard, *An Economic Interpretation of the Constitution of the United States* (New York: Macmillan, 1962); Michael Parenti, *Democracy for the Few*, 9th ed. (Boston, MA; Wadsworth, 2011).

2 Howard Zinn, *A People's History of the United States,* Reissue ed. (New York: Harper Perennial Modern Classics, 2015).

3 Richard O. Boyer and Herbert M. Morais, *Labor's Untold Story*, 3rd ed. (New York: United Electrical, Radio, and Machine Workers of America, 1984).
4 Albert J. Szymanski, *Class Structure: A Critical Perspective* (New York: Praeger, 1983).
5 Berch Berberoglu, *Class and Class Conflict in the Age of Globalization* (Lanham, MD: Lexington Books, 2009).
6 Victor Perlo, *Super Profits and Crises: Modern U.S. Capitalism* (New York: International Publishers, 1988).
7 Brandon Weber, *Class War, USA: Dispatches from Workers' Struggles in American History* (Chicago, IL: Haymarket Books, 2018).
8 Albert J. Szymanski, *The Capitalist State and the Politics of Class* (Cambridge, MA: Winthrop, 1978).
9 Barry Bluestone, *The Deindustrialization of America: Plant Closings, Community Abandonment, and the Dismantling of Basic Industry* (New York: Basic Books, 1984). See also Brian Philipps, *Global Production and Domestic Decay: Plant Closings in the U.S.* (New York: Garland, 1998).
10 See Bennett Harrison and Barry Bluestone, *The Great U-Turn: Corporate Restructuring and the Polarizing of America* (New York: Basic Books, 1988).
11 U.S. Council of Economic Advisers, *Economic Report of the President 2006,* Table B-46, p. 336; U.S. Bureau of Labor Statistics, Employment Projections Program, https://www.bls.gov/emp/tables/employment-by-major-industry-sector.htm Table 2.1. Last Modified Date: September 1, 2020.
12 U.S. Council of Economic Advisers, *Economic Report of the President 2006,* Table B-46, p. 336 and *Economic Report of the President 2021*, Table B-29, p. 492.
13 See U.S. Council of Economic Advisers, *Economic Report of the President, 2006*, Table B-47, p. 338 and *Economic Report of the President 2021*, Table B-30, p. 494.
14 U.S. Department of Labor, Bureau of Labor Statistics, 2020.
15 Edward N. Wolff, "Changes in Household Wealth in the 1980s and 1990s in the United States," *Working Paper No. 407* (May 2004), p. 13.
16 Institute for Women's Policy Research, *Fact Sheet,* No. C478 (March 2019), p. 1.
17 Stephen J. Rose and Heidi I. Hartmann, *Still a Man's Labor Market: The Slowly Narrowing Gender Wage Gap* (Washington, DC: Institute for Women's Policy Research, 2019). https://iwpr.org/publications/still-mans-labor-market/ (accessed March 2019).
18 Institute for Women's Policy Research. November 2017. "Women's Median Earnings as a Percentage of Men's, 1984-2017 (Full-time, Year-Round Workers) with Projections for Pay Equity, by Race/Ethnicity," IWPR Quick Figures #Q075 https://iwpr.org/publications/womens-median-earnings-1984-2017/ (accessed March 2019).
19 Perlo, *Super Profits and Crises: Modern U.S. Capitalism*, pp. 35–54.
20 Perlo, *Super Profits and Crises*, Appendix, Table 2A, p. 512; the rates for the year 2000 and 2011 were calculated by the author, with the assistance of Jason King. See Berch Berberoglu (ed.), *The Global Capitalist Crisis and Its Aftermath* (Burlington, VT: Ashgate, 2014), Figure 2.9a and 2.9b, p. 49.
21 U.S. Council of Economic Advisers, *Economic Report of the President 2021*, Table B-54, p. 519.
22 Denny Braun, *The Rich Get Richer: The Rise of Income Inequality in the United States and the World* (Chicago, IL: Nelson-Hall Publishers, 1991); Frank Ackerman, Neva R. Goodwin, Laurie Dougherty, and Kevin Gallagher (eds)., *The Political Economy of Inequality* (Washington, DC: Island Press, 2000); Stephen M. Caliendo, *Inequality in America* (Boulder, CO: Westview Press, 2015); and Edward N. Wolf, *A Century of Wealth in America* (Cambridge, MA: The Belknap Press of Harvard University Press, 2017).

23 U.S. Bureau of the Census, *Statistical Abstract of the United States, 2007*, p. 458; *ProQuest Statistical Abstract of the United States 2021 Online Edition*, Table 747.
24 U.S. Bureau of the Census, *Statistical Abstract of the United States, 2007,* p. 458; *ProQuest Statistical Abstract of the United States 2021 Online Edition*, Table 747.
25 Rick Fantasia, *Cultures of Solidarity: Consciousness, Action, and Contemporary American Workers* (Berkeley: University of California Press, 1988).
26 Berch Berberoglu, *Political Sociology in a Global Era: An Introduction to the State and Society* (New York: Paradigm, 2013).
27 Ira Katznelson and Al Zolberg (eds.), *Working Class Formation: Nineteenth-century Patterns in Western Europe and the United States* (Princeton, NJ: Princeton University Press, 1986).
28 Boyer and Morais, *Labor's Untold Story.*
29 Boyer and Morais, *Labor's Untold Story.*
30 Gil Green, *What's Happening to Labor* (New York: International Publishers, 1976), pp. 27–51; Judith Stepan-Norris and Maurice Zeitlin, "'Who Gets the Bird?' or, How the Communists Won Power and Trust in America's Unions," *American Sociological Review* 54, no. 4 (August 1989), pp. 505–523.
31 Green, *What's Happening to Labor*, pp.178–179.

4 The American Century

The Postwar Rise of the American Empire

There are two major turning points in the postwar history of the United States: one that marked the rise to world prominence of the United States at the conclusion of World War II, when the emerging American Empire came to lead the world in the immediate postwar period, and the other that signaled the end of "the American Century" less than three decades later, when the United States descended into an irreversible decline in the aftermath of the oil crisis in the early 1970s, compounded by the U.S. defeat in Vietnam and the economic slump that followed in the mid-1970s. Thus, the period from 1945 to the mid-1970s has been characterized as the heyday of America's dominant position in the world, which came to a definitive end in the early years of the new millennium. The September 11, 2001 attacks, the subsequent wars in Afghanistan and Iraq in 2001 and 2003 onward, and the "Great Recession" of 2008–2009 brought to an end the global prominence of the United States, and with it the gradual decline of the American Empire from the mid-1970s to the end of the second decade of the new millennium and continuing—spanning a period of over four decades, as of this writing in early 2022.

In this chapter, I examine the rise of the American Empire, the role of the U.S. state in promoting the development and expansion of U.S. capital abroad in the postwar period to the new millennium and beyond, and increasing monopoly control in the U.S. and global economy that led to the emergence of a new set of irreversible contradictions in the late 20th-century and early 21st-century U.S. and global capitalism.

The Rise of U.S. Capital onto the World Scene

The origins of U.S. capitalist expansion on a world scale go back to the early 20th century. Initially, U.S. direct investment abroad amounted to less than $1 billion, reaching a mere $1.6 billion by 1908; even by 1920, total U.S. direct investment abroad came to less than $4 billion.[1] But the post-World War I prosperity, which ushered in the "Roaring Twenties," set U.S. capital on its way to a prominent position within the global economy starting in the 1920s.

Although the Great Depression of the 1930s dramatically slowed down this expansion and greatly affected the rate of growth of the U.S. economy,

DOI: 10.4324/9781003282105-4

both domestically and globally, U.S. entry into World War II and the accompanying wartime contracts provided by the U.S. state to the emerging U.S. transnational corporations in the early 1940s once again propped up the U.S. economy and turned it into a giant productive machine with extensive operations in distant corners of the world. Thus, by 1950, U.S. foreign direct investments reached $12 billion.[2]

With the decline of the British Empire and the devastation of rival European powers during World War II, the United States clearly emerged as the leading center of the capitalist world and came to establish its dominant position as a global superpower. U.S. control and domination of the global economy and policy in the postwar period went virtually unchallenged for nearly three decades, as both Western Europe and Japan as well as most underdeveloped peripheral regions of the world came under direct U.S. economic and/or political-military hegemony.[3]

During the period from 1950 to 2020, U.S. foreign direct investment increased immensely, climbing from $12 billion in 1950 to $75 billion in 1970, to $617 billion in 1990, to $5.5 trillion in 2010, to $9.4 trillion in 2020, the latest year for which we currently have data (see Table 4.1).

Table 4.1 Growth of U.S. Private Investment Abroad, 1950–2020 (in Billions of Dollars)

		Value of Assets[a]	
Year	*Total*[b]	*Long Term*	*Direct*
1950	19.0	17.5	11.8
1955	29.1	26.8	19.4
1960	49.4	44.4	31.8
1965	81.1	70.9	49.3
1970	118.8	104.2	75.5
1975	237.6	174.9	124.2
1980	516.6	298.1	215.4
1985	821.8	346.8	232.7
1990	1,920.0	959.3	616.7
1995	3,225.1	2,089.4	885.5
2000	6,025.2	3,957.1	1,531.6
2005	9,743.1	6,527.9	2,453.9
2010	18,116.0	7,160.0	5,486.0
2015	20,989.0	9,570.0	7,057.0
2020	29,711.0	14,606.0	9,405.0

Sources: U.S. Department of Commerce, *Survey of Current Business* (monthly) annual articles on U.S. foreign investment; U.S. Bureau of the Census, *Statistical Abstract of the United States: 1968*, p. 791; *1978*; p. 864; *1987*, p. 779; *2006*, p. 823; *2012*, p. 796; ProQuest *Statistical Abstract of the U.S.* 2022 Online Edition, Table 1306.

a At year end and at current cost, excluding financial derivatives.

b In addition to direct investments, the total figure represents such items as foreign dollar bonds, foreign corporate stocks, and claims reported by U.S. banks (these are all forms of "portfolio" investments).

Together with all other types of private investment, total U.S. private investments abroad surpassed $29.7 trillion in 2020.[4]

U.S. economic expansion abroad during the postwar period was a logical outcome of the process of capitalist development in the United States for nearly a century; it also coincided with changes in the global balance of forces that permitted U.S. capital to enter the world stage.[5] Thus, while the decline of British and more generally West European power at the conclusion of World War II provided new opportunities for U.S. capital in previously colonized peripheral regions of the world, it also opened up vast areas of economic expansion within Western Europe itself through the Marshall Plan (the rebuilding of Western Europe through extensive U.S. aid).[6]

The Marshall Plan provided an unprecedented impetus for U.S. corporate expansion in Western Europe in the postwar period. It effectively subsidized and promoted the growth and development of U.S. capital in Western Europe and set the stage for subsequent capitalist expansion throughout the rest of the world.[7] Michael Tanzer states that:

> [s]ince war-torn Europe and Japan were heavily dependent upon U.S. assistance for reconstruction, the [U.S.] oil companies and the U.S. government used this opportunity to virtually ram American-controlled oil down the throats of the world to replace coal. Thus, Walter Levy, head of the Marshall Plan's oil division, and previously an economist for Mobil, noted in 1949 that "without ECA [the Marshall Plan] American oil business in Europe would already have been shot to pieces," and commented that "ECA does not believe that Europe should save dollars or even foreign exchange by driving American oil from the European market." Some $2 billion of total Marshall Plan assistance of $13 billion was for oil imports, while the Marshall Plan blocked projects for European crude oil production and helped American oil companies to gain control of Europe's refineries.[8]

Similarly, the establishment by U.S. capital of large-scale production, distribution, and communication networks on the continent strengthened the hand of the United States in Western Europe and thereby helped U.S. business dominate the West European economies throughout the postwar period. Thus, U.S. direct investment in Western Europe increased from a mere $1.7 billion in 1950 to $6.6 billion in 1960, to $25 billion in 1970, to $96 billion in 1980; by the early 21st century, U.S. direct investment in Europe had climbed to $2 trillion in 2010 and $3.7 trillion in 2020.[9] This expansion by U.S. capital was accompanied by an infusion of other investments into Canada, Australia, Japan, and less-developed countries, which, together with all other investments, including those in Europe, surpassed $6.1 trillion in 2020.[10] Europe alone accounted for more than half of all U.S. direct investments in the world in 2020, indicating the region's central role in the global operations of the U.S. corporations, especially in the most recent stage of the latter's postwar expansion throughout the world.

Whereas total U.S. foreign direct investment from 1960 to 1970 more than doubled, from $31.8 billion in 1960 to $75.5 billion in 1970, it nearly tripled during the 1970s, reaching $215.4 billion in 1980; by 2000, it had reached $1.5 trillion (see Table 4.1). And while petroleum and manufacturing investments accounted for the same proportion of the total, at $11 billion each in 1960, and petroleum investments roughly doubled twice during the following two decades, reaching $19.8 billion in 1970, $47 billion in 1980, and then $105 billion in 2000, manufacturing investments nearly tripled twice during this same period, reaching $31 billion in 1970, $89 billion in 1980, and $344 billion in 2000.[11]

More significantly, while total aggregate investment dollars in these sectors continued to flow into the developed capitalist countries (primarily Canada and Western Europe), the manufacturing sector of both developed and less-developed countries received a disproportionate share of total investments, far surpassing those in the petroleum industry throughout this period. Thus, investments in manufacturing increased from $9.2 billion in 1960 to $25.6 billion in 1970, to $71.4 billion in 1980, to $254 billion in 2000 in the developed capitalist countries, and from $1.9 billion in 1960 to $5.5 billion in 1970, to $17.7 billion in 1980, to $89.7 billion in 2000 in the less-developed countries.[12] Moreover, these investments were concentrated in few key countries within each region. In the developed capitalist world, Canada, Britain, Germany, the Netherlands, and France accounted for the bulk of these investments; in the less-developed capitalist periphery, Brazil, Mexico, and Singapore accounted for the bulk of these investments.

Historically, in the earlier stages of capitalist development, imperial investments have generally tended to be concentrated in the raw materials sector. And this was true for the United States up until the early 1960s. During the period since 1960, a shift in emphasis from raw materials to manufacturing investments has taken place, and the manufacturing sector has clearly emerged as *the* major category of U.S. direct investment abroad.[13]

Focusing on the less-developed countries, we see that in 1960, U.S. foreign raw materials investments amounted to $7 billion while manufacturing investments totaled less than $2 billion. However, from the early 1960s on, the relative share of the raw materials sector began to decline significantly as manufacturing investments began to rise very rapidly. This trend began to take effect during the 1960s and especially since the early 1970s, when the relative share of raw materials investments declined from 60.7 percent of the total in 1960 to 12.1 percent in 2000, while the share of manufacturing investments rose from 17 percent of the total in 1960 to 27.6 percent in 2000. This was accompanied by a major increase in the amount of financial investments, which rose from $1.5 billion in 1970 to $166.7 billion in 2000, reaching 35.7 percent of all U.S. direct investments in the less-developed countries in 2000.[14]

These data have clearly shown a shift in U.S. direct investments in the less-developed countries from raw materials to manufacturing (and financial) investments during the last three decades of the 20th century. As has been the case in the developed capitalist countries for a long time, a number of less-developed countries have reached a stage of economic development where manufacturing investments now represent the single largest category of U.S. foreign direct investment in these countries.

In line with this process of expansion in manufacturing investments in Western Europe, Canada, and some regions of the less-developed periphery, U.S. transnational capital has made inroads in acquiring an increasing number of local corporations in these regions in an attempt to reduce or eliminate any resistance to their monopoly of the production, distribution, and accumulation process. Thus, we have seen a growing number of U.S. corporate takeovers of prominent European, Japanese, Canadian, Brazilian, and other firms in steel, auto, aerospace, electronics, communications, banking, and other sectors of the world economy over the past several decades.

With the infusion of large sums of investment into Western Europe beginning in the 1960s, U.S.-based transnationals obtained a dominant position in the European computer and electronics industries by the end of the decade, producing 80 percent of the computers, 95 percent of the integrated circuits, and 50 percent of the semiconductors.[15] Throughout the 1970s, the centralization of capital in Western Europe, Canada, and Japan (under U.S. majority ownership and control) intensified, as U.S. firms in other sectors of the economy expanded their operations in a bid to monopolize them as well. Thus, by the late 1970s, U.S. foreign direct investment in West Germany reached a predominant position in oil refining (80 percent), glass and cement (54 percent), foods (54 percent), and electrical machinery (51 percent). It also obtained a strong position in iron and metals (50 percent), plastic and rubber (48 percent), pulp, paper, and boards (40 percent), automobiles (37 percent), and chemicals (33 percent) as well as in a number of other sectors at various rates.[16] The United States maintained a prominent position in these investments as the leading country in control of the largest share of the total. As of the late 1970s, among West Germany's 30 largest corporations were nine foreign subsidiaries, of which six (Exxon, General Motors [GM], Ford, International Business Machines [IBM], Texaco, and Mobil Oil) were U.S. owned. Between 1961 and 1978, about 38 percent of all new foreign direct investment in West Germany was from the United States. In Britain, U.S. transnationals obtained an even better position than in West Germany. In 1977, about 110 of Britain's 500 largest nonfinancial corporations were foreign owned, and two-thirds of the total capital invested in Britain by these corporations was controlled by U.S. and Canadian firms.[17]

In Japan in 1970, of the $7 billion in total foreign assets, the U.S. share was between 60 percent and 70 percent. U.S. firms accounted for 477 of the 776 foreign companies operating in Japan.[18] In the early 1970s, IBM controlled about 70 percent of Japan's computer market through a wholly owned subsidiary National Cash Register Company (Japan). In the petroleum industry, foreign capital, predominantly U.S. capital, controlled over half the Japanese market, while the company with the biggest sales of petroleum products in Japan, Nippon Oil Company, was in partnership with the U.S. giant Caltex. By the end of 1971, U.S. capital had control over the supply of 80 percent of Japanese imports of crude oil. And in agriculture, United Fruit Company moved in late 1971 to raise its holding in the Far East Fruit Company (a joint venture) from 44 percent to 78 percent.[19] Finally, responding to the expansion of the Japanese car industry into the U.S. market, U.S. car manufacturers, such as GM and Chrysler, moved to buy into the Japanese motor vehicle industry, where GM tied up with Isuzu and Chrysler with Mitsubishi, both capturing over one-third of the stock of these companies, while Ford captured 25 percent of the stock of Mazda. Thus, throughout the 1970s, an increasing number of U.S. companies expanded into various branches of Japanese industry (e.g., steel, electronics, high technology) in an effort to control competitors at the source, while at the same time effecting protectionist measures through high tariffs to seal the U.S. market against the influx of massive imports from rival firms.[20]

In Canada, by the mid-1970s foreign capital controlled 54 percent of the manufacturing sector, including 69 percent of the electrical products industry, 73 percent of the chemical industry, 92 percent of the petroleum and coal industry, 67 percent of nonelectrical machinery, and 40 percent of paper and related products. U.S.-controlled companies accounted for about 75 percent of the total assets of all foreign-controlled corporations.[21]

In Brazil in the late 1970s, foreign firms (mostly U.S. firms) accounted for the production of 60 percent of heavy machinery, 80 percent of radio and television sets, 90 percent of pharmaceuticals, 95 percent of autos, and 100 percent of tire and rubber products; the situation is similar in a number of other less-developed countries.[22]

The penetration of U.S. capital into Western Europe, Canada, Japan, and selected less-developed countries in the 1970s resulted in the further centralization of local capital in the hands of U.S. transnationals, effecting greater control over these crucial markets as well as protecting the U.S. market from its competitors, while turning the West European, Japanese, Canadian, and Third World economies into appendages of a world economy dominated by the U.S. monopolies. In this way, the U.S. transnationals succeeded by the late 1970s in dominating the world's production, trade, and financial networks. This penetration and domination of the global economy by the U.S. transnationals in the postwar period set the stage for the prominence of U.S. imperialism across the world in the latter half of the 20th century through the 1980s and 1990s.

To facilitate its economic objectives in Western Europe, U.S. capital utilized the powers of the U.S. state to establish a permanent presence there through a military occupation force bolstered by the North Atlantic Treaty Organization (NATO) and other instruments of imperial power and domination that the United States set up to exert its global hegemony.[23] In this way, Europe was effectively turned into an outpost of the rising American Empire at the service of U.S. capital now operating on a global scale. Thus, during the immediate postwar period in the late 1940s and early 1950s, the United States rapidly established its dominant position in the world political economy and groomed itself as the leading global superpower exerting control and influence throughout much of the capitalist world through the end of the 20th century and into the 21st century.

The Role of the U.S. State in Promoting the Global Expansion of U.S. Capital

The massive nature of U.S. transnational corporate expansion abroad and the hundreds of billions of investment dollars tied up in distant lands during the past several decades have led the U.S. state to play a more active role in promoting the global expansion of U.S. capital and a more aggressive military role in foreign policy in order to protect U.S. transnational interests abroad. An important aspect of the state's supportive role toward capital in this process of global expansion was the close relationship between capital and the state resulting from the granting to U.S. corporations of lucrative government contracts for war production during World War II. Thus, by 1944, government purchases of goods and services were seven times greater than they had been in 1939. With the onset of the Cold War after the end of World War II, this relationship grew throughout the postwar period. More specifically, in 1958 military purchases accounted for 93.7 percent of the output of the aircraft industry, 60.7 percent of the ships and boats built, 38.5 percent of transportation equipment production, 38 percent of the output of radio and communications equipment industry, 20.9 percent of electrical machinery, 20.1 percent of instruments, 13.3 percent of primary metals production, and 10.4 percent of petroleum output.[24] Focusing on the industrial-commercial electronics industry, we find that:

> 40 percent of all computers installed up to 1959 were purchased directly by the military or by the weapons industry with government funds. In terms of dollar sales, military purchases were even more significant than the 40 percent figure indicates, since they mainly involved large computers. And in one sense, the entire computer market can be traced to the military, since military requirements financed and directed most of the research and development.
>
> What is true for computers applies equally to other large segments of the industrial-commercial electronics market, such as test and measurement equipment and industrial control instruments. Together with computers, these items make up 65 percent of the industrial market. . . .
>
> Altogether then, indirect and direct military demand may account for close to 70 percent of the total output of the $14-billion-a-year

> electronics industry. This is just the reverse of the market situation in 1950, when consumer products possessed over 60 percent of the market and military products about 20 percent. Since then consumer sales have increased only about $500 million while military sales have increased more than $7 billion.[25]

Clearly, it was through such increases in military purchases that a substantial portion of the postwar U.S. economic growth was sustained. Thus, as Paul A. Baran and Paul M. Sweezy point out, "the difference between the deep stagnation of the 1930s and the relative prosperity of the 1950s is fully accounted for by the vast military outlays of the 50s" as the U.S. state came to play a critical role in the growth and development of capitalism in the United States during this crucial period of the rise to world prominence of U.S. monopoly capital.[26] By the mid-1960s, U.S. big business became thoroughly transformed into what President Dwight D. Eisenhower had earlier called "the military-industrial complex": 20 percent to 30 percent of the annual sales of major electronics firms like RCA, Magnavox, Philco, Sylvania, Motorola, Westinghouse, and General Electric were in the military-space field; others, like Raytheon, Lear, and General Precision Equipment were selling over 80 percent of their output to the military.[27] Of the 500 largest industrial corporations in the United States in the mid-1960s:

> *at least* 205 [were] significantly involved in military production, either through their primary industry of production, through diversification into the defense sector, or through military research and development contracts. If we exclude from the top 500 the large number of food, apparel, and tobacco firms, then military production involves about 50 percent of the major firms in the economy.[28]

It is in this context that the U.S. state through its military might became the leading political force to expand the American Empire in support of the global expansion of U.S. capital first in postwar Europe through the Marshall Plan and the NATO as well as the Truman Doctrine and the Central Treaty Organization (CENTO) in the Middle East and other political and military pacts across the world on behalf of U.S. transnational capital in its effort to expand the American Empire on a global scale. Thus, hundreds of U.S. military bases were established across the globe to impose onto the world the political and military will of the United States as the premier imperialist power in the postwar period to the end of the 20th century and beginning of the 21st century.[29] By 2020, the American Empire had some 800 military bases in 80 countries and territories across the world, including 174 in Germany, 113 in Japan, 83 in South Korea, 50 in Italy, 47 in Guam, 37 in Puerto Rico, 27 in the United Kingdom, 21 in Portugal, and 17 in Turkey (see Figure 4.1),[30] with the threat of intervention or invasion of any country that did not comply with the dictates

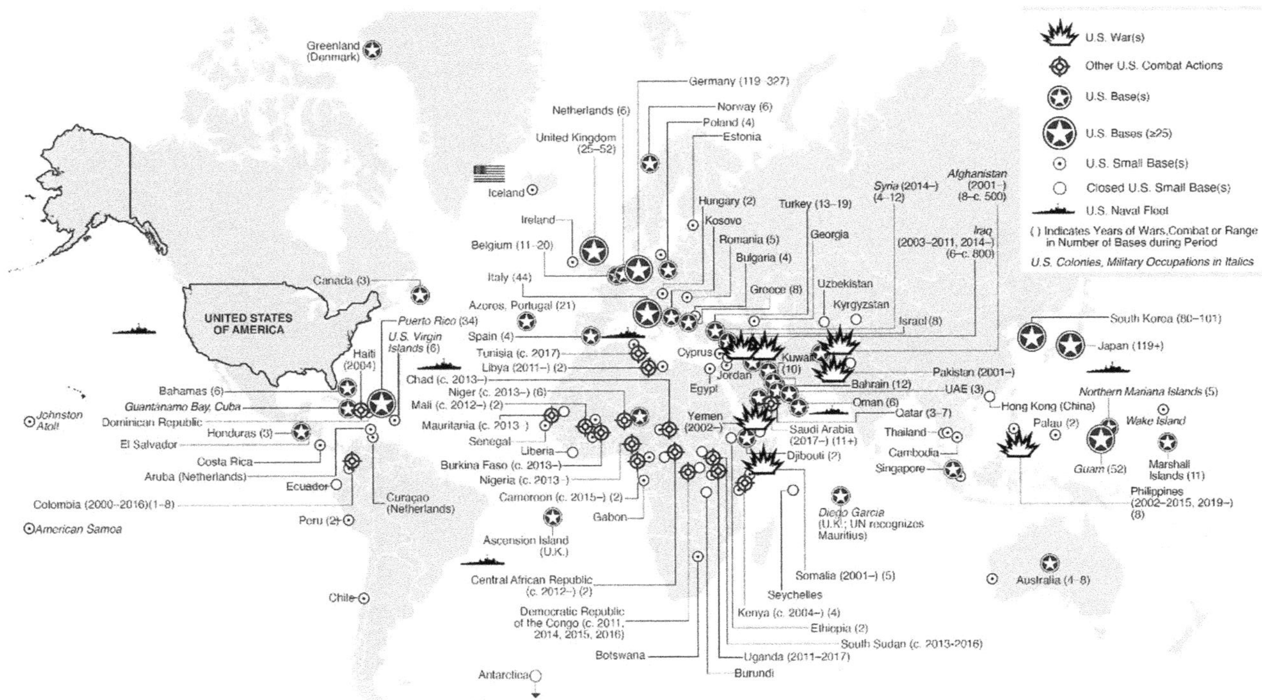

Figure 4.1 U.S. Wars, Military Bases, and Expansion Abroad, 2001–2020.

Source: David Vine, *The United States of War: A Global History of America's Endless Conflicts, from Columbus to the Islamic State* (Berkeley: University of California Press, 2020).

Notes: The map includes significant combat, bases, and expansion outside U.S. states. Some bases occupied only for part of this period. Base numbers range provided for countries with significant change during the period. During U.S. wars in Afghanistan and Iraq, there were over 2,000 bases abroad. There were around 800 in 2020. For ease of comparison, contemporary borders and a Mercator projection is used in the construction of the map.

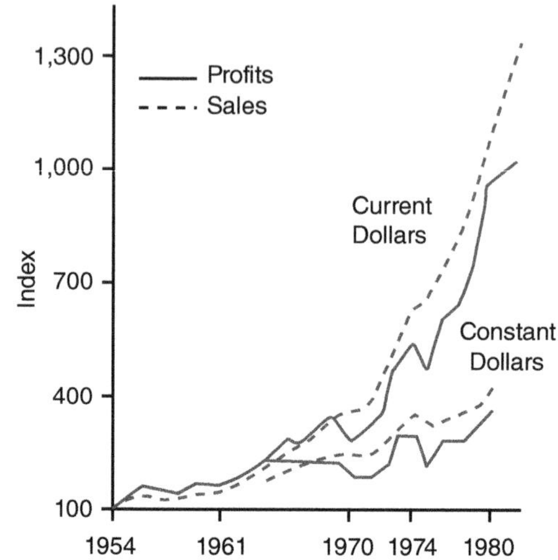

Figure 4.2 Sales and Profits of the 500 Largest U.S. Corporations, 1954–1980 (1954 = 100).

Source: Constructed with data from *Fortune*, April 24, 1989, p. 347.

of the American Empire in serving the interests of U.S. transnational corporations, at the cost of trillions of dollars.[31]

With the global expansion of U.S. capital and the U.S. state in the postwar period, the 1950s through the 1970s thus became the "golden age" of U.S. imperialism—a period that can be characterized as a bonanza for big business. The super-profits obtained from overseas investments, government contracts, and intensified exploitation of wage-labor at home and abroad resulted in record profits. Except for several short-term downturns in the business cycle, including five major recessions, this period was generally one of growth and expansion, especially for the largest and most viable U.S. corporations.

Taking the performance of the 500 largest industrial corporations as a yardstick for the overall sales and profit structure of U.S. big business from 1954 to 1980, we find that both in current and constant dollars, sales and profits showed a steady increase during this period (see Figure 4.2).

The rapid growth and expansion of U.S. capital during the 1950s through the 1970s strengthened the hand of big business and led to the demise of many smaller businesses, including family farms, thus resulting in the further monopolization of the U.S. economy.[32]

Increasing Monopoly Control in the U.S. Economy

As in most other sectors of the U.S. economy, the automobile industry is a prime example of increasing monopoly control through the concentration and centralization of capital in the United States since the late 19th century, when at least 1,900 different companies were producing over 3,000 makes of American automobiles.[33] By the turn of the 20th century, in 1908, the number of automobile producers had already declined to 253, and by 1929, there were only 44 companies remaining in this industry. Postwar accumulation of capital by big business led to further monopolization to a point when by the late 1950s all but four automakers disappeared and General Motors, Ford, Chrysler, and American Motors dominated the entire industry. The postwar period witnessed an accelerated monopolization in most sectors of the already heavily concentrated and centralized U.S. economy. The process of subsequent U.S. transnational economic expansion was largely the outcome of the growth and expansion of the giant monopolies in the United States, which, through mergers and acquisitions, came to account for a substantial share of the total assets, sales, and profits of U.S. corporations during this period.[34]

Postwar Monopolization in Industry and Finance

In a report on two decades of economic activity (1954–1974) by the 500 largest industrial corporations in the United States, an analyst for *Fortune* magazine wrote:

> The conglomerates . . . were rapidly piecing together vast empires of astonishing diversity and, in the process, taking over scores of well-known companies. . . . The merger boom meant, of course, that some companies were scoring tremendous sales gains.[35]

Moreover, "over the course of the two decades," the report continues, "the total annual sales of the 500 leaped from $136.8 billion to $834 billion—an average annual growth rate of 9.5 percent."[36] It is not surprising therefore that the assets of the 500 largest U.S. corporations increased from 55 percent of the U.S. total in 1955 to 75 percent in 1965, to 89 percent in 1980; likewise, sales of the 500 largest U.S. corporations increased from 58 percent of the U.S. total in 1955 to 65 percent in 1970, to 86 percent in 1980; and finally the profits of the 500 largest U.S. corporations rose from 45 percent of the U.S. total in 1955 to 54 percent in 1970, to 88 percent in 1980 (see Table 4.2).[37]

During the 1980s and in subsequent decades, the concentration of capital among the largest U.S. corporations continued to generate greater market share and higher profits both in industry and finance, domestically and abroad. Throughout the period from the 1980s to the turn of the 21st century, the concentration and centralization of capital continued unabated. The stock market crash of October 19, 1987, when the Dow fell by a then-record 508 points, which swept away nearly quarter of the value of stocks in one day, led to further consolidation of capital by the largest and most powerful corporations dominating the economy through the

Table 4.2 Assets, Sales, and Profits of the 500 Largest U.S. Corporations, 1955–1980 (as Percent of the U.S. Total).

Year	*Assets*	*Sales*	*Profits*
1955	54.6	57.9	44.6
1960	61.0	59.2	43.4
1965	74.9	60.6	40.0
1970	87.8	65.5	53.8
1975	88.1	81.2	56.7
1980	88.6	86.3	88.0

Sources: U.S. Council of Economic Advisers, *Economic Report of the President* (various years); *Fortune* (various issues).

acquisition of failed companies, which expanded the assets of the biggest monopolies.

Similarly, when the stock market crashed during the "Great Recession" of 2008–2009 and the Dow plunged from its pre-recession high of 14,164 on October 9, 2007 to a low of 6,594 on March 5, 2009, losing more than half its value in less than 17 months, the large corporations moved to take over bankrupt companies and thus further consolidated their position and expanded their assets to secure their place at the highest levels of the U.S. economy. Thus, the profits of domestic industries increased from $205 billion in 1980 to $315 billion in 1990, to $584 billion in 2000, to $1.4 trillion in 2010, to $1.9 trillion in 2020, while total corporate profits (domestically and abroad) surged from $241 billion in 1980 to $391 billion in 1990, to $730 billion in 2000, to $1.8 trillion in 2010, to $2.3 trillion in 2020 (see Table 4.3).

By 2020, after a decade of economic recovery, the concentration and centralization of capital in the United States had reached an unprecedented level and led to further monopolization of the U.S. economy, resulting in an enormous level of control and domination of the national economy by the 500 largest corporations in the United States. In looking at the data published by *Fortune* magazine on the 25, 50, 100, 200, and 500 largest corporations in 2020, we find that the top 25 corporations received $4.7 trillion in revenue, made $411.7 billion in profits, accumulated $13.7 trillion in assets, had a market value of $6.7 trillion, and employed 6,936,021 people; the top 50 corporations received $6.8 trillion in revenue, made $601.4 billion in profits, accumulated $23.1 trillion in assets, had a market value of $9.5 trillion, and employed 11,428,189 people; the top 100 corporations received $9.1 trillion in revenue, made $811.9 billion in profits, accumulated $31.1 trillion in assets, had a market value of $12 trillion, and employed 15,413,425 people; the top 200 corporations received $11.3 trillion in revenue, made $1 trillion in profits, accumulated $36.8 trillion in assets, had a market value of $16.1 trillion, and employed 21,458,448 people; and finally the top 500 corporations received $14.2 trillion in revenue, made $1.2 trillion in profits, accumulated $46.1 trillion in assets,

Table 4.3 Corporate Profits: Financial and Non-financial Industries, 1970–2020 (in Billions of Current Dollars)

Year[a]	Total Corporate Profits[b]	Domestic Industries[c]		
		Total	Financial	Non-Financial
1970	79.7	72.6	15.5	57.1
1975	144.2	129.6	20.4	109.2
1980	240.6	205.2	35.2	169.9
1985	289.7	251.6	46.5	205.1
1990	391.2	315.1	89.6	225.5
1995	667.0	574.0	140.3	433.7
2000	729.8	584.1	149.7	434.4
2005	1,629.2	1,403.4	409.5	993.9
2010	1,786.4	1,400.6	405.8	994.8
2015	2,184.6	1,789.4	447.2	1,342.1
2020[d]	2,337.9	1,914.8	495.8	1,419.0

Source: U.S. Department of Commerce, Bureau of Economic Analysis, as reported in U.S. Council of Economic Advisers, *Economic Report of the President 2021*, Table B-54, p. 519.

a Data on Standard Industrial Classification (SIC) basis for 1970–2000 include transportation and public utilities. Those on North American Industry Classification System (NAICS) basis include transportation and warehousing. Industry data on SIC basis and NAICS basis are not necessarily the same and are not strictly comparable.

b Includes domestic and foreign profits, with inventory valuation adjustment and without capital consumption adjustment.

c Domestic profits, with inventory valuation adjustment and without capital consumption adjustment.

d Data for 2020 is for the third quarter.

had a market value of $20.4 trillion, and employed 29,192,045 people (see Tables 4.4 and 4.5).

Despite the enormous amount of profits made by the top 500 corporations over the past several decades, especially after the corporate tax cuts enacted by the Trump Administration in December 2017 from 35 percent to 21 percent, an Institute on Taxation and Economic Policy (ITEP) report states that 379 of the *Fortune 500* companies paid an effective tax rate of only 11.3 percent in Federal corporate income tax and 60 of the *Fortune 500* companies paid no Federal corporate income tax on $79 billion in U.S. pretax income in the first year of the Trump tax cuts![38] These included Amazon.com, Netflix Inc., Chevron Corporation, Eli Lilly, and John Deere, among many others (see Table 4.6 for the complete list of the 60 companies that paid no Federal corporate income tax in 2018).

In a follow-up study by ITEP, released on December 16, 2019, when all companies released their 2018 financial filings, it was reported that altogether 91 corporations did not pay federal income taxes on their 2018 U.S. income and that another 56 corporations paid effective tax rates between 0 percent and 5 percent on their 2018 income.[39] Moreover, some of these corporate giants, in addition to paying zero in corporate income taxes, claimed that the Federal government owed them millions of dollars

Table 4.4 The 25 Largest U.S. Corporations by Revenues, Profits, Assets, Market Value, and Number of Employees, 2020

Rank	*Company Name*	*Number of Employees*	*Change in Rank*	*Revenues ($ millions)*	*Revenue Change*	*Profit ($ millions)*	*Profit Change*	*Assets ($ millions)*	*Market Value As of 3/31/20 ($ m)*
1	Walmart	2,200,000	-	523,964	1.9%	14,881.0	123.1%	236,495	321,803
2	Amazon.com	798,000	3	280,522	20.5%	11,588.0	15.0%	225,248	970,680
3	Exxon Mobil	74,900	−1	264,938	−8.7%	14,340.0	−31.2%	362,597	160,696
4	Apple	137,000	−1	260,174	−2.0%	55,256.0	−7.2%	338,516	1,112,641
5	CVS Health	290,000	3	256,776	32.0%	6,634.0	-	222,449	77,376
6	Berkshire Hathaway	391,500	−2	254,616	2.7%	81,417.0	1924.8%	817,729	442,897
7	UnitedHealth Group	325,000	−1	242,155	7.0%	13,839.0	15.5%	173,889	236,555
8	McKesson	70,000	−1	214,319	2.9%	34.0	−49.3%	59,672	21,845
9	AT&T	247,800	-	181,193	6.1%	13,903.0	−28.2%	551,669	209,388
10	AmerisourceBergen	21,500	-	179,589	6.9%	855.4	−48.4%	39,172	18,221
11	Alphabet	118,899	4	161,857	18.3%	34,343.0	11.7%	275,909	798,905
12	Ford Motor	190,000	-	155,900	−2.8%	47.0	−98.7%	258,537	19,151
13	Cigna	73,700	52	153,566	215.7%	5,104.0	93.6%	155,774	65,897
14	Costco Wholesale	201,500	-	152,703	7.9%	3,659.0	16.8%	45,400	125,908
15	Chevron	48,200	−4	146,516	−11.9%	2,924.0	−80.3%	237,428	136,176
16	Cardinal Health	49,500	-	145,534	6.4%	1,363.0	432.4%	40,963	13,988
17	JPMorgan Chase	256,981	1	142,422	8.4%	36,431.0	12.2%	2,687,379	276,750
18	General Motors	164,000	−5	137,237	−6.7%	6,732.0	−16.0%	228,037	29,695
19	Walgreens Boots Alliance	287,000	−2	136,866	4.1%	3,982.0	−20.7%	67,598	40,528
20	Verizon Communications	135,000	−1	131,868	0.8%	19,265.0	24.1%	291,727	222,220
21	Microsoft	144,000	5	125,843	14.0%	39,240.0	136.8%	286,556	1,199,550
22	Marathon Petroleum	60,910	9	124,813	28.5%	2,637.0	−5.1%	98,556	15,353
23	Kroger	435,000	−3	122,286	0.9%	1,659.0	−46.7%	45,256	24,114
24	Fannie Mae	7,500	−2	120,304	0.2%	14,160.0	−11.3%	3,503,319	1,841
25	Bank of America	208,131	-	113,589	2.7%	27,430.0	−2.5%	2,434,079	185,227
	Total for the top 25	6,936,021		4,729,550		411,723.4		13,683,954	6,727,405

Source: *Fortune 500* Special Issue (June 1, 2020). Online at https://www.fortune.com/fortune500/2020/search

Table 4.5 The 25, 50, 100, 200, and 500 Largest U.S. Corporations by Revenue, Profits, Assets, Market Value, and Number of Employees, 2020 (in Millions of Dollars)

U.S. Corporations	*Revenue*	*Profits*	*Assets*	*Market Value*	*Number of Employees*
Top 25	4,729,550	411,723.4	13,683,954	6,727,405	6,936,021
Top 50	6,845,503	601,418.1	23,088,910	9,538,717	11,428,189
Top 100	9,123,477	811,889.5	31,056,765	12,018,969	15,413,425
Top 200	11,330,923	1,003,402.7	36,798,344	16,072,556	21,458,448
Top 500	14,210,105	1,222,683.5	46,082,895	20,420,696	29,192,045
Top 25 as % of top 500	(33.3)	(33.7)	(29.7)	(32.9)	(23.8)
Top 50 as % of top 500	(48.2)	(49.2)	(50.1)	(46.7)	(39.1)
Top 100 as % of top 500	(64.2)	(66.4)	(67.4)	(58.9)	(52.8)
Top 200 as % of top 500	(79.7)	(82.1)	(79.9)	(78.7)	(73.5)

Source: *Fortune 500* Special Issue (June 1, 2020). Online at https://www.fortune.com/fortune500/2020/search

Table 4.6 Sixty Companies Avoiding All Federal Income Taxes in 2018 (U.S. Income and Federal Tax Figures in Millions of Dollars)

Company	*U.S. Income*	*Federal Tax*	*Effective Tax Rate*	*Industry*
Activision Blizzard	$447	$−228	−51%	Computers, office equipment, software, and data
AECOM Technology	$238	$−122	−51%	Engineering and construction
Alaska Air Group	$576	$−5	−1%	Transportation
Amazon.com	$10,835	$−129	−1%	Retail and wholesale trade
Ameren	$1,035	$−10	−1%	Utilities, gas, and electric
American Electric Power	$1,943	$−32	−2%	Utilities, gas, and electric
Aramark	$315	$−48	−15%	Miscellaneous services
Arrow Electronics	$167	$−12	−7%	Retail and wholesale trade
Arthur Gallagher	$322	—	—	Financial
Atmos Energy	$600	$−10	−2%	Utilities, gas, and electric
Avis Budget Group	$78	$−7	−9%	Motor vehicles and parts
Celanese	$480	$−142	−30%	Chemicals
Chevron	$4,547	$−181	−4%	Oil, gas, and pipelines
Cliffs Natural Resources	$565	$−1	0%	Oil, gas, and pipelines
CMS Energy	$774	$−67	−9%	Utilities, gas, and electric
Deere	$2,152	$−268	−12%	Industrial machinery
Delta Air Lines	$5,073	$−187	−4%	Transportation
Devon Energy	$1,297	$−14	−1%	Oil, gas, and pipelines

(*Continued*)

Company	*U.S. Income*	*Federal Tax*	*Effective Tax Rate*	*Industry*
Dominion Resources	$3,021	$−45	−1%	Utilities, gas, and electric
DTE Energy	$1,215	$−17	−1%	Utilities, gas, and electric
Duke Energy	$3,029	$−647	−21%	Utilities, gas, and electric
Eli Lilly	$598	$−54	−9%	Pharmaceuticals and medical products
EOG Resources	$4,067	$−304	−7%	Oil, gas, and pipelines
FirstEnergy	$1,495	$−16	−1%	Utilities, gas, and electric
Gannett	$7	$−11	−164%	Publishing and printing
General Motors	$4,320	$−104	−2%	Motor vehicles and parts
Goodyear Tire & Rubber	$440	$−15	−3%	Motor vehicles and parts
Halliburton	$1,082	$−19	−2%	Oil, gas, and pipelines
Honeywell International	$2,830	$−21	−1%	Industrial machinery
International Business Machines	$500	$−342	−68%	Computers, office equipment, software, and data
JetBlue Airways	$219	$−60	−27%	Transportation
Kinder Morgan	$1,784	$−22	−1%	Oil, gas, and pipelines
MDU Resources	$314	$−16	−5%	Oil, gas, and pipelines
MGM Resorts International	$648	$−12	−2%	Miscellaneous services
Molson Coors	$1,325	$−23	−2%	Food and beverages and tobacco
Netflix	$856	$−22	−3%	Retail and wholesale trade
Occidental Petroleum	$3,379	$−23	−1%	Oil, gas, and pipelines
Owens Corning	$405	$−10	−2%	Miscellaneous manufacturing
Penske Automotive Group	$393	$−16	−4%	Motor vehicles and parts
Performance Food Group	$192	$−9	−4%	Retail and wholesale trade
Pioneer Natural Resources	$1,249	—	—	Oil, gas, and pipelines
Pitney Bowes	$125	$−50	−40%	Computers, office equipment, software, and data
PPL	$1,110	$−19	−2%	Utilities, gas, and electric
Principal Financial	$1,641	$−49	−3%	Financial
Prudential Financial	$1,440	$−346	−24%	Financial
Public Service Enterprise Group	$1,772	$−97	−5%	Utilities, gas, and electric
PulteGroup	$1,340	$−44	−3%	Miscellaneous manufacturing
Realogy	$199	$−13	−7%	Miscellaneous services
Rockwell Collins	$719	$−16	−2%	Aerospace and defense
Ryder System	$350	$−23	−7%	Transportation
Salesforce.com	$800	—	—	Computers, office equipment, software, and data

(*Continued*)

Company	U.S. Income	Federal Tax	Effective Tax Rate	Industry
SpartanNash	$40	$−2	−4%	Retail and wholesale trade
SPX	$66	$−5	−8%	Industrial machinery
Tech Data	$203	$−10	−5%	Retail and wholesale trade
Trinity Industries	$138	$−19	−14%	Miscellaneous manufacturing
UGI	$550	$−3	0%	Utilities, gas, and electric
United States Steel	$432	$−40	−9%	Metals and metal products
Whirlpool	$717	$−70	−10%	Electronics and electrical equipment
Wisconsin Energy	$1,139	$−218	−19%	Utilities, gas, and electric
Xcel Energy	$1,434	$−34	−2%	Utilities, gas, and electric
TOTAL, These Companies	$79,025	$−4	−5%	

Source: Matthew Gardner et al., "Corporate Tax Avoidance Remains Rampant Under New Tax Law" Institute on Taxation and Economic Policy (April 11, 2019). ITEP analysis of SEC filings created with Datawrapper. https://itep.org/notadime/.

in tax credits. For example, a corporate giant, John Deere & Co., in addition to paying zero in Federal corporate income taxes, reported in 2018 that it was owed $268 million from the Federal government after various deductions and credits, according to its annual filing with the Securities and Exchange Commission, while the company reported global profits of $2.37 billion.[40] Other companies that paid zero corporate income tax and received a federal corporate income tax rebate include the computer maker IBM which earned $500 million in U.S. income and received a federal income tax rebate of $342 million; the retail giant Amazon, which reported $11 billion of U.S. income and claimed a federal income tax rebate of $129 million; the automaker GM reported a $4.3 billion of income and received a rebate of $104 million; beer maker Molson Coors made $1.3 billion of U.S. income and received a federal income tax rebate of $22.9 million; the streaming service Netflix, which reported $856 million of U.S. income and received a federal income tax rebate of $22 million; and the list goes on (see Table 4.6).[41] Moreover, in a report of the Institute on Taxation and Economic Policy, lead author Mathew Gardner writes: "Instead of paying $16.4 billion in taxes at the [new] 21 percent statutory corporate tax rate, these companies enjoyed a net corporate tax rebate of $4.3 billion [in 2018]."[42]

Monopolization in Agriculture

The process of postwar U.S. monopolization of the economy was not restricted to the industrial, financial, and service sectors alone; agriculture, too, experienced a similar process of consolidation, as fewer and fewer farming units (increasingly formed into giant agricultural conglomerates) came to control a larger and larger acreage, hence a disproportionate share

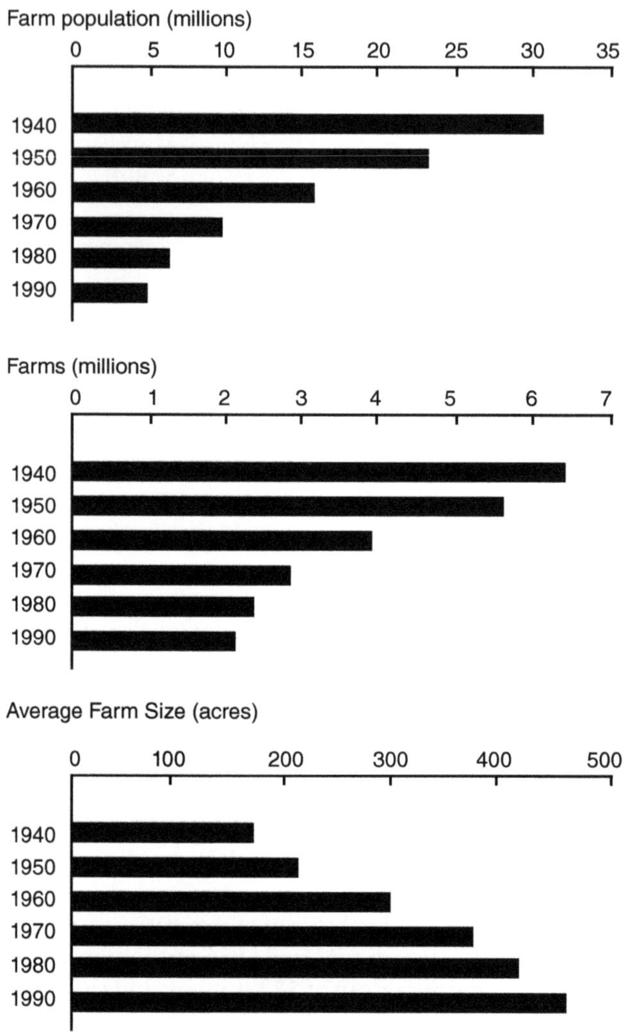

Figure 4.3 Changes in U.S. Farming, 1940–1990.
Source: Constructed with data from U.S. Bureau of the Census, *Statistical Abstract of the United States* (various issues).

of total assets and cash receipts from farming. In the 50-year period, from 1940 to 1990, the number of farms declined from 6.5 million in 1940 to just over 2 million in 1990 and the total population decreased from over 30 million in 1940 to less than 5 million in 1990, while the average size of farms rose from 170 acres in 1940 to 456 acres in 1990 (see Figure 4.3).

At century's end, the monopolization of U.S. agriculture was so complete that in 1988, less than 15 percent of all farms held 50 percent of all

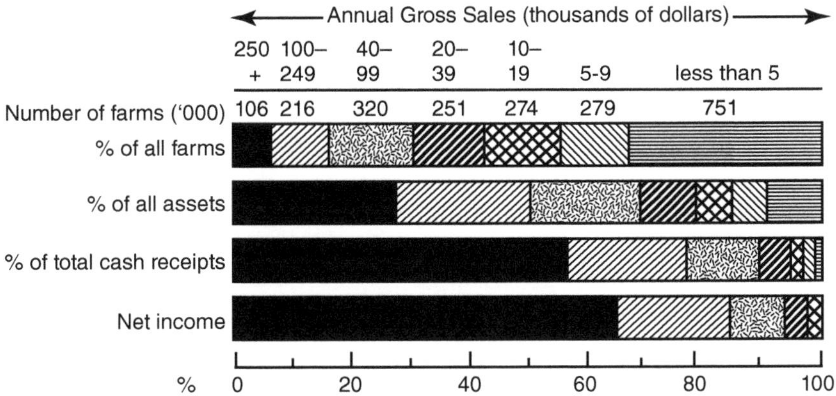

Figure 4.4 Farms, Farm Income, and Assets by Value of Sales, 1988.
Source: Constructed with data from U.S. Bureau of the Census, *Statistical Abstract of the United States: 1990*, p. 646.

farm assets and received 77 percent of total cash receipts and 85 percent of total net income in farming, while the lowest 34 percent of farms held 10.7 percent of total farm assets and received a mere 1.1 percent of total cash receipts and −1.4 percent of total net income. Moreover, nearly 50 percent of all farms held only 16 percent of total farm assets and received a mere 2.5 percent of the total cash receipts and −0.8 percent of total net income (see Figure 4.4).

By the early decades of the 21st century, the concentration and centralization of capital in U.S. agriculture had advanced so much that in 2018 there remained less than two million farms (accounting for 98 percent of all farms) of which 90 percent (with annual gross cash farm income before expenses of less than $350,000) accounted for 21 percent of total farm production, while the remaining 10 percent of farms (mainly large corporate farms) accounted for 79 percent of agricultural production in 2018 (see Figure 4.5).

Today, at the beginning of the third decade of the 21st century, we find that only 2.6 million people (or 1.3 percent of the employed population) remain in farming in 2020. Thus, with the largest industrial and agricultural corporations having reached a stage wherein they can be characterized as oligopoly or monopoly, the U.S. economy (in industry, finance, and agriculture as well) is now clearly operating through the logic of advanced capitalism dominated by big business. This has become increasingly evident over the past several decades in all sectors of the U.S. economy, such that by 2020 we find an extremely high level of concentration and centralization of capital and the consolidation of corporate control of the U.S. economy in the early 21st century.

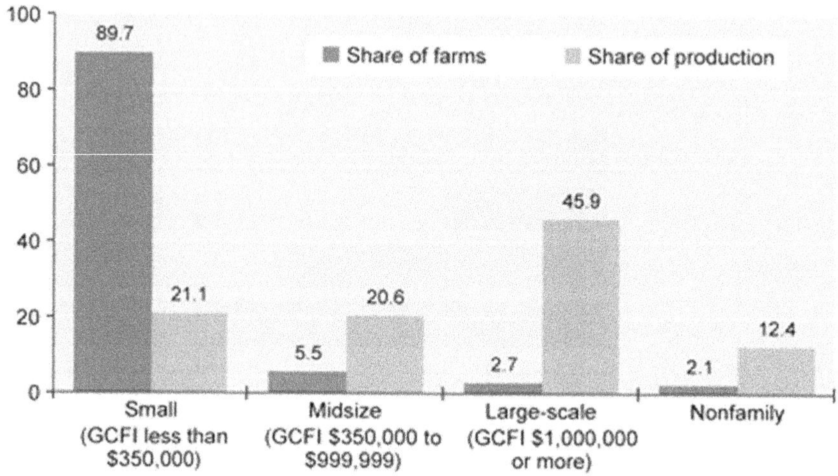

Figure 4.5 Farms and Their Value of Production by Farm Type, 2018.
Source: U.S. Department of Agriculture, Economic Research Service and National Agricultural Statistics Service. Agricultural Resource Management Survey. Data as of November 27, 2019.
Note: GCFI refers to annual gross cash farm income before expenses. Nonfamily are those where the principal operator and their relatives do not own a majority of the business.

New Contradictions

While the *effects* of accelerated monopolization in the United States and U.S. transnational expansion abroad began to appear in the U.S. domestic economy as early as the 1970s and became fully visible and felt by the early 1980s, competition from other rival centers of world capitalism began to pose a challenge to U.S. global economic dominance during this period, as a number of rising capitalist states emerged as serious contenders on the world scene.[43] Japan and West Germany, and the European Union as a whole, as well as a number of emerging economies in the 1970s and 1980s (e.g., South Korea, Taiwan, Hong Kong, and Singapore), began to make headway in production and worldwide trade, and together surpassed the traditional hold of the United States on the global economy as the pre-eminent global economic power in the postwar world economy.[44] Thus, beginning in the early 1970s and throughout the subsequent period, U.S. capital began to experience an entirely different process of global economic relations—one that was to set into motion a new set of contradictions that favored its global economic rivals.[45]

During the 1980s and 1990s, the global political economy went through a series of complex transformations from one region to another: accelerated U.S. global expansion during this period was accompanied by economic decline and class polarization in the domestic front; the collapse of the former Soviet Union and its associated East European states was in stark contrast to the economic boom in China through joint ventures and mass production for the world market; and the integration of European states into the European Union was in sharp contrast to the turmoil in the Balkans, the Middle East, and elsewhere in the less-developed regions where we have seen the rise of nationalism and ethno-national conflict that has torn apart the social fabric of entire societies.[46]

The culmination of these and other developments around the world during the final decade of the 20th and the early decades of the 21st century have brought to the fore a new set of contradictions and conflicts arising from the logic of transnational capitalist expansion, rivalries, wars, and crises that have led to the decline of the American Empire. These new contradictions and conflicts that have set into motion the end of U.S. global hegemony in the late 20th and early 21st century are discussed at length in Chapter 7 of this book.

Notes

1 Cleona Lewis, *America's Stake in International Investments* (Washington, DC: Brookings Institution, 1938), pp. 605–606.
2 U.S. Department of Commerce, *Survey of Current Business* (various issues, 1981).
3 Harry Magdoff, *Globalization: To What End?* (New York: Monthly Review Press, 1992).
4 ProQuest *Statistical Abstract of the U.S.*, 2022 Online Edition: Table 1306. Much of this increase was the result of reinvestment of earnings from pervious investments rather than of new capital flows from the United States to the recipient countries. In fact, outflow of capital from the United States has been only a small fraction of the increase in total foreign direct investment assets. While direct investment income of U.S. corporations was twice the value of outflows in the 1950s, by 2000 the gap between inflows and outflows reached such vast proportions that it became clear that direct investment income, totaling about $105 billion in 2000, was generated mainly through the internal processes of capital accumulation by the transnational subsidiaries within the host countries. Moreover, U.S. transnational monopolies through this process established a system of transnational production that no longer required the flow of capital from the parent to the subsidiaries for branch-plant expansion, and the direct investment income that has been generated abroad since 2000 has expanded the value of total U.S. assets across the globe immensely in the period from 2000 to the present.
5 Douglass Dowd, *The Twisted Dream: Capitalist Development in the United States Since 1776* (Cambridge, MA: Winthrop. 1977).
6 The Marshall Plan, proposed by then Secretary of State General George Marshall in June 1947, was implemented the following year as the European Recovery Program. In its four years of operation, the program gave $13 billion to 18 West European nations (including Greece and Turkey) for a broad variety of investment projects. Over 70 percent of the amount was spent for American goods. Dowd, *The Twisted Dream*, p. 235.
7 Michael Kidron, *Western Capitalism since the War* (Harmondsworth, England: Penguin Books, 1970).

8 Michael Tanzer, *The Energy Crisis: World Struggle for Power and Wealth* (New York: Monthly Review Press, 1974), pp. 17–18.
9 ProQuest *Statistical Abstract of the U.S.,* 2022 Online Edition, Table 1314. The figures for 2010 and 2020 include all of Europe (West and East).
10 ProQuest *Statistical Abstract of the U.S.,* 2022 Online Edition, Table 1314.
11 U.S. Bureau of the Census, *Statistical Abstract of the United States*, various issues; U.S. Department of Commerce, *Survey of Current Business* (July 2001), p. 27.
12 U.S. Department of Commerce, *Survey of Current Business* (September 2001), p. 90.
13 James Petras and Henry Veltmeyer, *Globalization Unmasked: Imperialism in the 21st Century* (London: Zed Books, 2001).
14 U.S. Department of Commerce, *Survey of Current Business* (August 1991), p. 88; (September 2001), p. 90. It must be noted that a large percentage of these financial investments went to a single country, Bermuda.
15 J. J. Servan-Schreiber, *The American Challenge* (New York: Atheneum, 1968), pp. 13–14.
16 Albert Szymanski, *The Logic of Imperialism* (New York: Praeger Publishers, 1981), pp. 501–502.
17 Stephen McBride and John Richard Wiseman (eds.). *Globalization and Its Discontents* (New York: Palgrave Macmillan, 2000); Steven Weber (ed.), *Globalization and the European Political Economy* (New York: Columbia University Press, 2001).
18 John Halliday and Gavan McCormack, *Japanese Imperialism Today* (New York: Monthly Review Press, 1973), p. 5.
19 Halliday and McCormack, *Japanese Imperialism Today*, p. 7.
20 Patrick O'Meara, et al. (eds.), *Globalization and the Challenges of the New Century: A Reader* (Indianapolis: Indiana University Press, 2000). Nevertheless, in the 1970s and 1980s, a growing number of Japanese corporations have been able to move part of their operations into the United States to supply the U.S. market from within, thus avoiding tariffs and other protectionist measures directed against them. Operating, in effect, as "American" corporations, some Japanese firms have thus escaped the problems associated with imports into the United States of goods manufactured abroad. The decline in U.S. wages relative to their increase in Japan during the past decade has been another important incentive for some Japanese firms to move part of their operations to the United States. See Glenn D. Hook and Hasegawa Harukiyo (eds.), *Political Economy of Japanese Globalization* (New York: Routledge, 2001).
21 Szymanski, *The Logic of Imperialism*, p. 502; Berch Berberoglu, *The Legacy of Empire: Economic Decline and Class Polarization in the United States* (New York: Praeger Publishers, 1992).
22 Berch Berberoglu "The Contradictions of Export-oriented Development in the Third World," *Social and Economic Studies* 36, no. 4 (December, 1987), p. 69; Priyatosh Maitra, *The Globalization of Capitalism in Third World Countries* (Westport, CT: Praeger Publishers, 1996).
23 NATO was established in 1949 as the military counterpart of the Marshall Plan.
24 Charles E. Nathanson, "The Militarization of the American Economy," in David Horowitz (ed.), *Corporations and the Cold War* (New York: Monthly Review Press, 1969), p. 211.
25 Nathanson, "The Militarization of the American Economy," p. 210.
26 Paul Baran and Paul Sweezy, *Monopoly Capital* (New York: Monthly Review Press, 1966), p. 176.
27 Nathanson, "The Militarization of the American Economy," p. 212.

28 Nathanson, "The Militarization of the American Economy," p. 231.
29 Chalmers Johnson, *The Sorrows of Empire: Militarism, Secrecy, and the End of the Republic* (New York: Henry Holt and Company, 2004).
30 David Vine, *The United States of War: A Global History of America's Endless Conflicts, From Columbus to the Islamic State* (Berkeley: University of California Press, 2020). See also, David Vine, *Base Nation: How U.S. Military Bases Abroad Harm America and the World* (New York: Metropolitan Books, 2015).
31 The U.S. wars in Iraq and Afghanistan alone, which lasted 20 years (from 2001 to 2021), cost $6.4 trillion by 2021, not to mention the U.S. war in Vietnam and other wars that the empire initiated and engaged in, which have drained the national budget and gained the U.S. new enemies around the globe. For the human and economic cost of these wars, see Watson Institute for International and Public Affairs, "Costs of War" Project at Brown University through this link: https://watson.brown.edu/costsofwar/costs (accessed August 28, 2021).
32 Bruno Amoroso, *On Globalization: Capitalism in the 21st Century* (New York: St. Martin's, 2001).
33 John B. Rae, "Why Michigan?" *Michigan History* Vol. 89, No. 2 (1996), pp. 6–13.
34 Howard J. Sherman, *Foundations of Radical Political Economy* (New York: M.E. Sharpe, 1987); Victor Perlo, *Super Profits and Crises: Modern U.S. Capitalism* (New York: International Publishers, 1988); Berch Berberoglu, *The Political Economy of Development: Development Theory and the Prospects for Change in the Third World* (Albany: State University of New York Press, 1992).
35 Linda Grant Martin, "The 500: A Report on Two Decades," *Fortune* (May 1975), p. 239.
36 Martin, "The 500: A Report on Two Decades," pp. 239, 241.
37 The relationship between monopolization based on asset size and the domination of markets and a tendency for profits to rise has been shown widely in a number of studies. One such study, conducted at Harvard University in the 1970s which covered 57 corporations involved in 620 separate businesses, found that the greater the share of the market for a given product that a company monopolized, the higher its rate of profit. Thus, according to the findings of this study, companies controlling less than 7 percent of the market share reported a 9.6 percent return on investment, while those controlling 22 percent to 36 percent of the market reported a 17.9 percent return, and companies controlling over 36 percent of the market showed a 30.2 percent profit. Joe Cappo, "A Little Closer Look at Free Enterprise," *Chicago Daily News* (17 May 1977), p. 28.
38 Matthew Gardner et al., "Corporate Tax Avoidance Remains Rampant Under New Tax Law" Institute on Taxation and Economic Policy (April 11, 2019). https://itep.org/notadime/ (accessed June 28, 2022)
39 Matthew Gardner, et al., "Corporate Tax Avoidance in the First Year of the Trump Tax Law" Institute on Taxation and Economic Policy (December 16, 2019). https://itep.org/corporate-tax-avoidance-in-the-first-year-of-the-trump-tax-law/ (accessed June 28, 2022)
40 Kathryn Kranhold, "Twice as Many Companies Paying Zero Taxes under Trump Tax Plan," The Center for Public Integrity, Washington, DC (April 11, 2019).
41 Gardner et al., "Corporate Tax Avoidance Remains Rampant Under New Tax Law". https://itep.org/notadime/ (accessed June 28, 2022)
42 Gardner et al., "Corporate Tax Avoidance Remains Rampant Under New Tax Law."

43 Nick Beams, *The Significance and Implications of Globalization: A Marxist Assessment* (Southfield: Mehring Books, 1998); O'Meara, et al. (eds.), *Globalization and the Challenges of the New Century*; Fred Halliday, *The World at 2000* (New York: St. Martin's Press, 2001).
44 Steven Weber (ed.), *Globalization and the European Political Economy* (New York: Columbia University Press, 2001); Hook and Harukiyo, *Political Economy of Japanese Globalization.*
45 Leslie Sklair, *Globalization: Capitalism and Its Alternatives* (New York: Oxford University Press, 2002).
46 Halliday, *The World at 2000.*

5 Wealth and Income Inequality in the Wealthiest Empire in History

The class divisions that exist in the United States since its founding over two centuries ago are so pervasive that they are prevalent in all spheres of life across the nation. The entrenched class relations that we discussed at length in the early chapters of this book are so deep that the divisions among Americans along class lines are now so divisive that we can no longer pretend we are one nation indivisible and part of a giant "melting pot" made up of a "middle class"—a myth we exposed at the beginning of this book. In fact, given the vast amount of wealth amassed by individuals and families at the top echelons of the U.S. class structure, it is no surprise that there exist immense inequalities in the United States along class lines, based on the unequal distribution of wealth and income that has reached unprecedented levels in the early 21st century.

Wealth and income inequality in America is the result of centuries of private accumulation of capital from the colonial period to the present. Wealthy interests from Europe brought over capital and continued to amass great fortunes and expanded their wealth through the exploitation of labor that facilitated the development of capitalism in the United States through the formation of trusts and cartels that in time came to dominate the U.S. economy. Thus, the further concentration of capital and its subsequent centralization through the emergence of monopolies and oligopolies led to the consolidation of class rule of the capitalists who came to establish family dynasties, such as the Rockefellers, the DuPonts, the Carnegies, the Mellons, and numerous other industrial and financial magnates. In time, this wealth, concentrated in the hands of a few capitalists, transformed the United States from a colonial outpost of Great Britain and other European powers to a new, rising imperialist power of its own with all the usual characteristics of empires abroad and massive wealth and income inequalities at home.

The recurring recessions and depressions of this initial period and subsequently the Great Depression of the early 20th century set back the continued concentration and centralization of capital over certain periods during the development and expansion of capitalism in the United States, which was the result of the capitalist business cycle during this period. However, the reign of the U.S. capitalist class was firmly established and

DOI: 10.4324/9781003282105-5

the U.S. state fully controlled by the wealthy in the aftermath of the Great Depression and subsequently following World War II when U.S. capital had reached its apex and had become thoroughly global. The U.S. transnational corporations that now came to dominate the national and global economy transformed the United States from a rising nation to a full-fledged Empire that embodied all the national and global inequalities that it came to represent, while continuing to propagate the false narratives of American democracy, equality, and prosperity for all, in attempting to hide the glaring *and widening* wealth and income inequalities that were there for all to see. The coalescence of economic wealth and political-military control of the state in the emerging empire by the now-established capitalist class in the postwar period led the five-star General and President of the United States Dwight D. Eisenhower to invoke his now-famous expression "the military-industrial complex," i.e., the coalescence and collusion of corporate capitalist and military/state interests promoting and advancing U.S. imperialist designs to expand the hegemony of the American Empire around the world.

This predicament of the United States under conditions of advanced capitalism and the capitalist state throughout the postwar period led to the emergence of irreversible social, economic, and political contradictions and crises that greatly affected the structure of American society and the American Empire, above all the nature and extent of wealth and income inequality in America today.

With the widening of the gap in the distribution of wealth and income in the United States in recent decades, especially in the aftermath of the Great Recession of 2008–2009, wealth and income inequalities have become central issues of concern in American society in recent years, which have led to increasing and sharper class divisions that are now threatening the social fabric of American society. Thus, concern over wealth and income inequality in the United States has become an urgent call, as the gap between the wealthy and the rest of the population has widened over the past several decades to an alarming level. Such wealth, accumulated by individuals and families, is often inherited and transmitted over generations. Great wealth brings in higher income from various sources and this leads to more wealth—a continuous process of private accumulation of assets in the hands of a small class of wealthy owners of capital that makes it possible for these capitalists to disproportionately own and control the vast resources of society for private profit.

This chapter explores the nature, sources, and extent of wealth and income inequality in America over the course of the 20th and early 21st century. After an overview of this serious societal problem, it provides detailed time-series data and analysis that illustrate the extent and depth of wealth and income inequality in the United States over the course of the past century, especially during recent decades, when the gap between the wealthy owners of capital and wage-labor has widened immensely.

Wealth and Income Inequality in America

Wealth and income inequality in capitalist society, such as the United States, stems from the ownership of private property in the means of production and the accumulation of private wealth (or capital) that it generates through the employment and exploitation of wage-labor. The wealth accumulated by the capitalists is, in fact, the portion of the value created by labor and kept by the capitalists as profit. Thus, the more workers a capitalist is able to employ and exploit, the more wealth the capitalist is able to accumulate and invest to generate further wealth through another cycle of production and accumulation that continues in perpetuity. Over time, as the income and wealth of this small owning-class increases as against that of the working class majority, so do wealth and income inequality widen in society.

The United States now has more wealth and income inequality than any other advanced capitalist country in the world. The gap between the very rich and everyone else in the United States is wider than at any time since the Great Depression of the 1930s.[1] One family alone owns more wealth than the bottom 150 million Americans. Growing wealth and income inequality based on the exploitation of labor under contemporary capitalism leads to class polarization and class conflict between capital and wage-labor. This becomes a source of tension between the working class and the capitalist class and leads to various forms of class conflict and class struggle that have important political implications, which open the way to potential social change and social transformation.

Wealth Inequality

Wealth (or net worth) is defined as the sum of a family's assets minus liabilities (or debt). Data on the concentration of wealth in the United States is hard to come by and is available only in irregular waves over a number of years. "The development of various data sets in the past 30 years (in particular the Survey of Consumer Finances)," write Marco Cagetti and Mariacristina De Nardi, "has allowed economists to quantify more precisely the degree of wealth concentration in the United States."[2] They write:

> The picture that emerged from the different waves of these surveys confirmed the fact that a large fraction of the total wealth in the economy is concentrated in the hands of the richest percentiles: the top 1% hold one third, and the richest 5% hold more than half of total wealth. At the other extreme, a significant fraction of the population holds little or no wealth at all.[3]

In looking at the share of total wealth in the United States during the course of the 20th century (Figure 5.1), we see an inverse relationship between the top 0.1 percent of families and the bottom 90 percent of families. The share of the 0.1 percent declined from 25 percent of the total in the aftermath of the Great Depression in the 1930s to below 10 percent in the 1970s, while the share of the bottom 90 percent rose from around 16 percent to 37 percent in the mid-1980s. However, over the course of the past four decades, the share of the top 0.1 percent has been rapidly increasing, from around 8 percent in 1978 to around 22 percent in 2012, while the share of the bottom 90 percent has been declining, from around 36 percent to 22 percent over the same period. This means that in 2012, the top 0.1 percent of families (about 160,000 families with net wealth above $20.6 million, according to Emmanuel Saez and Gabriel Zucman) owned as much wealth as the bottom 90 percent of families consisting of tens of millions of households in the United States (Figure 5.1).[4]

Similarly, the evolution of wealth distribution among the top percentiles of wealth holders in the United States (i.e., the top 0.01 percent and the top 0.1 percent as well as the top 1 percent) has followed the same pattern for the past 100 years—from 1913 to 2012 (Figure 5.2).

It is ironic to note that while the decline in the fortunes of capital during the Great Depression was accompanied by an improvement in the position of the working class due, in part, to favorable government policies toward labor in response to their deteriorating economic condition, the situation in the aftermath of the Great Recession of 2008–2009 was the reverse of the earlier experience. While the condition of the working class sharply declined, the position of the wealthy owners of capital greatly improved,

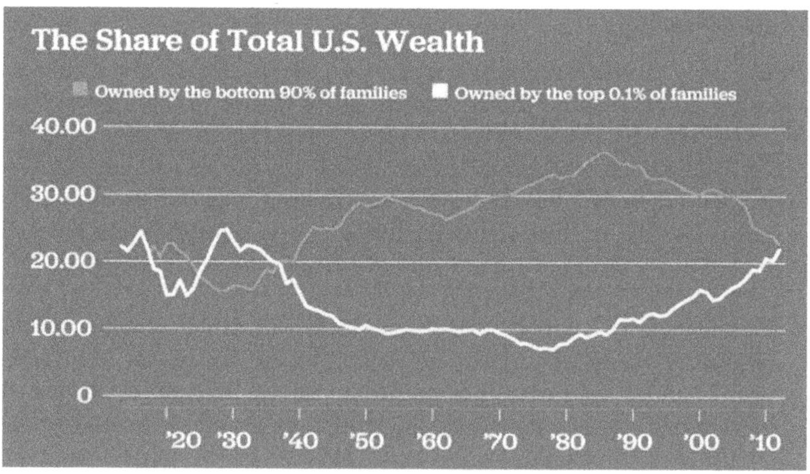

Figure 5.1 Distribution of Wealth in the United States, 1910–2012, Owned by the Top 0.1 Percent and the Bottom 90 Percent of Families (in Percent).

Source: https://gabriel-zucman.eu/files/uswealth/AppendixTables(Aggregates).xlsx

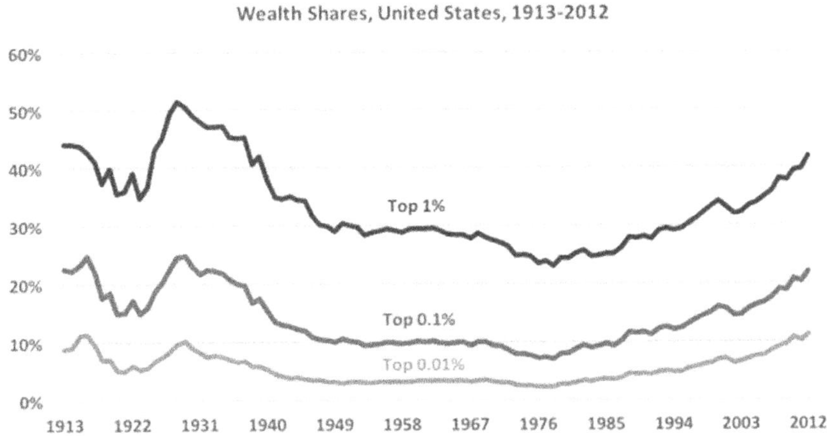

Figure 5.2 Wealth Shares of the Top 0.01 Percent, 0.1 Percent, and 1 Percent, 1913–2012 (in Percent).

Source: www.inequality.org/facts/wealth-inequality/

despite adverse conditions resulting from the severe economic downturn during this most recent episode in the business cycle.[5] In contrast to the deteriorating condition of the great majority of the population that experienced job loss, foreclosures, indebtedness, lack of health care, and overall decline, the wealthy owners of capital became even wealthier by cashing in on their questionable business transactions that immensely increased their family fortunes. Thus, the widening gap between labor and capital continued to grow—a trend that has been in place since the early 1990s. Data provided in Figure 5.3 show that the holdings of the richest 10 percent of families increased from $20 trillion in 1989 to $51 trillion in 2013, while the poorest 50 percent of families showed no change at $1 trillion. Families between top 10 percent and poorest 50 percent witnessed a modest increase from $9 trillion in 1989 to $15 trillion in 2013 (see Figure 5.3).

Data in Figures 5.4 and 5.5 illustrate the composition of the top 0.01 percent wealth share in the highest levels of the wealth pyramid and that of the bottom 90 percent during the 100-year period from 1913 to 2012, including fixed income claims, equities, business assets, and housing. In Figure 5.4, the category "other" includes business assets, net housing wealth, and pension wealth. Figure 5.5 combines the category of equities, fixed claims assets, and non-mortgage debt.

Figure 5.6 provides data on the real average wealth of the top 1 percent and bottom 90 percent of families since the mid-1940s. The figure depicts the average real wealth of the top 1 percent of families (left y-axis) and the bottom 90 percent of families (right y-axis) from 1946 to 2012. Wealth is expressed in constant 2010 U.S. dollars, using the GDP deflator.

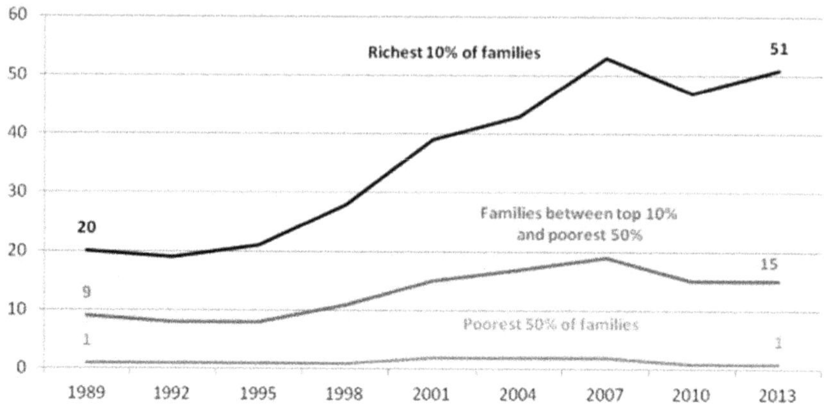

Figure 5.3 Holdings of U.S. Family Wealth, 1989–2013 (in Trillions of 2013 Dollars).

Source: Congressional Budget Office, "Trends in Family Wealth, 1989–2013" as reported in *www.inequality.org/facts/wealth-inequality/*

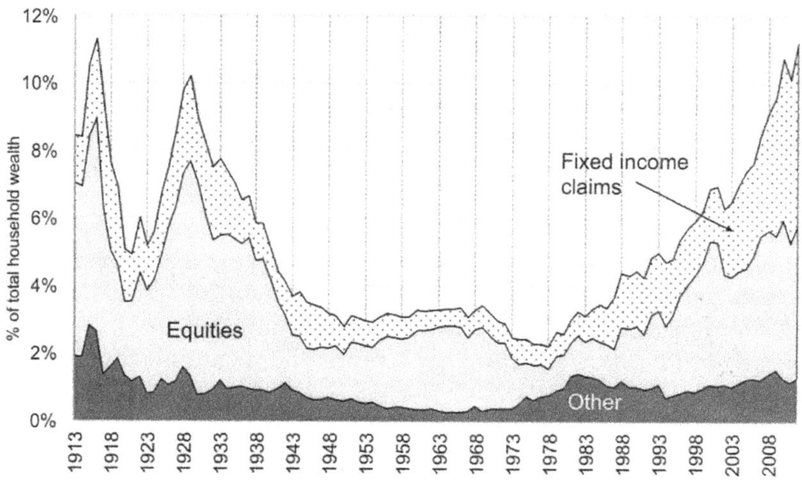

Figure 5.4 Composition of the Top 0.01 Percent Wealth Share in the United States, 1913–2012.

Source: Emmanuel Saez and Gabriek Zucman, "Wealth Inequality in the United States Since 1913: Evidence From Capitalized Income Tax Data," National Bureau of Economic Research Working Paper 20625 (October 2014). Appendix Table B5.

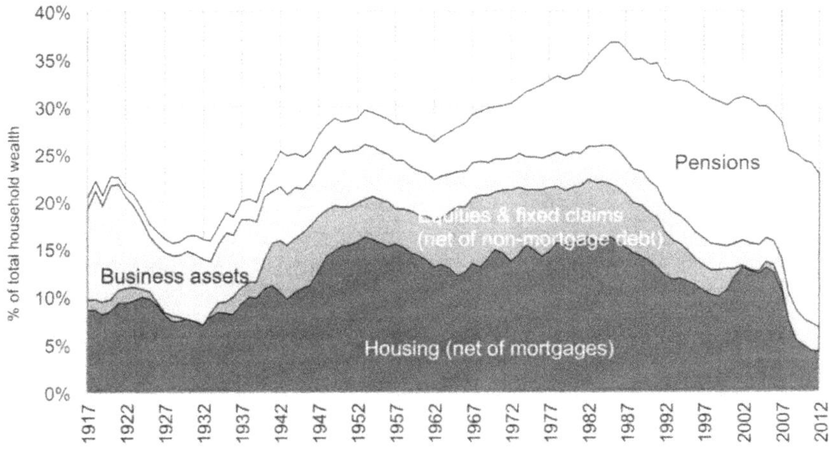

Figure 5.5 Composition of the Bottom 90 Percent Wealth Share in the United States, 1917–2012.

Source: Emmanuel Saez and Gabriek Zucman, "Wealth Inequality in the United States Since 1913: Evidence From Capitalized Income Tax Data," National Bureau of Economic Research Working Paper 20625 (October 2014). Appendix Table B5.

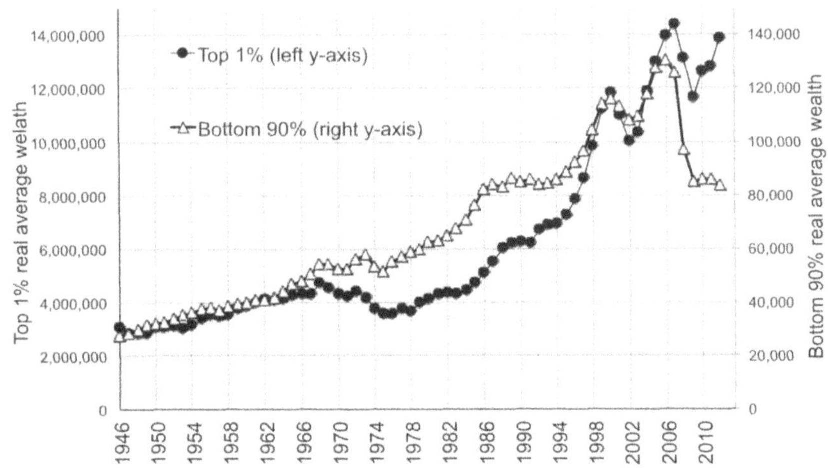

Figure 5.6 Real Average Wealth of Top 1 Percent and Bottom 90 Percent of Families in the United States, 1946–2012.

Source: Emmanuel Saez and Gabriek Zucman, "Wealth Inequality in the United States Since 1913: Evidence From Capitalized Income Tax Data," National Bureau of Economic Research Working Paper 20625 (October 2014). Appendix Table B3.

"The most striking aspect of the wealth distribution in the United States," write Cagetti and De Nardi, "is its degree of concentration."[6] Data on the concentration of wealth in the United States show the widening gap between the wealthy and the working class since the 1960s. Thus, according to available data, between 1963 and 1983, the richest 10 percent of families have increased their share of total wealth by nearly 7 percent, owning by 1983 nearly 72 percent of all assets, and the top 0.5 percent of families have increased their share by nearly 10 percent, owning 35 percent of all assets, while the remaining 90 percent of families have experienced a drop in their share of total wealth by nearly 7 percent.[7] Moreover, if we exclude from these data homes for personal use, the disparity in wealth becomes even more glaring: in 1983, the richest 10 percent of families owned over 83 percent of all assets and the top 0.5 percent of families owned nearly half of all assets, while the bottom 90 percent of families owned less than 17 percent of the total. Furthermore, the richest 10 percent of families owned 78 percent of real estate, 89 percent of corporate stock, over 90 percent of bonds, and nearly 94 percent of all business assets. More significantly, the top 0.5 percent of all families accounted for nearly or over half of all assets, corporate stock, bonds, and business assets.[8]

There is limited data on the distribution of wealth in the United States. The Federal Reserve Board has provided some data in its *Survey of Consumer Finances* for the period from 1983 to more recent years. These data suggest that there continues to be a great concentration of wealth among a small number of households. Table 5.1 provides data reported by Edward N. Wolff for the period 1983–2013, broken down by the top 1 percent, the top 20 percent, and the bottom 80 percent.[9] These data show that wealth is overwhelmingly concentrated in the top 1 percent and the top 20 percent, while it is virtually non-existent for the bottom 80 percent of households. Thus, according to this data, the top 1 percent accounted for more than one-third of total net worth and owned nearly one-half of all financial assets, the top 20 percent of households accounted for 81 percent to 89 percent of total net worth and 91 percent to 95 percent of all financial assets, while the bottom 80 percent of households accounted for 11percent to 19 percent of all wealth (including owner-occupied housing) and only 5 percent to 9 percent of total financial assets during the three decades from 1983 to 2013 (see Table 5.1). In looking at the data for the latest year (2013), we find that the top 1 percent accounted for 36.7 percent of total net worth and owned 42.8 percent of all financial assets, the top 20 percent of households accounted for 88.9 percent of total net worth and owned 94.7 percent of all financial assets, while the bottom 80 percent of households accounted for 11.1 percent of total net worth and owned a mere 5.3 percent of all financial assets (see Table 5.1).

Breaking down wealth by type of assets owned in 2001, 2007, and 2013, Table 5.2 provides data that show extreme concentration of wealth in the top 1 percent and the top 10 percent, with little to show for in the bottom

Table 5.1 Distribution of Net Worth and Financial Wealth of Households in the United States, 1983–2013 (in %)

	Net Worth[a]			*Financial Wealth*[b]		
Year	*Top 1%*	*Top 20%*	*Bottom 80%*	*Top 1%*	*Top 20%*	*Bottom 80%*
1983	33.8	81.3	18.7	42.9	91.3	8.7
1989	37.4	83.6	16.5	46.9	93.4	6.6
1992	37.2	83.8	16.2	45.6	92.3	7.7
1995	38.5	83.9	16.1	47.2	93.1	7.0
1998	38.1	83.4	16.6	47.3	90.9	9.1
2001	33.4	84.4	15.6	39.7	91.2	8.7
2004	34.3	84.6	15.3	42.2	92.5	7.5
2007	34.6	85.1	15.0	42.7	93.0	7.0
2010	35.1	88.6	11.4	41.3	94.8	5.2
2013	36.7	88.9	11.1	42.8	94.7	5.3

Source: Edward N. Wolff, *A Century of Wealth in America* (Cambridge, MA: Harvard University Press, 2017).

a Net worth (total assets) includes all of the following: the gross value of owner-occupied housing; other real estate owned by the household; cash and demand deposits; time and savings deposits, certificates of deposit, and money market accounts; government bonds, corporate bonds, foreign bonds, and other financial securities; the cash surrender value of life insurance plans; the cash surrender value of pension plans, including IRAs, Keogh, and 401(k) plans; corporate stock and mutual funds; net equity in unincorporated businesses; and equity in trust funds. Total liabilities include all of the following: mortgage debt; consumer debt, including auto loans; and other debts.

b Financial wealth includes all of the above, except owner-occupied housing.

90 percent. Thus, in 2001, the richest 1 percent of families owned 44.1 percent of stocks and mutual funds, 58.0 percent of financial securities, and 57.3 percent of business equity, in all accounting for nearly half of the total for the group of investment assets. The richest 10 percent of families owned 84.5 percent of stocks and mutual funds, 86.7 percent of trusts, 88.6 percent of financial securities, and 89.6 percent of business equity, in all accounting for 88.5 percent of the total for the group of investment assets. At the other end of the spectrum, the bottom 90 percent of families owned 15.5 percent of stocks and mutual funds, 13.3 percent of trusts, 11.3 percent of financial securities, and 10.4 percent of business equity, in all accounting for only 14.5 percent of the total for the group of investment assets.[10]

In 2007, the richest 1 percent of families owned 49.3 percent of stocks and mutual funds, 60.6 percent of financial securities, and 62.4 percent of business equity, in all accounting for half of the total for the group of investment assets. The richest 10 percent of families owned 89.4 percent of stocks and mutual funds, 93.3 percent of business equity, and 98.5 percent of financial securities, in all accounting for 87.8 percent of the total wealth in the group of investment assets. At the other end of the spectrum, the bottom 90 percent of families owned 10.6 percent of stocks and mutual funds, 6.7 percent of business equity, and a mere 1.5 percent of financial securities, in all accounting for only 12.2 percent of the total for the group of investment assets.

In 2013, the richest 1 percent of families owned 49.8 percent of stocks and mutual funds, 54.7 percent of financial securities, and 62.8 percent of business equity, in all accounting for more than half of the total for the group of investment assets. The richest 10 percent of families owned 91 percent of stocks and mutual funds, 93.8 percent of business equity, and 94.3 percent of financial securities, in all accounting for 88.5 percent of the total wealth in the group of investment assets. At the other end of the spectrum, the bottom 90 percent of families owned 9.1 percent of stocks and mutual funds, 6.2 percent of business equity, and 5.7 percent of financial securities, in all accounting for only 11.5 percent of the total for the group of investment assets (see Table 5.2).

Table 5.2 Distribution of Wealth in the United States, 2001, 2007, and 2013, by Type of Assets (in Percent)

	Top 1%			*Top 10%*			*Bottom 90%*		
Investment Assets	*2001*	*2007*	*2013*	*2001*	*2007*	*2013*	*2001*	*2007*	*2013*
Stocks; mutual funds	44.1	49.3	49.8	84.5	89.4	91.0	15.5	10.6	9.1
Financial securities	58.0	60.6	54.7	88.6	98.5	94.3	11.3	1.5	5.7
Trusts	46.3	38.9	49.5	86.7	79.4	83.5	13.3	20.6	16.5
Business equity	57.3	62.4	62.8	89.6	93.3	93.8	10.4	6.7	6.2
Nonhome real estate	34.9	28.3	33.7	78.5	76.9	77.8	21.5	23.1	22.2
Total for asset group	47.8	49.7	51.5	88.5	87.8	88.5	14.5	12.2	11.5

Source: Edward N. Wolff, "Changes in Household Wealth in the 1980s and 1990s in the United States," *Working Paper No. 407* (May 2004), p. 34 and Edward N. Wolff, "Recent Trends in Household Wealth in the United States: Rising Debt and the Middle Class Squeeze," *Working Paper No. 589* (March 2010), p. 51; Edward N. Wolff, *Household Wealth Trends in the United States, 1962–2013: What Happened over the Great Recession?* (Cambridge, MA: National Bureau of Economic Research, 2014).

The Racial Divide in the Distribution of Wealth

The racial divide in the distribution of wealth in the United States attests to the disparities in the patterns of ownership between the White and non-White population consisting of African Americans, Hispanics, and other racial/ethnic groups. "Between 1983 and 2001," reports Edward N. Wolff, "average net worth (in 2001 dollars) rose by a whopping 73 percent for Whites but only by 31 percent for Black households."[11] In looking at data over a period of three decades (from 1983 to 2013), we find that while during much of this period (from 1992 to 2004) the typical White family held a net worth six to seven times greater than the typical Black family, the disparity in ownership between the races has been exacerbated by the Great Recession, such that the gap has doubled to 13:1 in 2013, the latest year for which we have available data (see Figure 5.7).

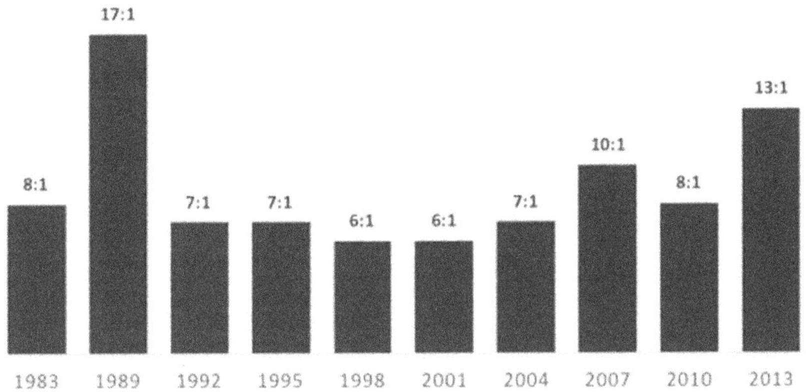

Figure 5.7 Ratio of Median U.S. White Household Wealth to Black Household Wealth, 1983–2013.
Source: Pew Research Center, as reported in www.inequality.org/facts/wealth-inequality/

The wealth gap between White and Hispanic households has widened as well. "What is also disturbing is that," writes Wolff, "the respective wealth gaps between African-Americans and Hispanics on the one hand and non-Hispanic Whites on the other were still much greater than the corresponding income gap."[12] Moreover, according to Wolff's calculations:

> While the income ratios were of the order of 50–55 percent, the wealth ratios were of the order of 12–17 percent. Median financial wealth among non-Hispanic Black and Hispanic households was still virtually zero in 2001 and the percent with zero or negative net worth was around a third, in contrast to 13 percent among non-Hispanic White households (a difference that appears to mirror the gap in poverty rates).[13]

Figure 5.8 provides data on median household net worth and financial wealth in the United States by race for the years 2007 and 2013 in adjusted 2013 dollars. It shows that in 2007, the average White household had a net worth (including an owner-occupied home) amounting to $161,400, the average African American household had a net worth of $10,400, and the average Hispanic household's net worth was $10,200. However, when the value of owner-occupied homes are removed from the figures, the median household financial wealth for Whites dropped to $49,000, for African Americans to $600, and for Hispanics to $400. The Great

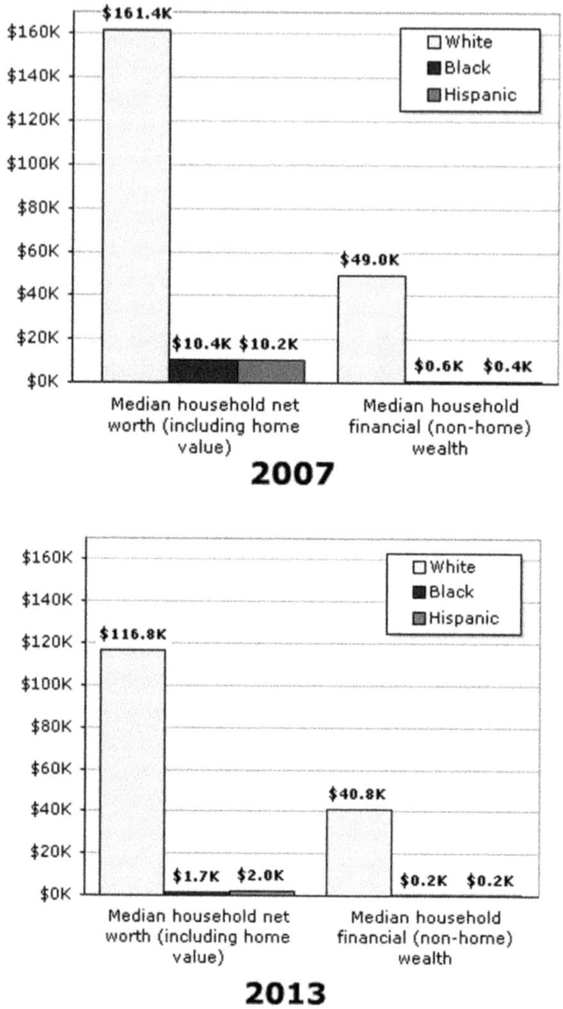

Figure 5.8 Median Household Net Worth and Financial Wealth in the United States by Race, 2007 and 2013 (in U.S. Dollars).

Source: Edward N. Wolff, *A Century of Wealth in America* (Cambridge, MA: Harvard University Press, 2017) reported by G. William Domhoff in url: http://www2.ucsc.edu/ whorulesamerica/power/wealth.html

Note: All amounts adjusted to 2013 U.S. dollars. The figure is modified from the original wealth and income data to show comparisons in household wealth for the two years, 2007 and 2013. For a similar comparison of data on household income distribution for the same years, see Figure 3.3 in Chapter 3 of this book.

Recession of 2008–2009 further exacerbated these disparities between White and non-White households, such that by 2013, when the full force of the recession hit many vulnerable households, the median household net worth (including an owner-occupied home) for Whites dropped to

$116,800, while it devastated Black households whose net worth was only $1,700 and for Hispanics it fell to $2,000. Finally, when looking at data on median household financial wealth (excluding an owner-occupied home), the figure for White households was $40,000 while for African American and Hispanic households was $200 each!

In his cogent analysis of the dire situation confronting African American and Hispanic households regarding median financial wealth in the United States, G. William Domhoff, who has spent many years in studying the social, economic, and political realities of contemporary American society, concludes: "In 2013, the average White household had more than 15 times as much total wealth as the average African-American or Latino household. If we exclude home equity from the calculations, and consider only financial wealth, the ratios are more than 200:1."[14] A decade later, in the post-COVID-19 Pandemic era in 2022, the situation has gotten worse not only for working people in general, but especially for those suffering from the racial divide and the rampant racism that has permeated American society in the early 21st century.

What these data show is that, both in terms of the composition and magnitude of wealth at the two opposite polls of the wealth distribution axis as well as the disparities in wealth by race, the United States is a highly divided society along class (and racial) lines—a situation that has dire consequences for future generations of Americans in terms of the implications of concentrated economic (and, as a result, political) power that would further threaten democratic governance and the equitable distribution of resources in the United States.

Income Inequality

Income inequality is a reflection of the amount of wealth and economic position one has in society, as wealth assures additional income in the form of profits, interest, dividends, and other sources of earnings that increases one's assets as well as access to resources that provide higher levels of earnings.[15] Wealthy people acquire positions in society that bring in greater income and benefits that separate them from their less fortunate counterparts in the income structure in the lower rungs of society.

The common way of measuring disparities in the distribution of income is through the division of the household population into quintiles (or fifths) and the top 1 percent and 5 percent of families in the United States. Data on the distribution of income among each fifth (20 percent) of households (as well as the top 1 percent and 5 percent of households) over a number of years would provide us a general view of patterns of income distribution. Looking at household income in quintiles, we see that much of the gains have occurred in the upper quintiles, while the lower quintiles have either stagnated or declined in terms of their share of the total national income.

This is evident in data on the distribution of income in the United States over much of the 20th century and into the 21st century, but especially over the past several decades, starting in the late 1970s (see Figure 5.9).

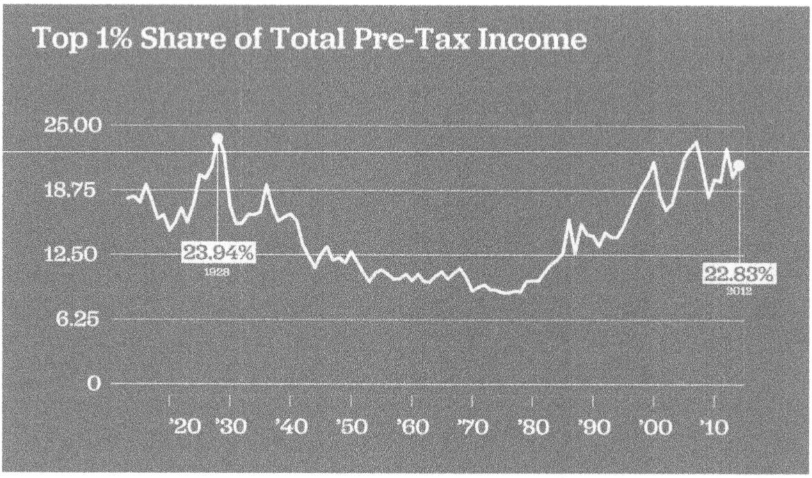

Figure 5.9 Top 1 Percent Share of Total Pretax Income, 1913–2012 (in Percent). Source: http://inequality.org/wp-content/uploads/2011/01/income-inequality-charts.pdf?aeaco

Table 5.3 Share of Aggregate Income Received by Each Fifth and Top 5 Percent of Families, 1970–2020 (in Percent)

	Share of Aggregate Income					
Year	*Lowest 20%*	*Second 20%*	*Third 20%*	*Fourth 20%*	*Highest 20%*	*Top 5%*
1970	5.4	12.2	17.6	23.8	40.9	15.6
1975	5.6	11.9	17.7	24.2	40.7	14.9
1980	5.3	11.6	17.6	24.4	41.1	14.6
1985	4.8	11.0	16.9	24.3	43.1	16.1
1990	4.6	10.8	16.6	23.8	44.3	17.4
1995	4.4	10.1	15.8	23.2	46.5	20.0
2000	4.3	9.8	15.4	22.7	47.7	21.1
2005	4.0	9.6	15.3	22.9	48.1	21.1
2010	3.8	9.4	15.4	23.5	47.9	20.0
2015	3.7	9.2	15.2	23.2	48.6	20.9
2020	3.7	9.1	14.7	22.6	49.8	21.6

Source: U.S. Census Bureau, *Historical Income Tables: Families*, Table F-2, https://www.census.gov/data/tables/time-series/demo/income-poverty/historical-income-families.html (accessed November 8, 2021).

Focusing on the latter period (late 20th and early 21st century—between 1970 and 2020), we find that while the shares in total income of the top 5 percent and the highest fifth of families have increased, the share of the bottom three-fifths of families has decreased. In looking at the data in Table 5.3, we find that the top 5 percent of families received 15.6 percent of the total aggregate income in 1970, 17.4 percent of the total in 1990, 20 percent of the total in 2010, and to 21.6 percent of the total in 2020. The highest 20 percent of families received 40.9 percent of the total aggregate income in 1970, 44.3 percent of the total in 1990, 47.9 percent of the total in 2010, and 49.8 percent of the total in 2020. However, the lowest 20 percent of families received 5.4 percent of the total aggregate income in 1970, dropping to 4.6 percent in 1990, to 3.8 percent in 2010, and to 3.7 percent in 2020 (see Table 5.3).

The Sources of Wealth and Income Inequality

While the distribution of both wealth and income are highly unequal in the United States, a look at data comparing wealth and income for a single year (2001) would highlight the fact that the distribution of wealth is much more unequal than the distribution of income (see Figure 5.10).[16] Thus, while the top 5 percent of households accounted for 22.4 percent of the total income, they accounted for 59.2 percent of the total wealth, and while the top 20 percent of households accounted for 50.1 percent of the total income, they accounted for 84.4 percent of the total wealth. In contrast, at the other end of the wealth and income distribution matrix, the bottom 40 percent of households accounted for 12.2 percent of the total income, but only 0.3 percent of the total wealth (see Figure 5.10).

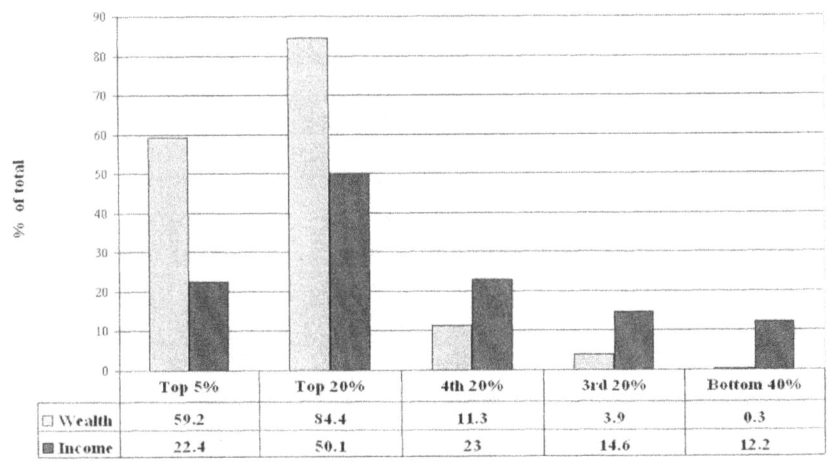

Figure 5.10 Total Wealth and Total Income of Households in the United States, 2001 (in Percent).

Source: https://www.faculty.fairfield.edu/faculty/hodgson/Courses/so11/stratification/income&wealth.htm

The key factor in the increase in wealth and income inequality in the United States has been the rise in productivity of labor, hence the rise in the rate of surplus value (or profits attained through the exploitation of labor)—which is the source of all wealth that is created by labor in society—and a consequent drop in labor's share over the years.[17] "From 1972 through 2009," writes James Cypher, "'usable' productivity – *that part of productivity growth that is available for raising wages and living standards* – increased by 55.5%. Meanwhile, real average hourly pay *fell* by almost 10% (excluding benefits)."[18] He goes on to point out:

> Had compensation matched *'usable'* productivity growth, the (adjusted) 84 million non-supervisory and production workers in 2009 would have received roughly $1.91 *trillion* more in wages and benefits. That is, 13.5% of the nation's Gross Domestic Product in 2009 was transferred from non-supervisory workers to capitalists (and managers) via the gap of 44.4 percent that had opened up between compensation and 'usable' productivity since 1972.[19]

Thus, as production and productivity per labor hour consistently increased during the postwar period, labor's share declined consistently during this period – from 40 percent in 1950 to 25 percent in 1984, to 18 percent in 2000, to 14.7 percent in 2011.[20] At the same time, the rate of surplus value in U.S. manufacturing industry nearly quadrupled during this same period – from 150 percent in 1950 to 302 percent in 1984, to 453 percent in 2000, to 580 percent in 2011 (see Figures 5.11A and 5.11B).[21]

This, together with favorable government policies toward large corporations (e.g., capital gains tax cuts), has resulted in record corporate profits. As a result, total corporate profits have increased immensely during the past several decades, from $80 billion in 1970 to $290 billion in 1985, to $730 billion in 2000, $1.8 trillion in 2010, to $2.3 trillion in 2020; likewise, total profits of domestic industries have increased several-fold during this period, from $73 billion in 1970 to $252 billion in 1985, to $584 billion in 2000, to $1.4 trillion in 2010, to $1.9 trillion in 2020, with the nonfinancial sector accounting for much of the profits, which reached $1.4 trillion in 2020 (see Table 4.3 in Chapter 4).[22]

While immense wealth has been accumulated by the wealthy owners of the giant corporations and banks, even during periods of economic crises, such as the Great Recession of 2008–2009, more and more workers have been struggling to hold on to their meager pay to maintain their standard of living at the other end of the class divide.[23] The resultant class polarization between labor and capital has thus become crystallized through the disparities in the distribution of wealth and income in the United States over the past several decades.[24] This disparity is also manifested in cumulative changes in real annual income between those on top of the income ladder and those on the bottom. As Figure 5.12 illustrates, between 1979

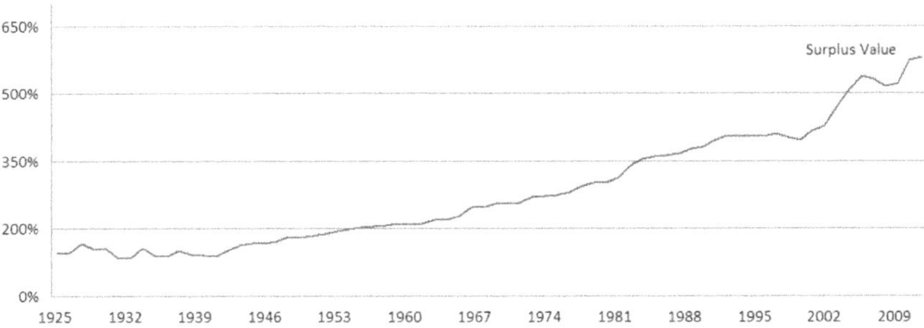

Figure 5.11A The Rate of Surplus Value, 1925–2011 (in Percent).

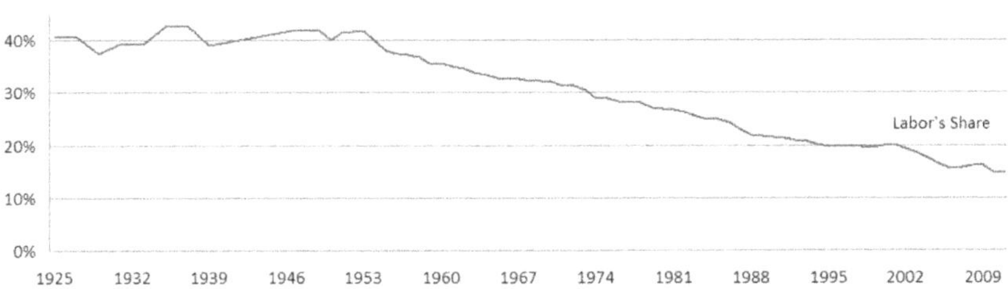

Figure 5.11B Labor's Share in Production, 1925–2011 (in Percent).

Source for Figure 5.11A and 5.11B: Victor Perlo, *Super Profits and Crises: Modern U.S. Capitalism* (New York: International Publishers, 1988), p. 43. Data for 1984–2011 updated by the author.

and 2013, the real annual income of the top 1 percent of income earners increased by 138 percent; that of the top 5 percent increased by 60 percent; and that of the bottom 90 percent increased by only 15 percent (see Figure 5.12).

Looking at the ratio of CEO compensation to workers' wages between 1965 and 2013, we find that it went from 20 times in 1965 to 59 times in 1990, to 383 times in 2000, dropping to 188 times during the 2000–2002 recession, climbing up to 351 times in 2007, dropping to 228 times during the Great Recession of 2008–2009, and finally climbing back up to 296 times by 2013 (see Figure 5.13).

Rising productivity of labor, through the intensified exploitation of wage-labor, has resulted in a tremendous expansion of corporate profits and the extended accumulation of capital by the capitalists and their CEOs, who have significantly benefited from the process of capitalist expansion based on the exploitation of the working class in the United States. This process has led to class polarization, class conflict, and class struggle throughout the history of capitalism in the United States, with

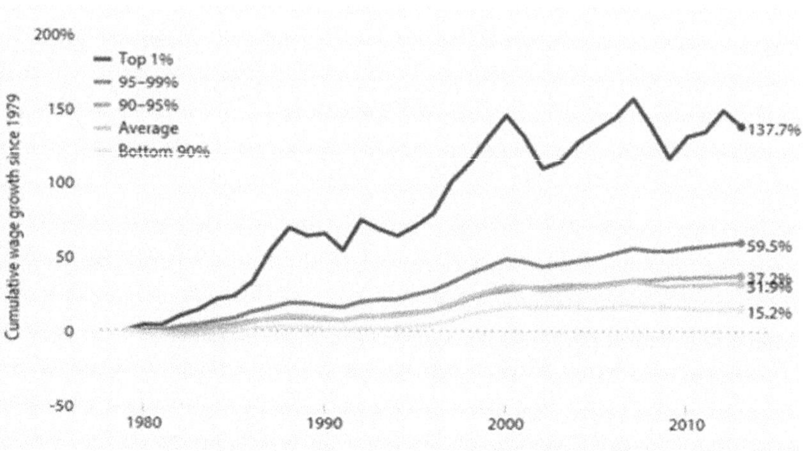

Figure 5.12 Cumulative Change in Real Annual Income by Income Group, 1979–2013 (in Percent).

Source: Economic Policy Institute analysis of data from Kopezuk, Saez, and Song (2010) and Social Security Administration wage statistics. Reproduced from Figure F in *Raising America's Pay: Why It is Our Central Economic Policy Challenge.*

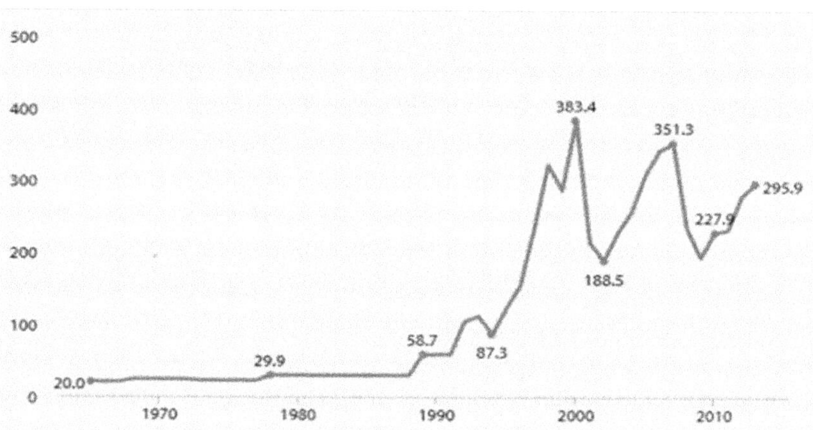

Figure 5.13 CEO-to-worker Compensation Ratio, 1965–2013.

Source: Economic Policy Institute analysis of data from Compustat's ExecuComp database, Bureau of Labor Statistics, Current Employment Statistics, and Bureau of Economic Analysis NIPA Tables.

changes in the balance of class forces that has maintained the continuation of the exploitation and repression of labor on one hand and resistance and struggle against that repression throughout the 20th and early 21st centuries on the other. This predicament has been and will continue to be the case as long as private property and the private accumulation of capital prevail and are transmitted to future generations of the wealthy through inheritance. Thus, to reduce and ultimately eliminate wealth and income inequality, both private property and inheritance of that property will need to be abolished. This is an important issue that will have immense political implications for American society in the 21st century.

Inequality, Class Conflict, and Social Transformation

Given the immense wealth and income inequality in the United States, it should come as no surprise to anyone that class conflict and class struggle are bound to re-emerge from such a volatile situation in the years ahead, just as they have in previous periods in U.S. history. While the weakening of labor unions and radical working-class organizations has made them ineffective in their fight against the capitalist system in the United States at the moment, nothing prevents labor from strengthening its ranks in the future. As the balance of class forces become increasingly in favor of U.S. workers in the years ahead, especially when the ruling capitalist class and its conservative and reformist political parties lose their legitimacy and fail to meet the workers' demands under deteriorating economic conditions that are bound to continue in the coming years, there is a good chance for labor to reorganize and revitalize its power to take on the system.[25]

The critical factor in turning the class struggle around in favor of the U.S. working class under accelerated economic crises and decline of the capitalist system is the centrality of the political organization of labor through class-conscious leadership with experience in past struggles against capital and a track record in scoring victories against their class antagonists, including the state that capital dominates and controls to serve its own class interests. Hence, as the U.S. working class becomes increasingly radicalized and class-conscious, led by a dedicated leadership prepared to win the class war in the struggle against capitalism and the capitalist state, its success to transform and replace the prevailing capitalist system becomes more and more possible. As the present social order begins to crumble and as the balance of class forces increasingly favor the working class, it becomes more and more possible for it to take power and rule over American society in the not too distant future.

This is not an argument based on some flimsy theoretical speculation on the prospects of an exploited class to capture the reigns of state power in an imaginary way to establish a utopia. It is a scientific, empirical observation of the impending class struggle that is based on the reality of contemporary U.S. capitalism embedded in class-based wealth and income inequalities that are fundamentally a product of the exploitation and oppression of wage-labor. These inequalities have, in turn, generated irreconcilable class antagonisms that will eventually require the resolution of the contradictions and conflicts that are part and parcel of modern capitalism that cannot be resolved through reforms and minor adjustments to the existing system. They require a revolutionary transformation of society based on the interests and will of the exploited and oppressed working class that is ready to put into action its growing collective power to reclaim its historic mission and responsibility to bring about the transformation that it is capable of bringing to save humanity from the impending catastrophe. That is what is in store for us if workers fail to realize this important chance they have to set humanity on a peaceful course to finally end all forms of injustice, including class, race, and gender oppression, which has been and continues to be the hallmark of the American Empire—the most exploitative and oppressive empire in history.

Notes

1 Michael D. Yates, *The Great Inequality* (New York: Routledge, 2016).
2 Marco Cagetti and Mariactristina De Nardi, "Wealth Inequality: Data and Models," (Chicago, IL: Federal Reserve Bank of Chicago, 2005), p. 1.
3 Cagetti and De Nardi, "Wealth Inequality: Data and Models," p. 1.
4 Emmanuel Saez and Gabriel Zucman, "Wealth Inequality in the United States since 1913: Evidence From Capitalized Income Tax Data," *Working Paper 20625* (Cambridge, MA: National Bureau of Economic Research, 2014). http://www.nber.org/papers/w20625 (accessed June 28, 2022).
5 Berch Berberoglu (ed.), *The Global Capitalist Crisis and Its Aftermath* (New York: Routledge, 2014).
6 Cagetti and De Nardi, "Wealth Inequality: Data and Models," p. 5.
7 Jerry Kloby, "The Growing Divide: Class Polarization in the United States in the 1980s," *Monthly Review* 39, no.1 (September 1987), p. 7.
8 Joint Economic Committee of the U.S. Congress, cited in Kloby, "The Growing Divide: Class Polarization in the United States in the 1980s," pp. 4–6; Jerry Kloby, "Increasing Class Polarization in the United States: The Growth of Wealth and Income Inequality," in Berch Berberoglu (ed.), *Critical Perspectives in Sociology: A Reader*, 2nd ed. (Dubuque, Iowa: Kendall/Hunt Publishing Company, 1993), pp. 30–35.
9 Edward N. Wolf, *A Century of Wealth in America* (Cambridge, MA: Harvard University Press, 2017).
10 Edward N. Wolff, "Changes in Household Wealth in the 1980s and 1990s in the United States," *Working Paper No 407* (May 2004), p. 34.
11 Wolff, "Changes in Household Wealth in the 1980s and 1990s in the United States," pp. 13–14.
12 Wolff, "Changes in Household Wealth in the 1980s and 1990s in the United States," p. 15.
13 Wolff, "Changes in Household Wealth in the 1980s and 1990s in the United States," p. 15.
14 G. William Domhoff, http://www2.ucsc.edu/whorulesamerica/power/wealth.html (accessed June 28, 2022).
15 Thomas Piketty, *The Economics of Inequality* (Cambridge, MA: Belknap Press, 2015). See also Thomas Piketty, *Capital in the Twenty-first Century* (Cambridge, MA: Belknap Press, 2017).
16 Javier Diaz-Gimenez, et al., "Dimensions of Inequality: Facts on the U.S. Distributions of Earnings, Income, and Wealth," *Federal Reserve Bank of Minneapolis Quarterly Review* 21(2) (Spring 1997), pp. 3–21; Santiago Budria et al., "Updated Facts on the U.S. Distribution of Earnings, Income, and Wealth," *Federal Reserve Bank of Minneapolis Quarterly Review*, 26 (3) (2002), pp. 2–35.

17 Victor Perlo, *Super Profits and Crises: Modern U.S. Capitalism* (New York: International Publishers, 1988), pp. 35-54; Berch Berberoglu (ed.), *Labor and Capital in the Age of Globalization: The Labor Process and the Changing Nature of Work in the Global Economy* (Boulder, CO: Rowman and Littlefield, 2002).

18 James M. Cypher, "Nearly $2 Trillion Purloined From U.S. Workers in 2009" in Linda Pinkow and Sam Pizzigati (eds.), *The Wealth Inequality Reader* (Boston, MA: Dollars & Sense – Economic Affairs Bureau, 2012), p. 47.

19 Cypher, "Nearly $2 Trillion Purloined From U.S. Workers in 2009," p. 49.

20 Data for the years 1950 and 1984 are provided in Perlo, *Super Profits and Crises: Modern U.S. Capitalism*, pp. 35-54. Data for the years 2000 and 2011 were calculated by the author from U.S. Census Bureau statistics.

21 Perlo, *Super Profits and Crises*, Appendix, Table 2A, p. 512. The rates for the years 2000 and 2011 were calculated by the author from the U.S. Census Bureau statistics.

22 U.S. Council of Economic Advisers, *Economic Report of the President 2021,* Table B-54, p. 519.

23 Michael Perelman, "The Corrosive Qualities of Inequality: The Roots of the Current Meltdown," *Challenge,* 51 (5) (2008), pp. 40–64; Raghuram G. Rajan, "Let Them Eat Credit: How Inequality Is at the Root of the Great Recession" *The New Republic* (August 27, 2010); Levin Welch, "The Global Capitalist Crisis and the 2008 Financial Meltdown in the United States," in Berch Berberoglu (ed.), *The Global Capitalist Crisis and Its Aftermath* (New York: Routledge, 2014).

24 Denny Braun, *The Rich Get Richer: The Rise of Income Inequality in the United States and the World* (Chicago, IL: Nelson Hall, 1991); Kloby, "Increasing Class Polarization in the United States: The Growth of Wealth and Income Inequality"; Wolff, "Changes in Household Wealth in the 1980s and 1990s in the United States" and Edward N. Wolff, "Recent Trends in Household Wealth in the United States: Rising Debt and the Middle Class Squeeze," *Working Paper No. 589* (March 2010); Welch, "The Global Capitalist Crisis and the 2008 Financial Meltdown in the United States"; Saez and Zucman "Wealth Inequality in the United States since 1913: Evidence From Capitalized Income Tax Data"; Yates, *The Great Inequality.*

25 Lee H. Adler, Maite Tapia, and Lowell Turner (eds.), *Mobilizing Against Inequality: Unions, Immigrant Workers, and the Crisis of Capitalism* (Ithaca, NY: ILR Press, 2014).

6 The "Great Recession" and the Beginning of the End for the American Empire

The "Great Recession" of 2008–2009, as it has been called, was the worst and most severe economic crisis in the United States since the Great Depression of the 1930s. It spread beyond the United States and unfolded in varying degrees across many regions of the global capitalist economy. It had a devastating effect on millions of working people around the world, while a small minority of wealthy capitalists profited from the downfall of their economies, bringing to bear their monopoly power over the means of production *and destruction* through speculative financial misdeeds and military misadventures that have bankrupted their former rivals (corporations and countries alike) in their imperial overreach to dominate and pillage the world. They have done this with impunity under the guise of neoliberalism and neoliberal economic policies that promote privatization, "free trade," and foreign investment that have led to the outsourcing of production and jobs—policies that governments controlled by capital have championed as a solution to their economic problems. But, in reality they have enriched a tiny fraction of the Empire's population, with most of the rest living paycheck to paycheck, if they are lucky enough to have a job that meets their minimum daily consumption needs.

As the Empire's misguided economic policies came under mounting criticism in many countries across the world and as the global capitalist crisis took on depression-era characteristics, neoliberalism and neoliberal economic policies became thoroughly discredited in countries affected by these calamities around the globe. Whereas millions of unemployed people were looking for a job to pay for basic necessities, governments throughout the world spent hundreds of billions of taxpayer dollars to bail out failed commercial and financial institutions, with more than a trillion dollars of economic stimulus program by the U.S. government alone and hundreds of billions of dollars by other governments in Europe, Asia, and elsewhere spent to counter the devastating effects of the system to save global capitalism from total collapse.[1]

The severity of the 2008–2009 capitalist crisis and its magnitude led analysts to conclude that this severe crisis of global capitalism centered on the United States can certainly be classified as the worst and deepest economic downturn and collapse since the Great Depression of the early 20th

DOI: 10.4324/9781003282105-6

century—a predicament that had and will continue to have serious economic, political, and social consequences for years to come. The capitalist state, finding itself in the midst of an economic crisis that is the product of a system it has long supported and cultivated through the protection of private profit at public expense, realized that the heaviest burden of this economic catastrophe fell on its shoulders to resolve. It is in this context that the state went to great lengths to salvage the failed corporations and financial institutions through the use of the public purse to save the global capitalist system—one that came very close to imploding through the unfolding of its own inherent contradictions.

The Stock Market Crash of 2008–2009 and the Collapse of Major U.S. Corporations

Despite the active role of the state in intervening in the economy to reverse its decline and collapse, corporations and banks, ranging from General Motors and Chrysler to Citigroup and Bank of America as well as financial and brokerage firms (such as Lehman Brothers), insurance companies and real estate underwriters (such as American Insurance Group, Fannie Mae, and Freddie Mack), came to a virtual halt, with some declaring bankruptcy while others threatened to take down with them the entire global capitalist economy.[2] As a result and with a ripple effect across the U.S. economy, the DOW plunged more than 50 percent from its highs of 14,000 in late 2007 to below 6,500 in early 2009, with more than a trillion dollars of value lost in the stock market—a development that threatened economies across the globe and resulted in similar losses in stock markets throughout the capitalist world during this period. The best examples of this impact are what happened to the once-powerful icons of U.S. big business—General Motors, American International Group (AIG), Citigroup, and other big corporations and banks—in the aftermath of the "Great Recession."

Let us take a closer look at six of these major U.S. corporate and financial institutions to assess the magnitude of the damage they suffered. Figure 6.1 documents the dramatic collapse of the once-powerful financial icon of Wall Street, Lehman Brothers brokerage house, which triggered the panic that, compounded by the enormous housing bubble, led to the banking and financial crisis and resulted in the "Great Recession" of 2008–2009.

Although it was officially announced that the recession had actually begun in December 2007, the sharp fall in the stock market in 2008, led by the financials, banks, and key industrial corporations, such as General Motors which declared bankruptcy in June 2009, signaled the beginning of the "Great Recession" (see Figure 6.2 for the collapse and liquidation of General Motors, as its stock stopped trading in March 2011 at 4 cents per share). The period 2008–2009 thus marked the beginning of the "Great

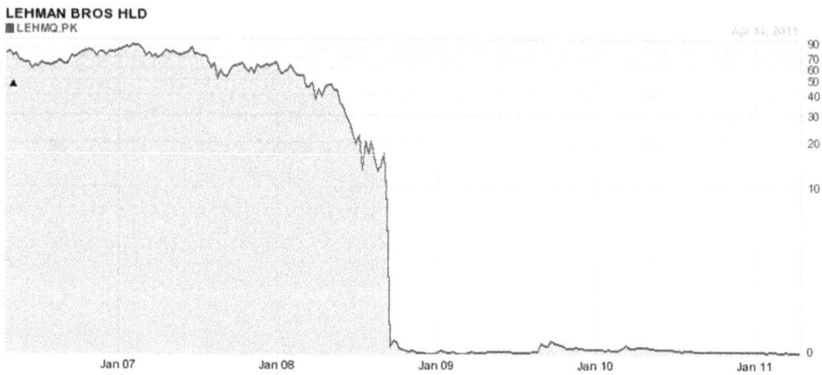

Figure 6.1 Lehman Brothers Stock, 2006–2011 (in Dollars).
Source: Yahoo Finance http://finance.yahoo.com (accessed April 14, 2011).

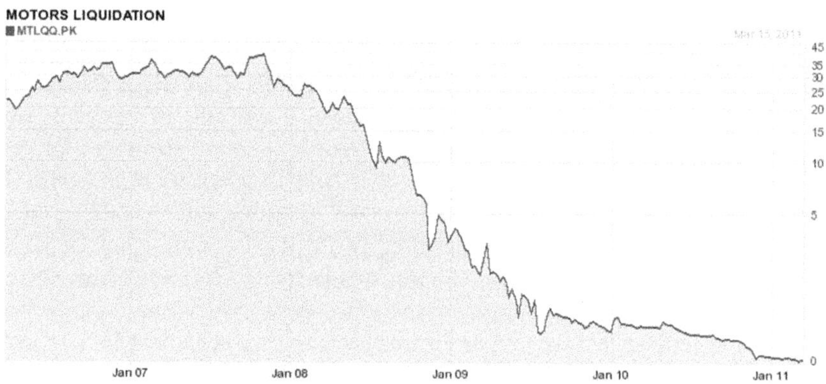

Figure 6.2 General Motors Corporation Stock, 2006–2011 (in Dollars).
Source: Yahoo Finance http://finance.yahoo.com (accessed March 15, 2011).

Recession" in the United States, which continued across the globe well into the mid-2010s.

Figure 6.3 shows one dimension of the collapse of the banking system in 2008–2009 in what happened to the Citigroup, which went from a $55 stock to one that traded for 96 cents in February 2009, before it went up some to the $2.80 level (adjusted for a 1-for-10 reverse stock split in May 2011 that artificially made it a $28 stock in August 2011). Looking at Citigroup in long-term perspective and situating its fall in broader context since the 1980s, Figure 6.4 shows its dramatic rise from the mid-1990s through the 2000s (to 2007), followed by its collapse in 2008–2009 from

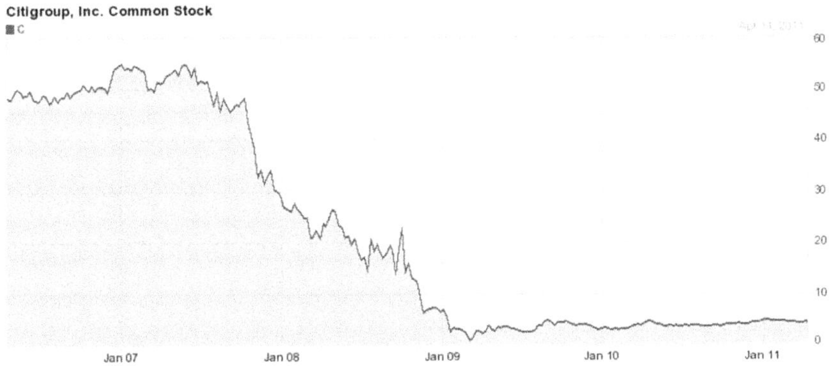

Figure 6.3 Citigroup Inc. Stock, 2006–2011 (in Dollars).
Source: Yahoo Finance http://finance.yahoo.com (accessed April 14, 2011).

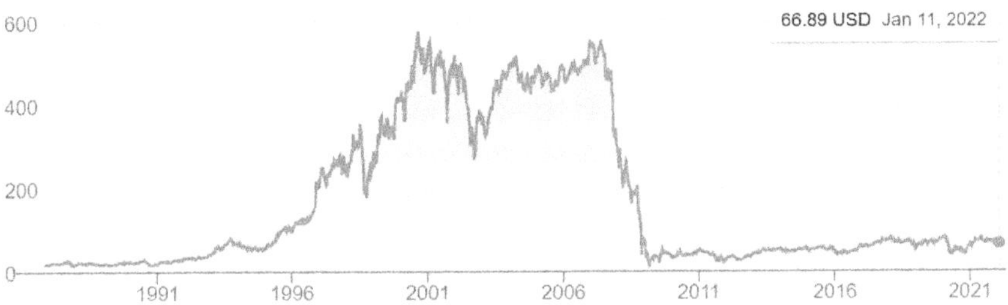

Figure 6.4 Citigroup Inc. Stock, 1986–2022 (in Dollars).
Source: https://google.com (accessed January 11, 2022).
Note: The dollar value of the stock for the period 1986–2022 is adjusted to the 1-for-10 reverse stock split in 2011.

which it has not been able to recover, when its stock traded at $66.89 per share in January 2022 (which is equivalent to $6.69 per share before the 1-for-10 reverse stock split in 2011).

The predicament of the AIG was even more dramatic. The once-giant global insurance company went through a total collapse, with its stock price crashing from above $1,400 a share in mid-2007 to below $9 a share in March 2009 (see Figure 6.5).

AIG was able to avoid bankruptcy only through massive government loans and bailout to prevent a meltdown of the entire U.S. economy. Here was a stock which traded at $1,971 per share in December 2000 had fallen so sharply to under $9 a share during the "Great Recession" that even

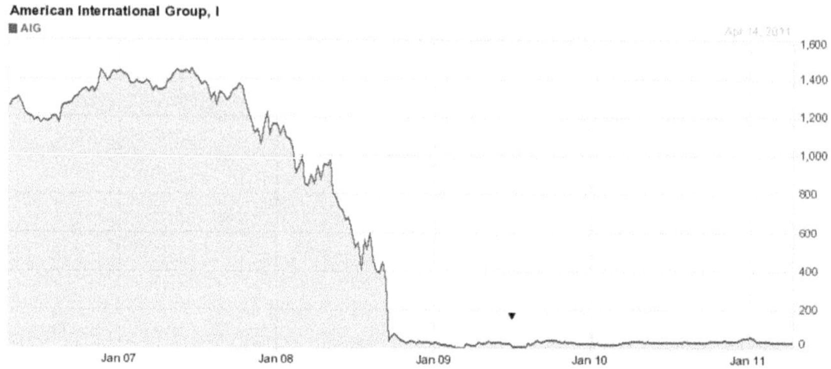

Figure 6.5 American International Group Stock, 2006–2011 (in Dollars).
Source: Yahoo Finance http://finance.yahoo.com (accessed April 14, 2011).

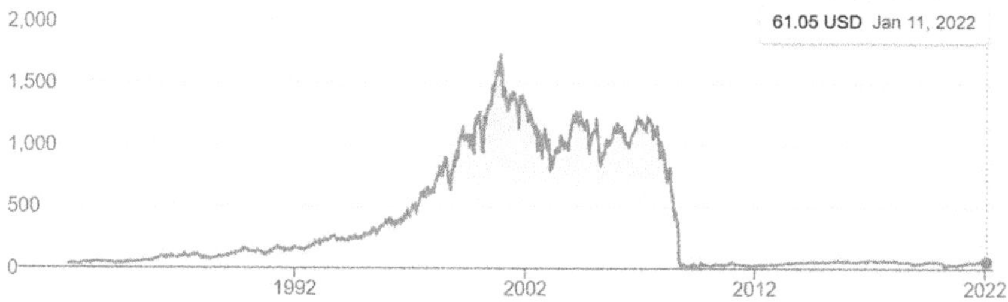

Figure 6.6 American International Group Stock, 1980–2022 (in Dollars).
Source: https://google.com (accessed January 11, 2022).

after more than a decade of "recovery," it rose to only $61.05 per share by January 2022 (see Figure 6.6).

Looking at AIG stock in longer historical perspective since the mid-1980s, we see a sharp rise in its price from the mid-1990s to the early 2000s, when it traded around $1,800 per share in late 2000 and early 2001, stabilizing between $1,000 and $1,500 per share until 2007, and then falling off the cliff in early 2009 and remaining at the $30–$60 per share range during the decade from 2012 to 2022 (see Figure 6.6).

The "Great Recession" of 2008–2009 was precipitated by a number of factors related to the economic crisis that was in the making, above all the collapse of the real estate and housing market which, together with the financial debacle, was one of the central contributing causes. In this context, one need only to review the total devastation of the home mortgage system through decimation of the popularly known Fannie Mae and Freddie Mac federally backed corporate mortgage arrangement. As the stock price of both of these giant housing mortgage institutions illustrate, the sharp drop of Fannie Mae stock from the $50 range in mid-2007 to pennies in October 2008 and the similarly devastating drop in value of Freddie Mac stock from the $68 range in mid-2007 to pennies in October 2008 (see Figures 6.7 and 6.8) show the impact of the "Great Recession" on the economy, especially the housing and mortgage industry, which without government intervention would have seen its total collapse.

By early 2022, these two stocks were each valued at a mere 90 cents per share—a far cry from their heyday of $50 and $68 a share, respectively, not too long ago. Looking at Fannie Mae and Freddie Mac stocks from a

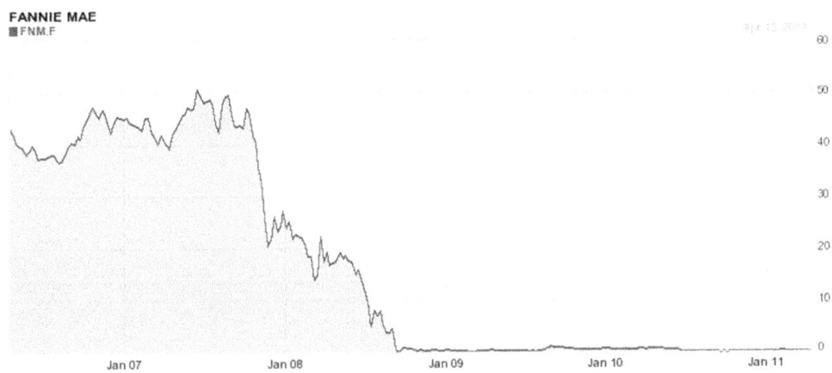

Figure 6.7 Federal National Mortgage Association (Fannie Mae) Stock, 2006–2011 (in Dollars).

Source: Yahoo Finance http://finance.yahoo.com (accessed April 13, 2011).

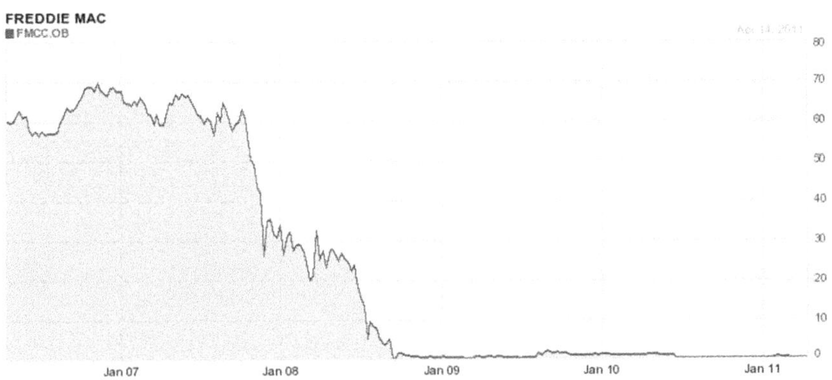

Figure 6.8 Federal Home Loan Mortgage Corp. (Freddie Mac) Stock, 2006–2011 (in Dollars).

Source: Yahoo Finance http://finance.yahoo.com (accessed April 14, 2011).

long-term perspective (Figures 6.9 and 6.10), we see that their stock price greatly increased during the 1990s, stabilized during the early to mid-2000s, and crashed in 2008, and have never recovered since.

The global economic crisis was the main topic of discussion among the heads of the world's leading economies at the G-20 meetings in London in April 2009, which resulted in guarded optimism that through substantial reforms in global financial institutions and an active interventionist state that monitors the situation with greater regulation of the economy, the evolving economic situation might provide the basis for a mild recovery and a new global economic order. However, today, as of this writing in early 2022, more than a decade after the 2008–2009 "Great Recession" had "officially" been declared as "ended" in late 2009, the news about the U.S. and the world economy is not very promising. The economic impact of the COVID-19 lockdown that led to the stock market crash of March 2020 and the subsequent economic downturn with rising unemployment and inflation, with U.S. consumer prices jumping 8.3 percent in May

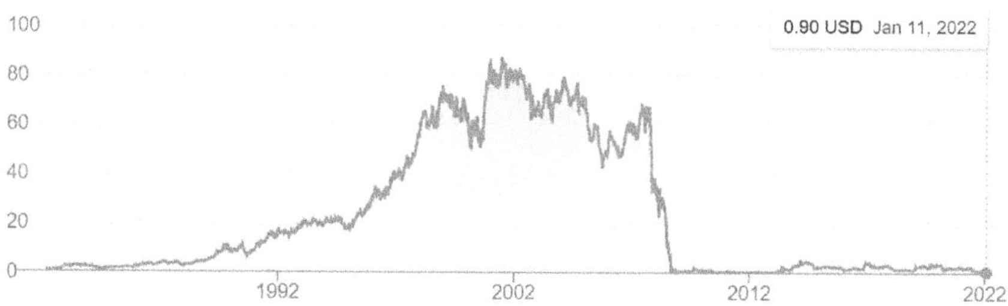

Figure 6.9 Federal National Mortgage Association (Fannie Mae) Stock, 1980–2022 (in Dollars).

Source: https://google.com (accessed January 11, 2022).

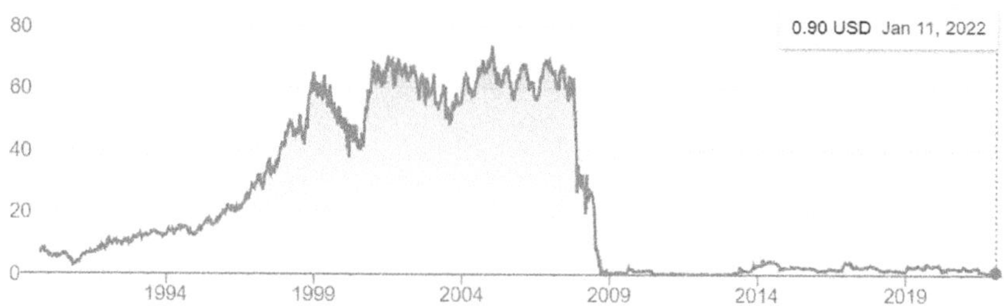

Figure 6.10 Federal Home Loan Mortgage Corp. (Freddie Mac) Stock, 1989–2022 (in Dollars).

Source: https://google.com (accessed January 11, 2022).

2022—the biggest surge in inflation in more than 40 years, with energy 30.3 percent, gasoline 43.6 percent, and fuel oil 80.5 percent.[3]

What the future of the U.S. and global economy will look like and what role the United States will play in it are questions that remain open and depend on the solutions adopted at the national and global level, especially in Europe, East Asia (China), and other emerging centers of global economic power, in the period ahead. But clearly we are going through a very volatile period, and what happens in the next decade will determine the future course of the U.S. and the global economy for a long time to come.

Contradictions and Crises of the Global Capitalist Economy

The development of capitalism over the past 100 years has formed and transformed the U.S. economy in a crucial way, one characterized by periodic crises resulting from the capitalist business cycle that now unfolds at the global level. The current crisis of the global economy is an outcome of the consolidation of economic power that the globalization of capital has secured for the transnational corporations over this period.[4] This has led to a string of problems associated with the contradiction between the expanded forces of production (technology) and existing social relations, which are manifested in a number of ways, including:

1 The problem of overproduction, resulting from the imbalance between wages and prices of commodities fueled by low purchasing power;
2 Increasing unemployment and underemployment, resulting from outsourcing of production to low-wage sweatshops in export processing zones abroad, compounded by the continued application of technology in production (i.e., automation);
3 Sub-prime mortgage and credit card debt and rising home foreclosures and bankruptcies as the unemployed become unable to pay off their debts;
4 Intensification of control and exploitation of labor through expanded production and profits by further accumulation of capital on a world scale;
5 Increased polarization of wealth and income at the national and global level between capital and labor and growth in numbers of the poor and marginalized segments of the population throughout the world.

These and other related contradictions and crises of the global economy define the parameters of capitalist globalization and provide us the framework for discussion on the nature and dynamics of this process that has been unfolding for a number of decades.

Given the logic of global capital accumulation in late capitalist society and the nature of global capitalist expansion on a world scale, it is no accident that the decline of the domestic economy of advanced capitalist countries over the past three decades corresponds to the accelerated export of capital abroad in search of cheap labor, access to raw materials, new markets, and higher rates of profit. The resulting deindustrialization of the domestic economy has had a serious impact on working people and other affected segments of the laboring population and has brought about a major dislocation of national economies.[5] This has necessitated increased state intervention on behalf of the large corporations and has heightened the contradictions that led to the global economic crisis in the early 21st century.

The widening economic gap between labor and capital (within a deteriorating national economy and the state's budgetary crisis) has led to the ensuing political crisis within the state apparatus and has sharpened the conflicts in a new political direction. As the crisis of the global economy has brought the state to center stage of economic life and revealed its ties to the corporations, thus exacerbating the state's legitimization crisis, the anger of the working people and the masses in general are becoming directed not only against capital, but against the state itself.

Global Capitalist Crisis and the Crisis of the Capitalist State

The crisis of the capitalist state on the global scene is a manifestation of the contradictions and crises of the global economy, which in the early 21st century has reached a critical point in its development. The massive flow of U.S. transnational investments throughout the world, especially in Western Europe, Japan, and other advanced capitalist regions, has led to the post-World War II reemergence of rivalry between the major capitalist powers, while fostering antagonisms between them in the scramble for the peripheral regions of the global economy—Latin America, Asia, Africa, and the Middle East.[6] This has created a situation where the state has become a key player to address the problems generated by such rivalry in the global economy. The current COVID-19-induced global economic crisis has made the state's role even more difficult, as it confronts forces that are increasingly hostile to it.

With the integration of the economies of Western Europe into the European Union and the emergence of Japan as a powerful economic force in the late 20th century as well as the rise of China as a global contender in the early 21st century, the position of the United States in the global economy has declined relative to both its own postwar supremacy in the 1940s and 1950s and to other economies since that time. Despite the fact that U.S. capital continues to control the biggest share of overseas markets and accounts for the largest volume of international investments, its hold on the global economy has recently been slipping in a manner similar to Britain's in the early 20th century. This has, in turn, led the U.S. state to play a more aggressive role in foreign policy to protect U.S. corporate interests abroad. Its massive deployment of troops in the Middle East in the early 1990s, which led to the Persian Gulf War of 1991, and subsequently its invasion of Afghanistan in 2001 and war against Iraq in 2003, has resulted in immense military expenditures that have placed an enormous burden on the American people, who have come to shoulder the colossal cost of maintaining a global Empire whose vast military machine encircles the world.[7]

In the current phase of the crisis of the U.S. economy and the state, the problems the state faces are of such magnitude that they threaten the supremacy of the United States in the global political economy and by extension the global capitalist system itself. Internal economic and budgetary problems have been compounded by ever-growing military spending propped up by armed interventions abroad, which have greatly contributed to the rise in the national debt to $30 trillion by 2022.[8] Moreover, a declining economic base at home is further complicated by global rivalry between the major capitalist powers as well as China, which has not been restricted to the economic field alone, but have immense political (and even military) implications that are global in magnitude.[9]

Global Economic Rivalry and Capitalist Crises

The growing prospects of economic rivalry between the major capitalist powers, backed up by their states, are effecting changes in their relations that render the global political economy an increasingly unstable character. Competition between the United States, the European Union, China, and Russia as well as other rival states are setting them on a collision course for world supremacy, manifested in struggles for markets, raw materials, and spheres of influence in geopolitical—as well as economic—terms, which may, in fact, lead to a new configuration of forces and consequently alliances that will have serious political implications in international relations. As the continuing economic ascendance of the major rivals of the United States, like China, take their prominent position in the global economy, pressures will build toward the politicization and militarization of these states from within, where the leading forces in the world economy will press forward with the necessary political and military components of their growing economic power in the global system.[10]

These developments in global economic and geopolitical shifts in the balance of forces among the major powers will bring to the fore new and yet untested international alliances for world supremacy in the 21st century. Such alliances will bring key powers like China and Russia into play in a new and complicated relationship that holds the key for the success or failure of the new rising centers that will emerge as the decisive forces in the global economic, political, and military equation and could lead to a new Cold War in the early decades of the 21st century.[11] Thus, the contradictions and conflicts embedded in relations between rival states of the world may again surface as an important component of international relations in the years ahead.

Such developments are part and parcel of the restructuring of the global economy and the international division of labor through the transfer of production to overseas territories in line with the globalization of capital on a worldwide basis—a process that has serious consequences for the economies of both the advanced and less-developed capitalist countries. Economic crisis and decline in the advanced capitalist centers (manifested in plant closings, unemployment, and recession) and super-exploitation of workers in sweatshops abroad (maintained by repressive authoritarian regimes) yield the same combined result that has a singular global logic: profits. It is in this context of the changes that are taking place on a world scale that the state is beginning to confront the current crisis of global capitalism.

Focusing on the most recent economic crisis in the United States—the "Great Recession" of 2008–2009—Richard D. Wolff, Professor Emeritus of Economics at the University of Massachusetts at Amherst, points out that empowered by the persistent struggles of trade unions from the 1820s to the 1970s, U.S. workers experienced a rising level of wages every decade; this came to an end, however, in the 1970s, as real wages stopped rising and they have never resumed since.[12] U.S. workers became more productive, but got paid the same; wages began to stagnate and decline, while the profits of the capitalists multiplied many-fold.

Given this process which favored capital and capitalists over labor, the large corporations made huge profits and had much money at their disposal. They bought other corporations (through mergers and acquisitions) and they put their money into banks. The banks loaned that money (with interest!) to workers who didn't have money to consume. This was done to raise the workers' purchasing power because their wages weren't enough to buy things. Since employers no longer raised workers' wages, the workers had to go into debt to survive. Debt began to rise and things got out of control. As corporations increasingly began to invest abroad (outsourcing production and services), U.S. workers lost their jobs, and this led to greater unemployment and underemployment.[13] Unemployed workers with a lot of debt were unable to make their mortgage and credit card payments, and were forced to go into foreclosures and bankruptcies. This, in turn, led to the collapse of the banking system, necessitating a government bailout of the banks. Wolff points out that it is only through the nearly trillion-dollar stimulus funds that the U.S. government poured into the economy to save the banks from default that a financial collapse like the Great Depression was averted.

Extent of the Capitalist Crisis in the United States during the "Great Recession"

The global capitalist crisis during the "Great Recession" of 2008–2009 has been deep and widespread, especially in the United States, the epicenter of the crisis. At the height of the "Great Recession," unemployment reached unprecedented levels, from seven million in December 2007 to 16 million in October 2010; counting the discouraged and part-time workers, the unemployment rate reached 18 percent in 2010. Foreclosures were running at over one million a year. Poverty rose to 44 million people, as one in seven Americans lived at or below the poverty line. A decade later, with the economic problems compounded by the COVID-19 lockdown, the situation has become much worse, with unemployment levels reaching depression-era figures as more than 25 percent of the labor force (or 42.6 million people) claimed unemployment benefits in mid-2020—an economic situation characterized by the mainstream media as being the worst since the Great Depression of the 1930s and the "Great Recession" of 2008–2009.[14]

Over the course of the late 20th and early 21st centuries, the decline in manufacturing through shifts in production to overseas territories, where cheap labor is employed in sweatshops across East and Southeast Asia, and the rise in finance capital has resulted in much lower levels of manufacturing employment after the 1970s compared to earlier periods going back to the postwar 1950s, as the share of domestic manufacturing began to sharply decline after the mid-1960s (see Figure 6.11).

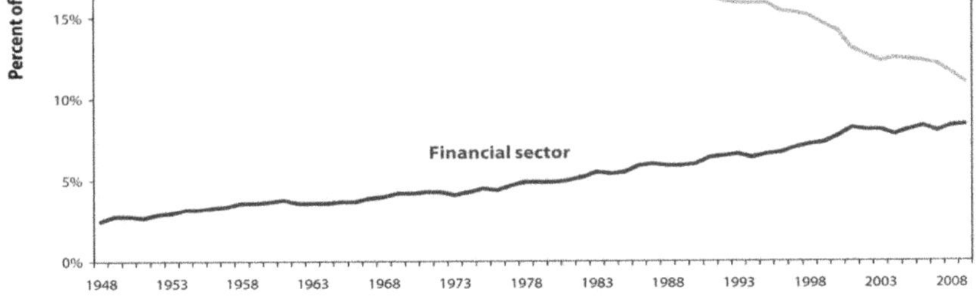

Figure 6.11 Manufacturing and Finance Sectors as Share of the Overall U.S. Economy, 1948–2008.

Source: Bureau of Economic Analysis data compiled by the Economic Policy Institute.

Gone are the days of the auto and steel industries and the smoke-stacked factories of the industrial age through the 20th century. These are now replaced by a service industry that is based on low-wage, low-skill, non-union, part-time, contingent labor, which has enriched wealthy capitalists and impoverished working men and women in the United States and around the world into the 21st century, with all the social and economic consequences for the fate of the American Empire across the globe. With the steady decline of the manufacturing sector in the United States through outsourcing of production to cheap labor areas abroad, 2.9 million well-paying manufacturing jobs disappeared in the period 2005–2008 alone. And that's on top of a loss of more than three million jobs in manufacturing from 1998 to 2003, with millions more lost in the entire postwar period. This has greatly transformed the labor force structure in the United States from a traditionally industrial economy to a new service economy, with all the associated implications for labor, the central one of which is its impact on employment.

In looking at unemployment data for 2007 through 2010, in the depth of the "Great Recession," we see that the unemployment rate was 4.6 percent in 2007, climbing to 5.8 percent in 2008, rising sharply to 9.3 percent in 2009, and remaining at 9.6 percent in 2010 (see Figure 6.12). During the two years following the onset of the recession, the official unemployment rate continued to hover above the 9 percent level.

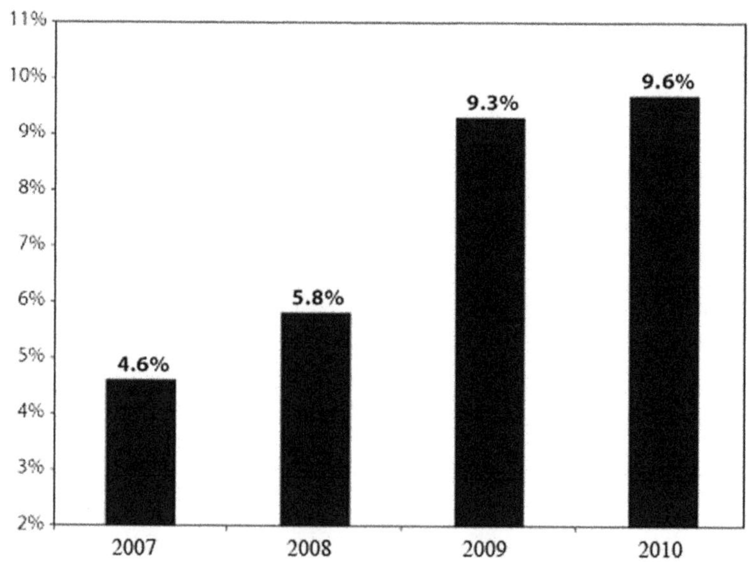

Figure 6.12 Average Annual Unemployment Rate, 2007–2010 (in Percent).
Source: Bureau of Labor Statistics.

Writing in July 2011 on the deteriorating unemployment situation in the United States, Associated Press economics writer Paul Wiseman observed: "booming profits have allowed Corporate America to leave the Great Recession far behind. But millions of ordinary Americans are stranded in a labor market that looks like it's still in recession."[15] He went on to point out that "unemployment is stuck at 9.2 percent, two years into what economists call a recovery. Job growth has been slow and wages stagnant."[16] Citing recent research by Andrew Sum, Director of the Center for Labor Market Studies at Northwestern University, Wiseman reported that:

> wages and salaries accounted for just 1 percent of economic growth in the first 18 months after economists declared that the recession had ended in June 2009… . In the same period after the 2001 recession, wages and salaries accounted for 15 percent. They were 50 percent after the 1991–92 recession, and 25 percent after the 1981–82 recession. Corporate profits, by contrast, accounted for an unprecedented 88 percent of economic growth during those first 18 months. That's compared with 53 percent after the 2001 recession, nothing after the 1991–92 recession and 28 percent after the 1981–82 recession.[17]

In elaborating on this theme in his article "A Boom in Corporate Profits, a Bust in Jobs, Wages," which he called an "economic disconnect" in referring to the surge in corporate profits while jobs and wages remained at recession levels, Wiseman listed several factors that contributed to this predicament:

- U.S. corporations are expanding overseas, not so much at home… . In the 2000s, they added 2.4 million jobs in foreign countries and cut 2.9 million jobs in the United States, according to the Commerce Department.
- Back in the United States, companies are squeezing more productivity out of staffs thinned by layoffs during the "Great Recession." They don't need to hire. And they don't need to be generous with pay raises; they know their employees have nowhere else to go.
- Companies remain reluctant to spend the $1.9 trillion in cash they've accumulated, especially in the United States, which would create jobs.[18]

The grim economic situation affecting millions of workers across the nation during the "Great Recession" prompted others like Simon Johnson, the former chief economist at the International Monetary Fund, to ask: "A Second Great Depression, or Worse?" Writing in *The New York Times* of August 18, 2011, Johnson warned of a prolonged period of economic crisis that may afflict the U.S. economy in the aftermath of the "Great Recession"; although "the main features of the Great Depression have not yet manifested themselves and still seem unlikely," he wrote, "it is increasingly likely that we will find ourselves in the midst of something nearly as traumatic, a long slump of the kind seen with some regularity in the 19th century."[19]

Data on unemployment, released in September 2011 by the Bureau of Labor Statistics and reported by the Economic Policy Institute, revealed that the unemployment rate in August 2011 was 9.1 percent (still above 9 percent). This amounted to 14 million workers who were still unemployed (6.3 million more than in December 2007), many of whom were concentrated in 11 states with double-digit unemployment rates. The *under*employment rate (i.e., those who are unemployed, marginally attached, or working part time involuntarily) was 16.2 percent. Altogether, there were 25.3 million workers who were either unemployed or underemployed in August 2011. Whites had an unemployment rate of 8.0 percent, Blacks 16.7 percent, and Hispanics 11.3 percent. In July 2011, seasonally adjusted underemployment was 13.2 percent for Whites, 25.3 percent for Blacks, and 22.0 percent for Hispanics. And the youth unemployment rate for all 16–24 years old was 17.7 percent and for all 16–19 years old it was 25.4 percent, while for 16–19 years old Blacks it was 46.5 percent and for 16–19 years old Hispanics it was 37.4 percent in August 2011.[20]

Looking at the unemployment situation in broader perspective, data for the period 2005–2010 show that the gap in the labor market due to the rise in unemployment from the fourth quarter of 2007 to the fourth quarter

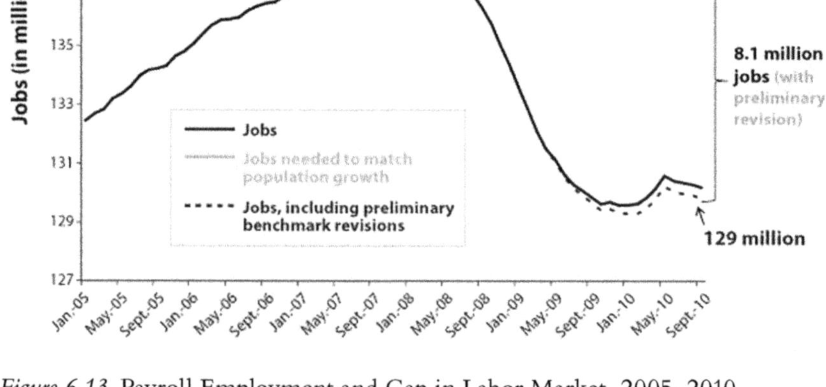

Figure 6.13 Payroll Employment and Gap in Labor Market, 2005–2010.
Source: Bureau of Labor Statistics data compiled by Economic Policy Institute.

of 2010, the worst period of the "Great Recession," was 11.5 million jobs. Thus, while jobs needed to match population growth would have put employment at the 141 million level in September 2010, the actual number of people working in September 2010 (129 million) put the total *deficit* in jobs at 11.5 million (see Figure 6.13).

Despite the slight improvement in the unemployment rate by August 2011, down to the 9.1 percent level, the economy still needed 11.2 million jobs to regain its pre-recession level of unemployment. A decade later, in March 2020, the U.S. economy was to come to terms with an unexpected global health crisis, the Coronavirus Pandemic, which effectively shut down the economy in the COVID-19 lockdown that triggered another recession in 2020.

The Continuing Global Capitalist Crisis Compounded by the COVID-19 Pandemic

The global expansion of capital has had a great impact on the continuing global capitalist crisis. This impact is the result of the globalization process, which has undermined national economies in the interests of transnational capital that profits from its global operations on a world scale, thus generating contradictions at a dual level: global and national.

At the global level, it has meant first and foremost the ever-growing use of cheap labor across the world, hence high rates of exploitation of labor. In addition, it has caused a depletion of resources that could be used for national development; environmental pollution and other health hazards; a growing national debt that tie many countries to the World Bank, the International Monetary Fund, and other global financial institutions; and a growing militarization of society through endless wars and the imposition of military and civilian dictatorships that violate basic human rights. The domination and control of countries for transnational profits through the instrumentality of the imperial state has at the same time created various forms of dependence of less-developed countries on the advanced capitalist centers that has become a defining characteristic of globalization today.[21]

Domestically, the globalization of capital and global economic expansion has had immense dislocations in the national economies of advanced capitalist states. Expansion of manufacturing industry abroad has meant a decline in local industry, as plant closings in the United States and other advanced capitalist economies have worsened the unemployment situation. The massive expansion of capital abroad has resulted in hundreds of factory shutdowns with millions of workers losing their jobs; hence the surge in unemployment in the United States and other advanced capitalist countries. This has led to a decline in wages of workers in the advanced capitalist centers, as low wages abroad have played a competitive role in keeping wages down at home. The drop in incomes among a growing section of the U.S. working class has thus lowered the standard of living of Americans in general and led to further polarization between labor and capital in the United States.[22]

The globalization of capital and the integration of national economies into the global system, a process that has been developing over the past several decades and its intensification under neoliberal capitalist policies over the past 40 years, had a direct impact on the extent and depth of the current global economic crisis. Previously nationally based economies, now under the control of transnational corporations and international financial institutions, have become appendages of the global economy that operates under the logic of global capital accumulation for the benefit of the transnationals while at a great cost to those who have become its victims.

Merely a decade after the "Great Recession" of 2008–2009 that plunged the global economy into a severe economic crisis, the COVID-19 Pandemic that spread across the world starting in December 2019 led to a global lockdown that triggered another severe economic crisis on a world scale, leading to the stock market crash in March 2020 when the Dow Jones Industrials dropped 2,997 points in a single day on March 16, the worst one-day drop in history.[23] Overall, the Dow dropped from nearly 30,000 in mid-February 2020 to just over 18,000 in late March 2020 (a drop of 38 percent), signaling the start of a second "Great Recession" or worse, as by June 2020 over 56 million workers had become unemployed, with millions more in danger of losing their jobs. By the end of February 2022, the COVID-19 Pandemic had already taken the lives of over 930,000 Americans, and by May 2022 the death toll had surpassed one million in the worst public health crisis since the Spanish Flue Pandemic of 1918-1919 when over 600,000 Americans had died. And one of the worst global economic crises since the Great Depression of 1929, triggered by COVID-19 in 2020, caused havoc around the globe, with devastating consequences for working people in the United States and other countries across the world.

A major global economic crisis, such as the Great Depression nearly a century ago and the "Great Recession" of a decade ago compounded by a global health crisis—the Spanish Flue Pandemic of a century ago and the COVID-19 Pandemic that we have experienced in 2020–2022—have greatly affected the economies of those nations that have become part of the global capitalist system. Thus, all the known consequences of such economic downturn (rising unemployment and underemployment, inflation and declining purchasing power, growing consumer debt, home mortgage foreclosures, small-business bankruptcies, and a host of other economic problems) are the very ingredients of a system-wide crisis. Such crisis has affected not only the advanced capitalist countries (where these crises have originated or are exacerbated), but all others integrated into the global capitalist system—more so in the latter, as they are more vulnerable to the forces of the global economy and its periodic cyclical crises.

The contradictions of global economic expansion, which have caused so many problems in both the periphery and the imperial centers, have, in turn, created the conditions for the decline and fall of the global capitalist system. Economically, these contradictions have afflicted the system with recessions, depressions, and associated realization crises; politically, it has set in motion an interventionist imperial state that through its presence in every corner of the world has incurred an enormous military expenditure to maintain an empire, while confronting the resentment of millions of people across the globe who are engaged in active struggles against it.[24]

The imperial state, extending its rule across vast territories, has dwarfed the militaristic adventures of past empires. Through its political and military supremacy, it has come to exert its control over many countries. As a result, acting on behalf of capital, it has reinforced the domination of capital over labor across the globe. This, in turn, has greatly politicized the conflict between labor and capital and led to a direct clash between these forces. Such clash takes on special significance during global economic crises, as labor and other affected segments of society increasingly become conscious of their interests and begin to take political action that directly confront capital and the capitalist state; in effect, the Empire and all its dependent states that embodies the entire global capitalist system.

Which Way Out of the Crisis of America's Global Capitalist Empire?

Economic remedies to save the Empire from collapse are bound to fail so long as they remain within the framework of the existing global capitalist system. Changes that are required to revitalize the global economy and to turn things around point to a redistribution of wealth and income to increase mass consumption on a global scale. This would increase demand for consumer goods, hence increase production, and create well-paying jobs for the unemployed as well as raising revenue for the state. All these would require a restructuring of the economy away from failed neoliberal corporate capitalist policies and toward a new set of priorities that promote the interests of the working people. Such restructuring requires the transformation of the capitalist-imperialist system. This would provide greater rights and benefits to working people and, in turn, benefit society greatly and set us on a prosperous course that would vastly improve living standards and pull us out of recurring capitalist economic crises.

However, these are not things that can readily be adopted within the framework of the prevailing capitalist order. As vested economic interests lie at the heart of any class-based system, the capitalist system too is based on powerful class forces that control, dominate, and benefit from the policies of the state and major social, economic, and political institutions of capitalist society that promote the accumulation of capital and secure the wealth of the capitalist class through the powers of the capitalist state.[25]

Thus, to change the existing societal order, it becomes incumbent upon the working class and its allies to take charge of their political destiny and carry out the transformation of capitalist society, especially capital's supportive political arm, the capitalist state, to dismantle the Empire that has caused so much harm to many across the globe.

The ongoing global capitalist crisis that we are experiencing today is a product of decades of neoliberal capitalist policies of privatization, deregulation, tax cuts for the rich, speculative investments, financialization, and profiteering of unimaginable proportions. Through such practices, most capitalists became very wealthy and amassed great fortunes during this period, while working people were super-exploited through extremely low wages in the sweatshops of the giant capitalist corporations that have spread their tentacles across the globe.

In 2008, global capitalism came very close to destroying the very system that it had created not so long ago. Cyclical crises of recessions and depressions, economic rivalry, political and military conflict, war, and other forms of disruptions and catastrophes have been the characteristics of global capitalism ever since its inception in Europe and the United States a few centuries ago. In my book *Beyond the Global Capitalist Crisis: The World Economy in Transition*, published in 2012, I pointed out that:

> Tracing the evolution of the capitalist economy and the capitalist business cycle historically, it becomes clear that the ups and downs—"booms and busts"—of the capitalist economy is the result of the "normal" process of evolution of the capitalist system, and that economic crises (i.e., recessions and depressions) are a recurrent aspect of capitalism at the national and now the global level.[26]

I went on to argue that therefore:

> the crisis-ridden business cycle of capitalism—one that is to be found *only under capitalism*—is the life-blood of the capitalist system in that capitalism cannot grow and prosper without such a 'correction' (crisis) in the economy every few years. And this can be seen as part of the process of capitalist expansion and contraction over its life-course.[27]

The contradictions of the unfolding process of global capitalist expansion and accumulation have brought to the fore new political realities: as the crisis unfolds and leads to further political organizing and mobilization by labor, the institutional forces that support the global capitalist power structure intensify renewed repression at home and abroad. This is done to control and neutralize an increasingly frustrated labor movement in the center states and militant mass movements of popular forces in the less-developed states of the periphery that are poised to resist neoliberal capitalist globalization.[28] This has occurred most visibly in Latin America,

Southeastern Europe, the Middle East, North Africa, and other regions where neoliberal policies have come under sharp attack and where popular alliances of oppressed classes have managed to come to power or are in the process of mobilizing their forces for such an eventuality.

The continuation of the economic crisis in the advanced capitalist countries is bound to lead to the emergence of similar movements that will seek a political solution to the persistent economic problems that they now confront in the imperial heartlands. And as the social and economic position of the affected populations become threatened in a more severe way across these regions, one can expect the resurgence of grassroots political movements to enter center stage and play a critical role in the coming period of crises and conflicts that will continue to unfold in the years ahead. Clearly, the inherent contradictions of global capitalism are making it increasingly difficult for the imperial state and the American Empire in general to control and manage the global political economy, as the continuing global capitalist crises are making things worse for the state to halt the process from further decline and decay. At the same time, such recurring crises are preparing the conditions for the international solidarity of labor in confronting global capital to address the many social, economic, and political inequities that characterize the global capitalist system dominated by the American Empire. Thus, while the prospects for positive change in the United States and the world appear to be good in the period ahead, it can only come through mass political action by the global working class *after* the dismantling of the American Empire.

Notes

1 Berch Berberoglu (ed.), *Beyond the Global Capitalist Crisis: The World Economy in Transition* (Burlington, VT: Ashgate, 2012) and Berch Berberoglu (ed.) *The Global Capitalist Crisis and Its Aftermath: The Causes and Consequences of the Great Recession of 2008-2009* (Burlington, VT: Ashgate, 2014).

2 Michael Chossudovsky and Andrew Gavin Marshall (eds.), *The Global Economic Crisis: The Great Depression of the XXI Century* (Montreal: Global Research Publishers, 2010); Howard Sherman, *The Roller Coaster Economy: Financial Crisis, Great Recession, and the Public Option* (Armonk, NY: M.E. Sharpe, 2010).

3 U.S. Bureau of Labor Statistics, "Consumer Price Index Summary" Table A, https://www.bls.gov/news.release/cpi.nr0.htm (accessed June 19, 2022).

4 Saskia Sassen, "Too Big to Save: The End of Financial Capitalism," *Open Democracy News Analysis* (April 2, 2009); Sherman, *The Roller Coaster Economy.*

5 Brian Phillips, *Global Production and Domestic Decay: Plant Closings in the U.S.* (New York: Garland, 1998); Berch Berberoglu, *Globalization of Capital and the Nation-State: Imperialism, Class Struggle and the State in the Age of Global Capitalism* (Lanham, MD: Rowman and Littlefield, 2003); Gerald Friedman, Fred Moseley, and Chris Sturr (eds.) *The Economic Crisis Reader* (Boston, MA: Dollars and Sense, 2009). This paradox of growth and expansion of capital on a world scale simultaneously with the decline and contraction of the domestic economy is a central feature of globalization at its highest and most intense

stage of worldwide expansion—a natural outcome of the operations of capitalist imperialism. See Berch Berberoglu (ed.), *Globalization and Change: The Transformation of Global Capitalism* (Lanham, MD: Lexington Books, 2005) and Berch Berberoglu (ed.), *Globalization in the 21st Century: Labor, Capital, and the State on a World Scale* (New York: Palgrave Macmillan, 2010).

6 Jeffrey A. Hart, *Rival Capitalists: International Competitiveness in the United States, Japan, and Western Europe* (Ithaca, NY: Cornell University Press, 1992); Richard Falk, *Predatory Globalization: A Critique* (Malden, MA: Blackwell, 1999); Fred Halliday, *The World at 2000* (New York: St. Martin's Press, 2001).

7 Berch Berberoglu, *Turmoil in the Middle East: Imperialism, War, and Political Instability* (Albany: State University of New York Press, 1999) and Berberoglu, *Globalization of Capital and the Nation-State.* The costs of empire are further documented in Chapters 4 and 7 of this book.

8 U.S. Department of the Treasury, Fiscal Data: Debt to the Penny (updated daily) https://fiscaldata.treasury.gov/datasets/debt-to-the-penny/debt-to-the-penny (accessed February 2, 2022).

9 David Harvey, *The New Imperialism* (New York: Oxford University Press, 2003). See also Leo Panitch and Colin Leys (eds.), *The New Imperial Challenge* (New York: Monthly Review Press, 2003).

10 Hart, *Rival Capitalists*; Falk, *Predatory Globalization.*

11 Doug Guthrie, *China and Globalization: The Social, Economic, and Political Transformation of Chinese Society* (New York: Routledge, 2006); Philip Stephens, "A Summit Success That Reflects A Different Global Landscape," *Financial Times* (April 3, 2009). For most recent analyses of the rise of China and its prospects for global economic as well as political and military supremacy, see Martin Jacques, *When China Rules the World: The End of the Western World and the Birth of a New Global Order*, 2nd ed. (New York: Penguin, 2012) and Alfred McCoy, *To Govern the Globe: World Orders and Catastrophic Change* (Chicago, IL: Haymarket Books, 2021).

12 Richard D. Wolff, "Capitalism Hits the Fan," in Gerald Friedman et al. (eds.), *The Economic Crisis Reader* (Boston, MA: Dollars & Sense, 2009).

13 Wolff, "Capitalism Hits the Fan."

14 According to Anneken Tappe, "that's an unemployment rate not recorded since the Great Depression, and the highest monthly level since the data collection began in 1948." See Anneken Tappe, "Nearly 43 Million Americans Have Filed for Unemployment Benefits during the Pandemic," *Cable News Network* (June 4, 2020) https://edition.cnn.com/world/live-news/coronavirus-pandemic-06-04-20-intl/h_9a8b6c47799a094e5536b2a34a881727 (accessed August 8, 2020).

15 Paul Wiseman, "A Boom in Corporate Profits, A Bust in Jobs, Wages," *Associated Press* (July 22, 2011). https://www.timesfreepress.com/news/local/story/2011/jul/23/boom-corporate-profits-bust-jobs-wages/54630/ (accessed April 6, 2021).

16 Wiseman, "A Boom in Corporate Profits, A Bust in Jobs, Wages."

17 Wiseman, "A Boom in Corporate Profits, A Bust in Jobs, Wages."

18 Wiseman, "A Boom in Corporate Profits, A Bust in Jobs, Wages."

19 Simon Johnson, "A Second Great Depression, or Worse?" *The New York Times* (August 18, 2011).

20 Economic Policy Institute, *EPI Fact Sheet: Labor Day by the Numbers* (Washington, DC: Economic Policy Institute, September 5, 2011), pp. 1–2.

21 Michael Amaladoss (ed.), *Globalization and Its Victims as Seen by Its Victims* (Delhi: Vidyajyoti Education and Welfare Society, 1999); Leslie Sklair, *Globalization: Capitalism and Its Alternatives* (New York: Oxford University Press, 2002).

22 Berch Berberoglu, *The Legacy of Empire: Economic Decline and Class Polarization in the United States* (New York: Praeger, 1992); Berch Berberoglu (ed.), *Labor and Capital in the Age of Globalization: The Labor Process and the Changing Nature of Work in the Global Economy* (Lanham, MD: Rowman and Littlefield, 2002); Berch Berberoglu, *Class and Class Conflict in the Age of Globalization* (Lanham, MD: Lexington, 2009).

23 https://www.vox.com/2020/3/16/21182341/dow-jones-biggest-point-drop-coronavirus-3000 (accessed July 28, 2021).

24 While one consequence of neoliberal globalization has been domestic economic contraction and an associated class polarization, a more costly and dangerous outcome of this process has been increased militarization and intervention abroad, such that the defense of an expanding capitalist empire worldwide has come to require an increasing military presence and a permanent interventionist foreign policy to protect and advance the activities of transnational corporations. However, such aggressive military posture has had (and continues to generate) major problems for global capitalism and the imperial state, and thus is increasingly threatening its effectiveness and, in the long run, its very existence.

25 Berch Berberoglu, *Political Sociology in a Global Era* (Boulder, CO: Paradigm, 2013).

26 Berberoglu, *Beyond the Global Capitalist Crisis*, p. 179.

27 Berberoglu, *Beyond the Global Capitalist Crisis*, p. 179.

28 Francois Houtart and Francois Polet (eds.), *The Other Davos Summit: The Globalization of Resistance to the World Economic System* (London: Zed Books, 2001).

7 The Decline of the American Empire

Inter-Imperialist Rivalry, Wars, and the End of U.S. Global Hegemony

It is one of the great ironies of our time that imperialism, that is, advanced monopoly capitalism operating on a world scale, would promote the spread of capitalism throughout the world, while at the same time giving rise to a new set of contradictions at the global and national levels. In this chapter, I examine the decline of the American Empire as an outcome of the emergence of new centers of power, as inter-imperialist rivalries unfold, economic crises set in, and endless wars wear down its global reach, while the contradictions of this process begin to affect the U.S. economy and society at the national and global level.

One major result of the international expansion of U.S. capital during the postwar period, which was intensified and reached unprecedented levels by the mid-1970s, was the emergence of new centers of world capitalism (primarily Western Europe and Japan) and the resurgence of global rivalry among advanced capitalist centers. Such rivalry between the leading capitalist states of the world economy had its roots in U.S. postwar domination of the economies of Western Europe and Japan during the second half of the 20th century.[1]

Although the large-scale U.S. postwar global expansion ushered in a period of unquestioned U.S. supremacy over the world economy and polity during the 1950s and 1960s, the economic strength of U.S. capital over foreign markets through investment, production, and trade during the 1970s took on a new significance resulting from the restructuring of the international division of labor. U.S. transnational capital, in line with its transfer of large segments of the production process to the periphery, poured massive amounts of capital into select countries in less-developed regions of the world as well as into its traditional areas of foreign investment—Canada and Western Europe—and became the leading center of world capitalism in a new way, that is, by becoming the dominant force in the worldwide production process. Thus, not only did overall U.S. direct investment expand immensely during this period, as discussed at length earlier in Chapter 4, but also the political and military force the U.S. state brought to bear to enforce its supremacy in the global political economy—in effect as the dominant capitalist/imperialist superpower on the world stage.

DOI: 10.4324/9781003282105-7

Reacting to this situation during the 1980s and 1990s, Western Europe and Japan attempted to make a comeback to counter the domination of their economies by U.S. capital and their governments by the U.S. state, and thus entered center stage in a new round of global inter-imperialist rivalry for control of the financial lifeline of the world capitalist economy.[2]

The Resurgence of Inter-Imperialist Rivalry and Decline of the American Empire

The arena of this new rivalry between the major capitalist powers, which began to unfold in full force during the 1980s, extends from Western Europe to North America, to Japan, to select regions of the less-developed periphery, while new areas outside these regions, such as China, Russia, India, and other emerging powers, may become forces that tip the balance in favor of one or another of the capitalist rivals fighting it out on the global scene.

The decline of the U.S. economy, beginning in the mid-1970s, coincided with the rise of Europe organized into a viable economic force during this period. The expansion of the European Economic Community (EEC) via the Common Market on the continent during the 1970s set the stage for the emergence of Western Europe as a serious contender for the leadership of the global capitalist economy. Thus, while U.S. capital was in the process of becoming increasingly internationalized and spreading across a vast global territory constituting the boundaries of a new international market dependent on the U.S. monopolies, Europe focused on its home base in expanding the basis of a rival territory poised to take on the United States as its competitor in the global economy and polity.

A similar development in East Asia and the Pacific Rim brought about the rise to economic prominence of Japan and a number of newly industrializing countries such as South Korea, Taiwan, Hong Kong, and Singapore. Japan's entry into the global economic scene during this period resulted in big success, as Japanese banks captured, by 1988, a position where nine of the top ten banks in the world were Japanese—quite a contrast with the position of Japan in the world economy in the mid-1970s.

In 1974, the three largest banks in the world were American (BankAmerica Corporation, Citicorp, and Chase Manhattan) while only two of the top ten banks were Japanese (Dai-Ichi Kangyo, ranked fifth, and Sumitomo, ranked tenth). However, a little over a decade later, in 1988, nine out of the ten largest banks in the world were Japanese, while only one U.S. bank (Citicorp) remained in the top 25 list. In all, of the 25 largest banks in the world in 1988, 17 were Japanese, seven were European (four French, two British, and one West German), and one American. By 1991, all the top ten banks in the world were Japanese, while only one U.S. bank remained in the top 25 list. Clearly, by the end of the 1980s and early 1990s, Japanese banks came to dominate international finance capital and established themselves as the leading force in the world of finance.

A similar trend in the position of industrial corporations during this period resulted in a decline in the number of U.S. corporations and an increase in the number of Japanese and European corporations in the top 25 list. Thus, while in 1974 15 of the 25 largest industrial corporations in the world were U.S.-based, by 1988 this number was down to nine; conversely, while in 1974 there were only eight European corporations and only one Japanese corporation among the 25 largest industrial corporations in the world, by 1988 these numbers increased to 11 and four, respectively. Moreover, if we take European and Japanese corporations together as posing a challenge to U.S. dominance of the world economy, we see a complete reversal of the situation in 1988 as compared with 1974. Whereas the share of U.S. corporations in the top 25 list declined from 15 in 1974 to nine in 1988, the share of European and Japanese corporations increased from nine in 1974 to 15 in 1988. This trend continued to unfold during the 1990s, placing the European and Japanese corporations in an increasingly favorable position vis-à-vis their U.S. counterparts.

These developments clearly show that a shift in the centers of the world economy had taken place—away from the United States and toward Japan and Europe, and increasingly China, with Japan controlling the financial lifeline of the global capitalist economy and Europe (especially Germany) and Japan making inroads into industrial production, while China captured a growing share of world trade. With the increase in the number of European and Japanese corporations among the top 100 and with production moving in the direction of advanced electronics where Japan had clearly achieved an edge over its U.S. and European competitors, it is not difficult to see that Japanese capital came to play a critical role in the world economy and established itself as a viable competitor in subsequent decades. This, in conjunction with developments in Western Europe and the integration of Eastern and Western Europe during the first decade of the 21st century, ushered in a multipolar world economy in which the United States became a junior partner stripped of its postwar dominance.

The unprecedented economic and political changes that unfolded at full speed during the 1990s brought about a new international order in which superpower military tensions gave way to global economic competition and rivalry among the leading capitalist economies, which arose during this period over the control of oil in the greater Middle East region.

Inter-Imperialist Rivalry for Control of Oil in the Middle East

Over the course of the past several decades, the major imperialist powers of the late 20th and early 21st centuries (the United States, Germany, and Japan) attempted to use as their surrogate one or another of the major regional powers in the Middle East (Iran, Iraq, and Saudi Arabia) to advance their political and economic interests in the region—above all, in securing access to sources of oil to fuel the industrial engines of their economies and thus maintaining global hegemony over their economic rivals.[3] In this inter-imperialist competition between the major capitalist powers, the two rising capitalist states of the 1990s (Germany and Japan) attempted to establish independent access to sources of Middle Eastern oil, bypassing the United States' postwar grip over the region through its control of a string of satellite nations from Iran to Saudi Arabia and the Persian Gulf states. The German and Japanese challenge to U.S. domination of Middle Eastern oil prompted a swift response by the United States through massive U.S. military intervention in Saudi Arabia and the initial invasion of Iraq with the subsequent launching of the Persian Gulf War of 1991—a war that was ostensibly launched to drive the Iraqi Army out of Kuwait, but in fact was designed to punish Iraq for its role in cultivating close economic and geopolitical ties with the chief global economic rivals of the United States over access to and control of oil in the Middle East.[4]

The U.S. intervention in Afghanistan in the aftermath of the September 11, 2001, attacks on the World Trade Center in New York City and the overthrow of the Taliban regime for harboring al Qaeda as well as the subsequent invasion of and war against Iraq in March 2003 and threats against other regimes in what the Bush Administration called the "Axis of Evil," stretching from the Middle East through Southwest Asia to North Korea, was another expression of U.S. power imposed over the region to secure access to sources of oil in the Middle East and *beyond*.[5] Thus, while the flow of oil from the Middle East continues to play a prominent role in ensuring America's dominant position in the region and thereby the world economy, the breakup of the Soviet Union and the emergence of the post-Soviet newly independent states, such as Azerbaijan and Turkmenistan, opened access to alternative sources of oil for the U.S. transnational oil companies, such that a new oil pipeline from the Caspian Sea through Turkmenistan, Afghanistan, and Pakistan to the Indian Ocean would provide an alternative to the oil obtained from the volatile nations of the Middle East.[6] Still, the Middle East remained the centerpiece of U.S. transnational control of oil in the global economy, and Iran and Iraq continued to play an important role as the leading regional powers that were entangled in inter-imperialist rivalries among the advanced capitalist/imperialist states for control of oil in the Middle East throughout the postwar period to the late 20th and early 21st centuries.[7]

Iran, Iraq, and Inter-Imperialist Rivalry among the Advanced Capitalist Countries

In the period from the early 1950s to the late 1970s—a period of uncontested U.S. supremacy in the Middle East—the United States firmly established itself in Iran and other countries of the Persian Gulf to control the flow of oil from the Middle East.[8] By the 1970s, the United States became the chief importer of Iranian oil. Iranian exports to the United States, consisting primarily of crude oil, rose dramatically from $60 million in 1970 to $2.1 billion in 1974, to $4.3 billion in 1978, the final year of the Shah's regime; in turn, imports from the United States to Iran rose sharply from $359 million in 1970, to $974 million in 1974, to $4.1 billion in 1978.[9] However, in the latter half of the 1970s, inter-imperialist rivalries between the major capitalist powers began to reappear, as Japan, Germany, Britain, and other major powers began to expand their trade relations with Iran.

Although the U.S. grip over Iran in the postwar period strengthened the Shah's authoritarian rule and kept him in power for 25 years, it also prompted his regime to open up to other capitalist countries and to establish Iran as a regional sub-imperialist power in the Middle East.[10] Thus, in the latter half of the 1970s Iranian exports (mainly oil) to Japan, Germany, and other European countries dramatically increased, while imports of consumer goods from these countries similarly increased.[11]

To counter these developments, Iraq—Iran's chief rival in the region—attracted a number of European countries such as France and Italy as well as Japan to meet their energy needs in exchange for imported manufactured goods—a relationship Iraq sought to cultivate in building itself as an alternative regional power center in the Middle East. As a result, Iraqi exports to Japan, consisting primarily of oil, rose from $5 million in 1972 to $527 million in 1976, to $4 billion in 1980; to France, it increased from $268 million in 1972 to $1.5 billion in 1976, to $5.1 billion in 1980; and to Italy, it rose from $250 million in 1972 to $1.2 billion in 1976, to $2.6 billion in 1980.[12]

The overthrow of the Shah's regime in 1979 and the accession to power of a new Islamic regime in Iran, followed by the war with Iraq, brought import-export trade between Iran and the United States to a virtual halt; but, despite these developments, Iran's trade with Japan as well as with Germany and other European countries continued to be on a strong footing throughout the 1980s. Thus, while Iran's exports to the United States dropped from $4.3 billion in 1978 to $556 million in 1982, to a mere $2 million in 1990, exports to Japan made up the bulk of Iran's total exports, amounting to $3.9 billion in 1978, $2.3 billion in 1982, and $3.2 billion in 1990.[13] Likewise, while imports from the United States declined from $4.1 billion in 1978 to $209 million in 1983, to $140 million in 1990, imports from Japan totaled $3 billion in 1978, $3.1 billion in 1983, and $1.8 billion in 1990; imports from Germany were also an important part of total Iranian imports, totaling $3.7 billion in 1978, $3.3 billion in 1983, and $2.8 billion in 1990.[14]

Clearly, a major shift occurred during this period in the export of Iranian oil away from the United States and toward Japan and various European countries. This was also evident in the sources of Iranian imports, such that while there was a sharp drop in imports from the United States, imports from Japan, Germany, and other European countries substantially increased over the same period—indicating an apparent shift in patterns of political alliances manifested in the import-export trade.

In Iraq, during the early 1980s, we find a similar pattern of trade relations with rival advanced capitalist countries, where Japan, France, and Italy were the prime recipients of Iraqi oil exports and, together with Germany, the major sources of Iraqi imports of manufactured goods. However, by the late 1980s, the United States began to tilt away from Iran and toward Iraq and became the chief purchaser of Iraqi oil and the largest supplier of finished manufactured goods. Iraqi exports to the United States increased from $478 million in 1987 to $1.5 billion in 1988, to $2.3 billion in 1989, to $3 billion in 1990; imports of goods from the United States likewise rose from $752 million in 1987 to $1.3 billion in 1989, dropping to $704 million in 1990.[15]

The rivalry between the chief imperialist powers vis-à-vis access to and business with Iran and Iraq during the 1980s thus became intensified by the decade's end and led to an opening for greater regional power play between the two competing national centers vying for control over the Persian Gulf, hence an increase in their bargaining position vis-à-vis the rival imperialist powers. Iraq's invasion of Kuwait in August 1990, Bernard Headley points out, "had the potential to upset the balance of economic power in the Middle East and threatened the ability of Western (especially U.S. and British) powers to have a decisive influence over the terms and conditions of oil policy."[16] Thus, to counter such a development, Headley writes, the United States wanted to "use its military might to reassert Western control over the world's key resources and to reinforce U.S. strength in relation to its economic rivals."[17] Hence, "Iraq's invasion of Kuwait provided an opportunity to implement this militaristic strategy for making sure the U.S. would be the world's undisputed superpower."[18] And to this end, the United States asserted its control and domination of the Middle East as the center of its global empire through its vast network of military bases, interventions, and wars in this important region of the world to maintain its supremacy (see Figure 7.1 for the location of U.S. military bases, interventions, and wars led by the United States throughout the greater Middle East).

The Persian Gulf War of 1991

The United States went to war against Iraq in 1991 in order to "liberate" Kuwait, to "uphold freedom and the rule of law," and to take a stand against "international aggression"—so argued the U.S. administration, its Western allies, and its Arab collaborator regimes, which brutally ruled over the region for decades. In his State of the Union address, President George H. W. Bush proclaimed:

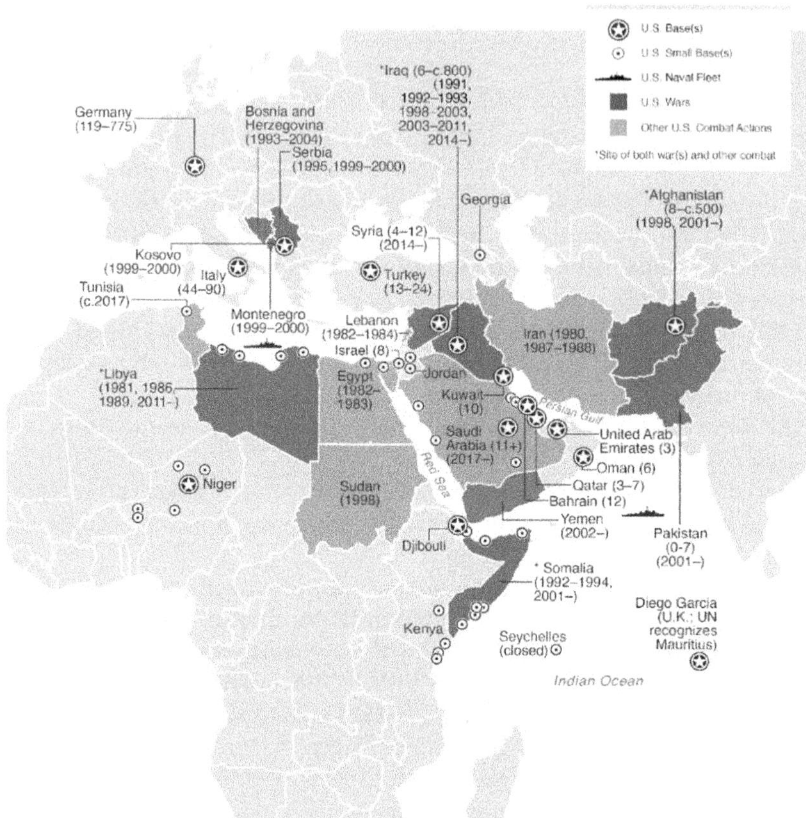

Figure 7.1 U.S. Military Bases, Interventions, and Wars in the Greater Middle East, 1980–2020.

Source: David Vine, *The United States of War: A Global History of America's Endless Conflicts, from Columbus to the Islamic State* (Berkeley, CA: University of California Press, 2020).

Notes: Bases in the Greater Middle East helped launch U.S. wars and other combats in at least 17 countries in the region between 1980 and 2020. For ease of comparison, contemporary borders and a Mercator projection is used in the construction of the map.

> What is at stake is . . . a new world order—where diverse nations are drawn together in common cause to achieve the universal aspirations of mankind: peace and security, freedom and the rule of law. . . . Saddam Hussein's unprovoked invasion . . . will not stand.[19]

If this could happen to the ruling al-Sabah family in Kuwait, the argument went, it could also happen to the Saudi royal family as well as the sultans and the emirs and their kind throughout the Persian Gulf. This would mean that Saddam Hussein would next march down the Arabian Peninsula and eventually take over Saudi Arabia, then the entire Persian Gulf region, and finally the whole Middle East. But as Edward Greer points out:

> The ground advanced to the American people to accede to attacking Iraq was that of the classical big lie: that the war to be waged was a collective and preemptive defense against a powerful regional criminal state, one with advanced means of mass destruction which it was in the process of deploying against world peace.
>
> In retrospect, the ascribed reasons were false, and known to be such by the president. Iraq was not targeted because Hussein had launched an unprovoked military attack on a neighboring state which has major oil deposits. Saddam Hussein had already done precisely that to Iran a few years before, with active U.S. support.
>
> Nor was Iraq targeted because it was defying United Nations resolutions condemning military aggression and occupation of another sovereign state or its territory. Neither the Turkish occupation of Cyprus, nor the Israeli occupation of the West Bank—both continuing to this day in contravention of similar resolutions—constituted a *casus belli* for the United States.
>
> Nor was Iraq targeted for American military attack because Kuwait's medieval regime . . . embodied any political or cultural value dear to Americans.[20]

The massive intervention by the United States in the Persian Gulf and the invasion of Iraq, despite proclamations to the contrary, was not for "democracy and freedom," "the rule of law," "liberating" Kuwait, "peace," "security," or a "new" world order. Interestingly enough, it was not for the continued supply of oil to the United States either, for the United States neither depends on nor needs any significant amount of oil from the Middle East, as less than 10 percent of total U.S. oil consumption originates there. Other more reliable and more secure sources, such as Mexico and the North Sea, for example, could easily take up the slack. So, why then was the oil question raised at all?

What seems to be a complicated issue becomes clear and revealing once we discover that the oil controlled by the U.S. transnational oil companies in the Middle East is supplied mainly *not* to the United States, but to Germany and Japan—to fuel and thereby control the industrial life of the United States' chief rivals in the world economy:

> Germany and Japan [were at the time] rising economic powers, while Britain and the United States declining. . . . As rising powers, Germany and Japan were not particularly threatened by Iraq's seizure of Kuwaiti resources. . . . Britain and the United States have had exactly the opposite reaction.[21]

As client states of the United States in the Persian Gulf, Kuwait, Saudi Arabia, and the oil emirates play a key role in securing U.S. hegemony in the Middle East, hence controlling the flow of oil from this region. "The abolition of American suzerainty over oil-producing states of the Persian Gulf," writes Tom Mayer, "would threaten . . . the position of the United States relative to its principal commercial rivals."[22] Thus:

> it is hardly surprising that the United States should resort to war to repel a challenge to the imperial status quo. In the traditional fashion of declining economic powers (e.g., fourth-century imperial Rome, late fifteenth-century Spain, pre-First World War Britain), U.S. leaders are continually tempted to compensate for economic weakness with military force.[23]

The significance of control of sources of oil in the Middle East by the United States becomes evident as soon as one considers the alternative: How different the world might actually have been if the oil fields now controlled by the U.S. oil companies were in fact controlled by the oil companies of Japan and Germany! And today, in the early 21st century, one could add China to the list as the newly emergent rival power to keep in check U.S. global imperialist hegemony.

The United States and its coalition partners succeeded in punishing Iraq for its invasion of Kuwait by forcing Iraq out of Kuwait and establishing a firmer control over sources of oil in the Middle East. At the same time, the regime of Saddam Hussein was kept intact, but a clear message was sent to him and his newly found European and Asian allies to halt their challenge to U.S. power in the Middle East in the post-Soviet "New World Order." The real challenge to U.S. global supremacy, however, was yet to occur. It came a decade later with the shock of the September 11, 2001, attacks against the symbol of U.S. global economic domination, the twin towers of the World Trade Center in New York City, and the command and control center of U.S. global military domination, the Pentagon in Washington, D.C. These events of major worldwide significance prompted the massive U.S. military responses, the invasions of Afghanistan in 2001 and Iraq in 2003, actions that were in the making well before the September 11 attacks, but the latter served as the pretext to reassert U.S. global supremacy in the new millennium.

The Afghan War of 2001

The U.S. military invasion of Afghanistan in late 2001 came in the aftermath of the September 11 attacks on the twin towers of the World Trade Center in New York City and the Pentagon in Washington, D.C. The invasion was carried out in retaliation to the perpetrators of the September

11 attacks, which, according to the U.S. government, were committed by a terrorist group known as *al Qaeda* based in Afghanistan.

Accusing the Taliban regime in Afghanistan of harboring the *al Qaeda* terrorists led by Osama bin Laden, the U.S. military launched the invasion, overthrew the Taliban, and carried out a massive bombing campaign that leveled large parts of the country suspected to be *al Qaeda* hideouts. Thousands of bombs that were dropped on this poor country have caused much devastation, destruction, and death. While several hundred *al Qaeda* members were killed through this operation, thousands of Afghan civilians also perished.

The war in Afghanistan and the United States' presence and engagement in the region did not start with the terrorist attacks on September 11. In fact, it goes back to a much earlier period when the United States was actively involved in shaping events in Afghanistan over the previous two decades, leading to the accession to power of the Taliban in the mid-1990s.[24] The origins of U.S. intervention in Afghanistan go back to the late 1970s, when in 1978 the corrupt and dictatorial government of President Mohammed Daoud was forced out of office by a leftist military coup that brought to power the People's Democratic Party (PDP). According to Parenti:

> The new government began to pursue much needed reforms. It legalized labor unions, and set up a minimum wage, a progressive income tax, a literacy campaign, and programs that gave ordinary people greater access to health care, housing and public sanitation.[25]

However, serious opposition arose against the government from several quarters—especially the feudal landlords and the Islamic clergy—and pressure was put on the government to halt the popular reforms and reverse its egalitarian policies:

> The feudal landlords opposed the land reform program that infringed on their holdings while benefitting poor tenant farmers. And tribesmen and fundamentalist *mullahs* [Muslim clergy] vehemently opposed the government's dedication to gender equality and the education of women and children.
>
> Because of its egalitarian economic policies, the government also incurred the opposition of the U.S. national security state.[26]

These were the precipitating events that put Afghanistan on the global map. "Almost immediately after the People's Democratic Party (PDP) coalition came to power," writes Parenti, "the CIA, assisted by Saudi and Pakistani military, launched a large scale intervention into Afghanistan on the side of the ousted feudal lords, reactionary tribal chieftains, mullahs, and opium traffickers"[27]:

> Over the years the United States and Saudi Arabia expended about $40 billion on the war in Afghanistan. The CIA and its allies recruited, supplied, and trained almost 100,000 radical Mujahideen from forty Muslim countries including Pakistan, Saudi Arabia, Iran, Algeria, and Afghanistan itself. Among those who answered the call was Saudi-born millionaire rightwinger Osama bin Laden and his cohorts.[28]

The constant pressure on the PDP and superior arms provided to the Mujahedeen by the Central Intelligence Agency (CIA) eventually succeeded in overthrowing the popular government of Afghanistan in 1992, installing in its place a brutal, right-wing Islamic dictatorship of the Mujahedeen who unleashed an official reign of terror on the people of Afghanistan that was the beginning of a dark period in Afghan history[29]:

> Upon taking over Afghanistan, the Mujahedeen . . . ravaged the cities, terrorized civilian populations, looted, staged mass executions, closed schools, raped thousands of women and girls, and reduced half of Kabul to rubble. . . . Ruling the country gangster-style and looking for lucrative sources of income, the tribes ordered farmers to plant opium poppy. The Pakistani ISI, a close junior partner of the CIA, set up hundreds of heroin laboratories across Afghanistan.[30]

Soon the Afghan-Pakistan border had become the biggest heroin-producing region in the world. Given its callous behavior and excesses in abuses of the Afghan people, the Mujahedeen government became very unstable and a liability to the U.S. and Pakistani states to maintain order under its control. Thus, in 1994, U.S. and Pakistani leaders devised a plan to support a group that might bring together the various reactionary elements in the country to form a stable right-wing government; that group was the Taliban.[31] "Within a year," writes Parenti:

> an extremist strain of Sunni Islam called the Taliban—heavily funded and advised by the ISI and the CIA and with the support of Islamic political parties in Pakistan—fought its way to power, taking over most of the country, luring many tribal chiefs into its fold with threats and bribes.[32]

Once the Taliban came to power, the country changed drastically, *for the worse*. "The Taliban unleashed a religious reign of terror, imposing an even stricter interpretation of Muslim Law than used by most of the Kabul clergy."[33] But, for the United States, the Taliban was a useful tool in its strategy to control the entire Central Asian region.[34]

While it has been revealed by the mainstream mass media that the United States had planned to invade Afghanistan to destroy *al Qaeda* nine months prior to the attacks on the World Trade Center and the Pentagon,[35] the September 11 events provided the rationale to declare an all-out war against *al Qaeda* and the Taliban and move in full force to occupy Afghanistan and to destroy *al Qaeda*'s terrorist network. In early October 2001, "the U.S. launched air strikes against Afghanistan with cruise missiles, stealth bombers, Tomahawks, 'bunker-busting' missiles, and Mark 82 high drag bombs."[36] By late 2001, after nearly three months of massive U.S. air strikes, the Taliban and *al Qaeda* forces were destroyed or had fled to Pakistan.

Although fighting against terrorism was the proclaimed aim of the United States in rationalizing its invasion and occupation of Afghanistan, "there were other compelling reasons that drew U.S. power into Afghanistan":

> The Central Asian region is rich in oil and gas reserves. The U.S. Department of Energy estimates that the Caspian basin holds 110 billion barrels, about three times the United States' own reserves. And Turkmenistan has immense natural gas supplies. Hence it should come as no surprise that U.S. policy elites were contemplating a military presence in Central Asia long before September 2001.[37]

"If one tries to make sense of the events that preceded or succeeded the terrorist attacks on the U.S.," writes Dimitris Yannopoulos in his article "Checkerboard of Oil, Minefields":

> one need only "follow the money"—particularly the petrodollars. . . . It's all the money poised to cash in on the prospective oil bonanza of Central Asia. But there's also all the money set in motion to scuttle, delay or divert the most competitive and economically viable Eurasian pipeline plans.
>
> The stakes are therefore very high and key parameters can easily be lost in the logistical maze of the alternative Eurasian pipeline routes that already exist around the Caspian Sea and those meant to expand, reroute or replace them.[38]

At the center of the competing oil pipeline projects lies the Central Asian Gas and Oil Pipelines project, which was planned:

> to transport oil and natural gas from Kazakhstan and Turkmenistan through Afghanistan and Pakistan all the way into India and the Arabian Sea. Each pipeline in this southbound route would be over 1,000 miles long, built at an estimated total project cost of $4.5 billion, with capacity to carry 700 billion cubic feet of gas and one million barrels of oil per day.[39]

"The discovery of vast oil and gas reserves in Kazakhstan and Turkmenistan," Parenti points out, "provided the lure, while the dissolution of the USSR removed the one major barrier against pursuing aggressive interventionist policy in that part of the world"[40]:

> U.S. oil companies acquired the rights to some 75 percent of these new reserves. A major problem was how to extract the oil and gas from the landlocked region: U.S. officials opposed using the Russian pipeline or the most direct route across Iran to the Persian Gulf. Instead, they and the corporate oil contractors explored a number of alternative pipeline routes, across Azerbaijan and Turkey to the Mediterranean or across China to the Pacific. The one favored by Unocal, a US-based oil company, crossed Afghanistan and Pakistan to the Indian Ocean. The intensive negotiations that Unocal entered into with the Taliban regime were still unresolved by 1998, as an Argentine company placed a competing bid for the pipeline. Bush's war against the Taliban rekindled Unocal's hopes for getting a major piece of the action.[41]

According to Ted Rall in his article "The New Great Game: Oil Politics in Central Asia," Unocal's plan was "to extend Turkmenistan's existing system west to the Kazakh field on the Caspian and Southeast to the Pakistani port of Karachi on the Arabian Sea. That project runs through Afghanistan."[42] The significance of the U.S. intervention in Afghanistan, then, was more to its relationship to the country's strategic location with regard to the oil pipeline project that has been in the works for some time than an immediate response to the September 11 events. As Parenti points out, what all these developments mean is that:

> the U.S. government had made preparations well in advance of September 2001 to move against the Taliban and create a compliant regime in Kabul and a direct U.S. military presence in Central Asia. The September 11 attacks provided the impetus, stampeding U.S. public opinion and reluctant allies into supporting military intervention.[43]

Following the U.S. intervention in Afghanistan in late 2001, a compliant regime supportive of U.S. policy in Central Asia was installed to carry out U.S. military, geopolitical, and economic interests. Shortly thereafter, in June 2002 the Afghan government signed an agreement with Turkmenistan and Pakistan for the construction of an oil pipeline from Turkmenistan through Afghanistan and Pakistan to the Arabian Sea in order to transport oil from the Caspian Sea to the Pakistani port city of Karachi on the Arabian Sea. Thus was sealed the fate of Central Asian oil for the profits of the U.S. transnational oil companies who succeeded in expanding their area of control of this vital resource from the Middle East to the former Soviet territories in Central Asia—an expansion that facilitates their central role in furthering U.S. imperialist designs to dominate the world economy.

The Iraq War of 2003

In the aftermath of the war in Afghanistan and the drive to root out terrorism directed at the United States in the post-September 11 world, the Bush Administration declared there was an "axis of evil"—a geopolitical area stretching from Syria and Iraq through Iran to North Korea; this concept came to define the nature of U.S. foreign policy, linking many of these states to the *al Qaeda* terrorist network.

The alleged links between Iraq and *al Qaeda*, implicating the Iraqi state in the September 11 attacks on the World Trade Center, provided the impetus to attack and disarm Iraq of "weapons of mass destruction" to prevent another terrorist act against the United States. Hence, with this argument, the United States tried to outmaneuver its long-time Western European allies by pushing for a United Nations resolution to declare war on Iraq through the U.N. Security Council. After failing to obtain the support of the council and threats of veto by France, Germany, and Russia, the United States and its coalition partners (primarily the British) launched a massive assault against Iraq by invading, bombing, and occupying Iraq in March 2003.

The ensuing "shock and awe" campaign of mass bombings launched several thousand tomahawk and cruise missiles against Iraqi targets, especially in Baghdad, including several presidential palaces, the Ministry of Information, command and control centers, and numerous other government buildings and bunkers. The bombings set the city ablaze for more than two weeks, causing much destruction and death. The U.S. and British troops engaged in bloody battles and met with stiff resistance from the Iraqi Army, the Republican Guard, and irregulars, including the *Fedayeen* and the paramilitary forces who fought to defend Umm Qasr, Basra, An Nasiriya, An Najaf, and Karbala as well as Baghdad and other cities across Iraq. But by early April 2003, the U.S. forces succeeded in entering Baghdad, taking control of much of Iraq, and toppling the regime of Saddam Hussein.

The war against Iraq by the sole global superpower, the United States (and its imperialist junior partner, Britain), which unleashed tens of thousands of troops and several thousands of missiles and threatened the region with nuclear war, was designed to expand to include Syria and Iran in order to redraw the map of the entire Middle East region in favor of U.S. and Israeli interests. The aim was to lay claim to the oil resources of the Middle East by toppling the Baathist regimes in Iraq and Syria as well as the regime of the Ayatollahs in Iran, to neutralize the Arab opposition, and to crush the Palestinian movement in Gaza and the West Bank, so that a new U.S.-Israeli joint control over the region could be exerted, with efforts to colonize the area and to link it across the Fertile Crescent to the Caspian Sea and the Central Asian oil fields to Afghanistan and beyond. It is through this latest high-tech imperialist onslaught that the United States planned to impose its colossal rule over the region to reshape the new post-Cold War realities of the Middle East and the rest of the world—realities that have been shaping up within the framework of decades-long rivalries that have been taking place among the chief imperialist states for control of oil in the Middle East and beyond.

The Political Economy of Post-Cold War Realities for the American Empire in the Middle East

As the decades-long hostilities between the United States and the former Soviet Union in the Middle East came to an end with the end of the Cold War, this important region of the world has reemerged as the arena for rivalries between the major capitalist-imperialist powers of the world over sources of oil that is vital for their economies. Locked in inter-imperialist competition for control of raw materials, cheap labor, new markets, and higher rates of profit across the globe, the chief imperialist powers found in Iraq and Iran the potential for an alternate power center to control and regulate the flow of oil, which has become the key strategic commodity that will determine the success or failure of one or another of the rival capitalist powers in the world economy into the 21st century.

Clearly, both Germany and Japan, and to a lesser extent other European powers like France, have been searching for a surrogate power in the Persian Gulf for over four decades. For a variety of reasons, including the financing of a decade-long war against Iran, Iraq became the power that could secure for U.S.'s rivals a future foothold in the Middle East. Decline in U.S. influence in the region in post-Shah power politics and the challenge posed by rival forces through an expanding Iraqi hegemony over the region was thought could thus secure for these forces direct access to sources of oil in the Middle East, bypassing the traditionally dominant position of the U.S. oil companies in the region.

This is exactly what happened in an earlier period of British imperial control over the Middle East, with U.S. encroachments to the region in direct rivalry to Britain's traditional hold over these territories, from Iran and Iraq to Jordan, Egypt, and down to the Arabian Peninsula, including the entire Persian Gulf region. A half century later and in the same strategic territories, the same superpower rivals became involved in conflict once again, at various levels, for the very same reason: control of oil.

The disintegration of the Soviet Union as a military superpower, which during the postwar period played a key role in keeping in check U.S. imperialist encroachments throughout the world, allowed the United States to intervene in the Persian Gulf and succeeded in outmaneuvering its archrivals, Germany and Japan, denying them direct access to sources of oil essential to their economic independence and emerging position in the world economy and forcing them to pay a substantial portion of the cost of an operation that was designed to suppress them![44] And now, as China expands to this region to secure its increasing energy needs in situating itself as a new economic rival of the United States in the 21st century, one hears the echoes of a new emerging Cold War between the United States and China in the period ahead.

The cost of the war against Iraq was enormous for the people of Iraq in both human and material terms: over 100,000 Iraqi soldiers and tens of thousands of innocent civilians were killed with billions of dollars' worth of destruction in a high-tech massacre inflicted on Iraq by the United States during its invasion and occupation of Iraq in the First Gulf War in 1991.[45] A decade later, in 2001, the United States launched a similar military operation in Afghanistan that caused much devastation, destruction, and death, culminating in the overthrow of the Taliban regime and the installation of a government subservient to the United States. This was followed by the second U.S. war against Iraq in 2003 and the massive invasion and occupation of that country by some 150,000 U.S. troops to topple the regime of Saddam Hussein. Thus, as a result, the United States became further entrenched in the Middle East, dominating the region by open military force to advance U.S. imperialist interests in the early 21st century.[46]

With the United States remaining in firm control of the oil fields in the Middle East through its close relations with Saudi Arabia and further expanding its influence over Central Asia, Europe moving ahead with its full integration in its own territory, and Japan continuing to expand its role and presence in the world economy through its economic relationship with China, especially in East Asia and the Pacific Rim, another clash of interests could erupt as part of the long-standing rivalry between the chief competitors of the global economy in the early decades of the 21st century. The U.S. war to disarm Iraq and to occupy its oil-rich territories in 2003 was more related to this ongoing rivalry between the chief imperialist powers for control over oil in the Middle East than the concern over "weapons of mass destruction" that Iraq was said to have possessed, which was proven by international inspectors to be non-existent, but to the extent it may have possessed in the past in some small quantity (e.g., mustard gas) were supplied to Iraq by the United States to use against Iran during the Iran-Iraq War in the 1980s.

For over two decades, since the overthrow of the Shah's regime in Iran in 1979, Iran and Iraq were at the center of the rivalry between the chief imperialist states of the global capitalist system—the United States, Japan, Germany, and several other major European countries. As the long and bloody war between Iran and Iraq from 1980 to 1988 failed to fully resolve the power struggle between these rival regional powers in the Middle East, the United States became the chief arbiter in determining the balance of forces between these two pivotal oil states by first siding with Iran, then with Iraq, and finally against both. Japan, Germany, France, Italy, and other countries have, in turn, built a commercial partnership by one or the other of these two states locked in a power struggle challenging the traditional dominance of this region by Egypt and Saudi Arabia under the tutelage of U.S. imperialism.

The Persian Gulf War of 1991 became a test case of territorial control within the larger context of Middle Eastern geopolitics. The direct intervention of the United States in its war against Iraq in 1991 thus became the decisive response to the political turmoil that engulfed the region in the aftermath of the Cold War. The muscle flexed by the U.S. military machine in the Persian Gulf was thus meant to send a clear message to its imperialist archrivals that the United States continues to play a key role in the political economy of the Middle East. This role, which had been a dominant one throughout the post-World War II period, was once again reestablished through the U.S. invasion of Afghanistan in 2001 and by the U.S. war against Iraq in 2003 (as well as threats against other noncompliant states like North Korea and Iran) culminating in new conflicts and destabilization of the world in the post-Soviet, post-Cold War "new world order" that came to define the parameters of great power politics in the Middle East and adjoining regions extending to Central Asia and beyond.

Nearly two decades after the invasion and occupation of Afghanistan and after the announcement by President Joe Biden in July 2021 that the United States will finally leave Afghanistan soon, the Taliban launched a major offensive and took over much of the country in a short period of time, and on August 15, 2021, marched into Kabul, the Afghan capital, and took over the government after the Afghan President fled the country and the Afghan Army collapsed.[47] In his address to the nation on the rapidly developing events as the United States rushed to evacuate its embassy in Kabul, which some have called it "Biden's Saigon moment," President Biden stated:

> We will end America's longest war after twenty long years of bloodshed. Events we're seeing now are sadly proof that no amount of military force would ever deliver a stable, united, secure Afghanistan, as known in history as graveyard of empires.[48]

Just as the U.S. defeat in Vietnam that brought down the mighty American Empire to its knees some four and a half decades earlier, when the U.S. embassy in Saigon evacuated in defeat amidst the onslaught of the People's Army of Vietnam and the Viet Cong on April 30, 1975, Taliban's aggressive nationwide offensive that swept across the country and led to the capture of the Afghan capital Kabul on August 15, 2021 resulted in a humiliating defeat of the United States in Afghanistan after two decades of occupation, bringing to an end America's longest war (Figures 7.2A and 7.2B).

Figure 7.2A Evacuation of U.S. Embassy in Kabul, Afghanistan (August 15, 2021).

Figure 7.2B Evacuation of U.S. Embassy in Saigon, South Vietnam (April 30, 1975).

Source: Photo comparison created by Sangeeta Nair (August 16, 2021). https://www.jagranjosh.com/current-affairs/saigon-kabul-comparison-why-us-withdrawal-from-kabul-is-being-compared-to-fall-of-saigon-what-is-saigon-1629103833-1.

The post-9/11 wars in Afghanistan, Iraq, and elsewhere have not only cost the American Empire an enormous amount of taxpayer dollars (to the tune of $8 trillion)[49] and contributed greatly to the downfall of the U.S. economy through the "Great Recession," but also nailed the coffin of the American Empire and brought to an end the global economic supremacy of the United States in the early 21st century. While the American Empire has been spending enormous amounts on its military to protect U.S. corporate capitalist interests to continue their domination of the global economy, China has been concentrating on developing its economy, ironically in collaboration with the same U.S. corporate capitalist interests who have made enormous investments in China through joint-ventures and other economic collaboration that have served them well, while continuing to use the U.S. military as their shield in their entanglements in the rest of the world where they confront forces of resistance. It is within this globalist view of the world economy in which the major U.S. corporations have prospered while the great majority of the American people have suffered from the overexpansion that has deprived them of the basic necessities of life—a decent job, affordable healthcare, good education, a dignified retirement, and a peaceful life in a livable clean environment.

Although the endless wars of the American Empire to safeguard a decaying crisis-ridden capitalist system across the globe has drained the resources of the nation and forced many of its people into a precarious social, economic, and political existence, the American people will ultimately be liberated from their present predicament, but only after the American Empire and U.S. imperialism come to a swift end—and this will happen as we usher in a new America, *after Empire*.

Notes

1 Although economic rivalry between the major capitalist powers has intensified in recent decades and surfaced as a major challenge to postwar U.S. hegemony over the global economy, the origins of such rivalry goes back nearly a century, when Britain, France, Germany, Japan, and the United States became part of the worldwide struggle for global supremacy—as manifested, for example, in the struggle over control of oil in the Middle East at the turn of the 20th century—that later led to World War I. Today, in the post-Soviet environment, a similar struggle between the chief imperialist powers has extended the boundaries of this rivalry to lands beyond the greater Middle East—to the oil fields of the Caspian Sea and the surrounding countries of Central Asia.

2 Nick Beams, *The Significance and Implications of Globalization: A Marxist Assessment.* (Southfield, MI: Mehring Books, 1998).

3 Berch Berberoglu, *Turmoil in the Middle East: Imperialism, War, and Political Instability* (Albany: State University of New York Press, 1999).

4 Haim Bresheeth and Nira Yuval-Davis (eds.), *The Gulf War and the New World Order* (London: Zed Books, 1991). For varied explanations on the nature and causes of the Persian Gulf War of 1991, see Robert Brenner, "Why Is the United States at War with Iraq?" *New Left Review*, no. 185 (1991); Tom Mayer,

"Imperialism and the Gulf War," *Monthly Review* 42, no. 11 (1991); Michael Tanzer, "Oil and the Gulf Crisis," *Monthly Review* 42, no. 11 (1991); Bernard Headley, "The 'New World Order' and the Persian Gulf War," *Humanity & Society* 15, no. 3 (1991); and Edward Greer, "The Hidden History of the Iraq War," *Monthly Review* 43, no. 1 (1991).

5 Roger Burbach and Ben Clarke (eds.), *September 11 and the U.S. War: Beyond the Curtain of Smoke* (San Francisco, CA: City Lights Books, 2002).

6 Ted Rall, "The New Great Game: Oil Politics in Central Asia," in Roger Burbach and Ben Clarke (eds.), *September 11 and the U.S. War: Beyond the Curtain of Smoke* (San Francisco, CA: City Lights Publishers, 2002), p. 49.

7 Berch Berberoglu, *Globalization of Capital and the Nation State: Imperialism, Class Struggle, and the State in the Age of Global Capitalism* (Lanham, MD: Rowman and Littlefield, 2003).

8 Fred Halliday, *Iran: Dictatorship and Development* (New York: Penguin, 1979).

9 International Monetary Fund, *Direction of Trade Statistics, Yearbook 1970-76* (Washington, DC: IMF, 1977), pp. 148–149; 1982, pp. 207–208; 1987, pp. 229–230; 1991, pp. 226–227.

10 Halliday, *Iran: Dictatorship and Development*; Patrick Clawson, "The Internationalization of Capital and Capital Accumulation in Iran and Iraq," *Insurgent Sociologist* 7, no. 2 (Spring 1977).

11 Kaoru Sugihara, "Japan, the Middle East, and the World Economy," in K. Sugihara and J. A. Allan (eds.), *Japan in the Contemporary Middle East* (London: Routledge, 1993), pp. 1–13.

12 International Monetary Fund, *Direction of Trade Statistics, Yearbook 1970-76*, pp. 150–151; 1982, pp. 210–211; 1987, pp. 231–232; 1991, pp. 228–229.

13 International Monetary Fund, *Direction of Trade Statistics, Yearbook 1970-76*, pp. 148–149; 1982, pp. 207–208; 1987, pp. 229–230; 1991, pp. 226–227.

14 International Monetary Fund, *Direction of Trade Statistics, Yearbook 1970-76*, pp. 148–149; 1982, pp. 207–208; 1987, pp. 229–230; 1991, pp. 226–227.

15 International Monetary Fund, *Direction of Trade Statistics, Yearbook 1970-76*, pp. 150–151; 1982, pp. 210–211; 1987, pp. 231–232; 1991, pp. 228–229.

16 Bernard Headley, "The 'New World Order' and the Persian Gulf War," *Humanity & Society* 15, no. 3 (1991), p. 322.

17 Headley, "The 'New World Order' and the Persian Gulf War," p. 323.

18 Headley, "The 'New World Order' and the Persian Gulf War," p. 323.

19 Quoted in Brenner, "Why Is the United States at War with Iraq?" p. 122.

20 Greer, "The Hidden History of the Iraq War," pp. 6–7.

21 Mayer, "Imperialism and the Gulf War," pp. 3–4.

22 Mayer, "Imperialism and the Gulf War," p. 4.

23 Mayer, "Imperialism and the Gulf War," p. 4.

24 Philip Bonosky, *Afghanistan: Washington's Secret War.* 2nd ed. (New York: International Publishers. 2001); Peter Marsden, *The Taliban: War and Religion in Afghanistan,* Rev. ed. (London: Zed Books, 2002).

25 Michael Parenti, *The Terrorism Trap: September 11 and Beyond* (San Francisco, CA: City Lights Books, 2002), p. 57.

26 Parenti, *The Terrorism Trap*, pp. 57–58.

27 Parenti, *The Terrorism Trap*, p. 58.

28 Parenti, *The Terrorism Trap*, pp. 58–59, 60.

29 Bonosky, *Afghanistan*; Marsden, *The Taliban.*

30 Parenti, *The Terrorism Trap*, p. 61.

31 M.J. Gohari, *The Taliban: Ascent to Power* (New York: Oxford University Press, 2001); Ahmed Rashid, *Taliban: Militant Islam, Oil and Fundamentalism in Central Asia* (Waterville, Maine: Thorndike, 2002); Marsden, *The Taliban.*

32 Parenti, *The Terrorism Trap,* p. 63.

33 Parenti, *The Terrorism Trap*, p. 63.
34 For this, the United States paid off the Taliban in a big way. According to Ted Rall's November 2, 2001, *San Francisco Chronicle* report cited by Parenti, "as recently as 1999, the U.S. government paid the entire annual salary of every single Taliban government official." Parenti, *The Terrorism Trap*, p. 64.
35 The lead headline of the August 12, 2002, issue of *Time* magazine, which devoted its cover story to a "Special Report: The Secret History—They Had a Plan" of the Afghan war, reads: "Nine months before 9/11 the U.S. had a bold plan to attack al-Qaeda. It wasn't carried out until the towers fell." See Michael Elliott, "Special Report: The Secret History—They Had a Plan," *Time* (August 12, 2002), pp. 28–43.
36 Arundhati Roy, "War Is Peace," in Roger Burbach and Ben Clarke (eds.), *September 11 and the U.S. War: Beyond the Curtain of Smoke* (San Francisco, CA: City Lights, 2002), p. 101.
37 Parenti, *The Terrorism Trap*, p. 67.
38 Dimitris Yannopoulos, "Checkerboard of Oil, Minefields," in Roger Burbach and Ben Clarke (eds.), *September 11 and the U.S. War: Beyond the Curtain of Smoke* (San Francisco, CA: City Lights, 2002), p. 51.
39 Yannopoulos, "Checkerboard of Oil, Minefields," p. 52.
40 Parenti, *The Terrorism Trap*, pp. 67–68.
41 Parenti, *The Terrorism Trap*, p. 68.
42 Rall, "The New Great Game: Oil Politics in Central Asia," p. 49.
43 Parenti, *The Terrorism Trap*, p. 69.
44 Japan was made to pay $13 billion and Germany $10 billion as part of "their share" of the cost of the war to secure U.S. victory! See Christopher Knowlton and Carla Rapaport. "Germany and Japan: Missing in Action," *Fortune* (March 11, 1991), p. 58.
45 See the *New York Times* (March 28, 1991) for a transcript of General Norman Schwarzkopf's interview "Talking with David Frost," in which the general said, "I would estimate . . . that we easily killed more than 100,000 [Iraqi soldiers]." Quoted in Greer, "The Hidden History of the Iraq War," p. 3.
46 The cost of the U.S. wars in Iraq in 1991 and 2003 and in Afghanistan in 2001, now estimated at $8 trillion, have greatly contributed to the onset of the recessions in 1992, 2001–2002, and 2008–2009 in the United States, with lasting damage to the financial stability of the American Empire which now, after three decades of wars in the Middle East, from 1991 to 2021, has practically bankrupted the United States with a Federal deficit of $27 trillion in 2021.
47 CNN Breaking News, "Taliban Enters Kabul as Afghan President Flees Country," (August 15, 2021).
48 See President Biden's full speech on August 15, 2021. YouTube/NBC News, "Full Speech: President Biden Addresses Nation on Afghanistan" (August 16, 2021). https://www.youtube.com/watch?v=RmioEI6tzCk (accessed on August 16, 2021).
49 See Brown University, Watson Institute for International and Public Affairs, "Costs of War" Project, "Estimate of U.S. Post-9/11 War Spending" https://watson.brown.edu/costsofwar/figures/2021/BudgetaryCosts (accessed September 11, 2021). See also Neta C. Crawford, "The U.S. Budgetary Costs of the Post-9/11 Wars" (Watson Institute for International and Public Affairs, Brown University and The Frederick S. Pardee Center for the Study of the Longer-Range Future, Boston University, September 1, 2021). https://watson.brown.edu/costsofwar/files/cow/imce/papers/2021/Costs%20of%20War_U.S.%20Budgetary%20Costs%20of%20Post-9%2011%20Wars_9.1.21.pdf (accessed September 11, 2021).

8 Awakening of the American People from the Shackles of a False Dream

At last, it is a new morning and a new day in America, after another night of a false and unattainable dream that had for many years turned into a nightmare in the dark hours of the night. Working people in America are, it seems, gradually awakening from the shackles of a false dream—the "American Dream"—that has chained them to the false promises of the capitalist Empire that has enriched a small number of wealthy industrialists, financiers, and profiteers while impoverishing the great majority of the people—working people.[1]

This was done at the expense of millions of hard working people of a "promised land" when none of the promises of the "founding fathers" to "we the people" materialized into a decent life, let alone for "the pursuit of happiness," for those who bought into the system that lured them into submission, while their masters controlled the wealth of the Empire and the government that they installed to serve their own class interests, leaving behind those struggling to survive from paycheck to paycheck in "the land of the free and the home of the brave" and other myths to keep the people subservient to a system that kept them in perpetual servitude. They did so to prevent working people from gaining class consciousness so they would continue to slave away for their bosses while still feeling they are "free"—an illusion spread across American society through the ideological hegemony of the capitalist class and the capitalist state to keep the masses in check and to prolong their subjugation to the powers that be, while those in control of much of the wealth and power in America and the world have succeeded in protecting and advancing their own interests.

The "American Dream" or an American Nightmare?

Every American child from his or her formative years in primary school through adulthood has been promised the realization of the "American Dream," and this promise has prevailed generation after generation without any significant change in the social position of working people in America who have struggled to make ends meet, notwithstanding the illusion under which they have lived their tormented lives, while yearning for better days ahead. This dream—and it is certainly only a dream—has

DOI: 10.4324/9781003282105-8

never become a reality for the vast majority of working Americans, despite their optimism that they will one day realize the fruits of their labor. All that has mattered has been the *hope* that one day they will get to "the promised land," despite all odds to the contrary.

This belief and this faith in something that in reality does not exist has prevailed as the cornerstone of the American psyche, so much so that people believe it to be true, even though there is no visible evidence of its existence that would explain the predicament of most Americans under conditions of late 20th-century and early 21st-century American society.[2] "The American Dream is dead; long live the American Dream" is the battle cry of those true believers that no amount of reality-check could convince them otherwise. Well, this is America and we are the "chosen people"; thus, we can do whatever we "wish" and whatever we "hope," because we are "free". "Whatever we wish?" "Whatever we hope?" "Whatever we dream?"

This illusion, this false reality has become so "real" for millions of Americans (at least for 74 million of them who voted for Donald Trump in the 2020 presidential elections) that it has become the basis of "alternative facts" that do not exist, but are "real" to many just the same, to a point when such illusions become delusional when many can no longer differentiate the truth from a lie, right from a wrong. While such a predicament has its redeeming value for its psychological effect for as long as it lasts in fantasyland, it also contains in itself a toxic residue that is both destructive and liberating—destructive for here and now and liberating in another world, if such exists—a wishful thinking over an impossible fate.

The "American Dream" of "rags to riches" has been just that—a dream—which has turned into a nightmare for many Americans on the edge of survival from paycheck to paycheck.[3] The dream, deferred and unfulfilled over the course of a lifetime, has become a symbol to many not of upward mobility to a better life, but a downward slide into poverty. Thus, the working poor without adequate food, shelter, healthcare, or a decent job to pay their bills have come to suffer here on earth while those in positions of wealth and power with their faithful servants in the state have offered to the unfortunate the assurances of a better life in "the promised land" *after* they die. A subversion of morality in the name of perpetuating wealth and income inequality, the powers-that-be have propagated the big lie of "pie in the sky after you die"—that things will get better not now here on earth but in the afterlife, while those in the upper rungs of American society have enjoyed the fruits of others' labor (*the labor of working people!*). All these propaganda have been disseminated in the name of profits for the capitalist class who have come to own, control, and rule over society to advance their particular class interests, while working people have continued to suffer through their life-long struggles to stay alive.

The Great Awakening of Working People in America

Through the control of the political and ideological superstructure of American society—by ownership and/or control of the mass media, public and private schools, the legal system and other institutions—the capitalist class has come to manipulate and shape the thinking of working people and of the American people in general in inculcating capitalist ideas and a capitalist outlook (in effect, indoctrination of the American people by capitalist ideology)[4] to convince them of the legitimacy of the capitalist system. This, despite the fact that most people in the United States do not own capital and are members of the wage-labor working class who are exploited by the capitalists and who struggle to survive their day-to-day lives from paycheck to paycheck. This has happened over a long period of time throughout the course of labor's long and turbulent history.[5]

The public school system, the mass media (radio, television, films, etc.), the churches, the laws and the legal system, and other spheres of capitalist society in which the owners of private property in the means of production and distribution reign over the people and rule over them, including the so-called "democratic" state which the wealthy control and use to advance their own class interests, while imposing the dominance of capital over labor and all other subordinate classes in every sphere of society.

But no more. As the capitalist system has been going through a series of economic, social, and political crises, and as the capitalist state has become increasingly unable to resolve these crises to restore order to the prevailing system, capitalism and the capitalist state are beginning to lose their legitimacy among the people, as has been occurring in recent decades.[6] In response, working people are not only becoming aware of these facts and developing class consciousness, but also beginning to look for alternatives to the system and envision new ways of resolving the prevailing societal crises.[7]

Likewise, sons and daughters of working people—the young millennial workers—are becoming critical of the capitalist system and are more sympathetic and open to alternative systems (such as socialism), exploring egalitarian solutions to inequalities under global capitalism. This new development, led by labor and other oppressed and exploited people of America and the world, is increasingly becoming the new reality, when tens of millions of working people are beginning to realize the potential for social change and social transformation in America and throughout the world.[8]

The class contradictions of contemporary American society are such that the struggle between labor and capital, which has been a continuing struggle since the inception of the capitalist system in the United States more than two centuries ago, is a *class struggle* between workers and the capitalists, which carries with it the potential for social transformation once the inevitable class contradictions of the system are revealed and exposed, leading the advanced class-conscious contingents of the working class to take the necessary actions to bring about the needed changes in favor of workers and all other affected populations in America and across the globe.[9]

The decline and fall of the American Empire is a manifestation of the capitalist nature of its economy and polity, in effect the nature of the economic and political system that the capitalists have installed from its inception, as we have documented in Chapter 2 of this book. Thus, while the capitalists of the British and French Empires were the original capitalists who set up the foundations of capitalism in North America during colonial times, the resurgent U.S. capitalists of the American Empire are the descendants of the same capitalists whose empire collapsed a century earlier.

But now, in the early 21st century, the American capitalists face the same fate as we witness the decline and fall of the American Empire through the same set of contradictions and conflicts that decimated its predecessors. And it is precisely this same logic of the contradictions of the capitalist system in the United States that will precipitate the fall of the American Empire on a global scale.[10]

This will at the same time ignite the forces of change when working people in America will of necessity develop the class consciousness and the radical leadership that it so desperately needs to wage battle against the entire capitalist system and become the agents of change to end the supremacy of U.S. capitalists over the American and global economy and polity to bring about the end of the Empire and to usher in a new, democratic, and egalitarian America, *after Empire.*

The Rise in Working-Class Consciousness, Class Struggle, and the End of the American Empire

The American Empire is not in the best interests of American workers and the American people in general. As the Empire has caused much harm to workers in the United States and to millions of others around the world, it will inevitably compel workers everywhere to confront it head on to bring it to an end. Clearly, as the persistence of the American Empire is not of any direct benefit to working people in the United States and across the globe, the lived experience of workers in America and the world (the material conditions that they experience and endure on a daily basis) will eventually force them to not only become aware of the conditions under which they live, but also to take the necessary steps to end these conditions under which they suffer.

The reality of the adverse effects of the American Empire on working people in the United States and the world are increasingly becoming obvious with each passing day, such that one can clearly see the impact of this "naked imperialism," as John Bellamy Foster calls it, on working people in their misery and poverty, while the beneficiaries of the Empire (the wealthy owners of the transnational corporations) enrich themselves at the cost of the great majority of the American people and millions of others around the world whose lives depend on their daily labor to sustain themselves on the edges of the Empire's distant territories.[11]

The dialectics of wealth and poverty, booms and busts, freedom and servitude show us that the prevailing social conditions that people experience in society are a product of the balance of social, economic, and political forces that determine the nature and consequences of the divisions and inequalities within which people are trapped; these divisions and inequities are socially created, and hence can be socially changed.[12] The realization of these conditions by working people is what propels them to develop class consciousness (i.e., awareness of their own place in society within definite class boundaries). It is this realization that will ultimately inform and lead workers to take action that will liberate them from the forces that keep them down. The empowerment of workers through this process of realization of their own inherent power is what will compel them to take the appropriate political action to set them free. It is in this way that the working people of America and the world will come to the realization of the necessity to end the American Empire and start building their lives and their societies anew.

This task of mobilization of working people in America and on a global scale will not be easy, as a number of factors need to be considered to unleash the power of labor against capital and the capitalist state to take state power. The rise in class consciousness of the working class will of necessity also mean awareness of the artificial divisions among the people that have been created and reinforced by capital and the capitalist state, most importantly racial/ethnic and gendered divisions among workers which have been created and perpetuated by capital and the capitalist state to divide and control the working class, setting them against each other and thus preventing class unity that would generate a strong multicultural and multiracial working class becoming a powerful force against capital, the capitalist state, and the entire capitalist system.[13]

As the American Empire operates at the global level and to maintain its power engages in repressive military action around the world to divide and conquer its subjects, the same kind of divisions and conflicts are promoted and sustained by the Empire across the world in creating racial, ethnic, and national conflicts through perpetual wars that are fought in distant lands (such as in Vietnam, Iraq, and Afghanistan, to name a few) where American and local blood is spilled to maintain the supremacy of the American Empire around the world—all in favor of U.S. and global capital that this empire represents. But here, too, the tide is beginning to turn, as millions of people across the world are coming together in struggle to resist the American Empire and U.S. imperialism in the global South.[14]

It is for all these reasons and for the future of an America without empire that the working people of America will finally come to the realization that such an empire is not in their best interests, and that not only the people of the world (the subjects of the American Empire), but also all ordinary (working) people of America lose from the empire and thus have a commonality of interests in terminating it to usher in a new America, *after empire.*

Such a large-scale global effort in dismantling the empire and empowering labor to promote peace and equality across the world will necessitate the close cooperation of workers on a global level, as the liberation of the people of the world from the American Empire will at the same time mean the *liberation of the American people from their masters as well.*[15] In the same way, the liberation of working people of color around the world (the victims of America's global Empire) will also mean *the liberation of working people of America as well.* Similarly, the liberation of women around the world (and in America itself) will mean the liberation of all men across the globe (and in America itself) from patriarchy that has been prolonging the oppression of women for so long. Thus, *ending the exploitation and oppression of labor by capital around the world is intimately related to ending the exploitation and oppression of labor by capital at home (in America itself).* And this requires the end of the American Empire to stop the pain that capitalism has been inflicting on working people across the world, for workers of the world "have nothing to lose but their chains," and it is in this sense that Marx and Engels's urgent call "workers of the world, unite!" translates into a call for the global solidarity of labor against capital on a worldwide basis. And it is for this reason that Lenin concluded "imperialism is the eve of the social revolution of the proletariat on a worldwide scale."[16]

Clearly, the global solidarity of the working class will become a formidable force in fighting imperialism (in particular, the American Empire) to liberate the workers of the world *and the people of America itself* to usher in a new workers' state and society based on an economy and a state that is equitable, democratic, and humanitarian—a development that will bring about a new world from the ashes of the old. And this we, too, will experience in America, *after empire!*

Legacy of Empires, Old and New

"Old habits die hard," as the saying goes. This is also true of old empires! It took a long time for the Roman Empire to die, as did for all previous empires and yet others since—the Egyptian, the Hindu, and many others before and the Byzantine, the Ottoman, the Spanish, the British, and others since. And the American Empire won't be an exception to the rule of the rise and fall of empires, nor its longevity in decline in the age of modern imperialism. While it is expected that it, too, will one day end up in the dustbin of history, it would be in the best interests of the American people and the people of the world for America to give up its empire, sooner rather than later, for the sake of its people and those subjected to its rule around the world. In fact, the survival of America as a nation depends on the dismantling of its empire now rather than later.

Distinguished British historian Paul Kennedy, in his book *The Rise and Fall of the Great Powers* (1987), argues that economic strength and military power have been highly correlated in the rise and fall of major empires over the past five centuries.[17] He contends that rising political and military commitments to police an empire lead to increases in military expenditures that eventually overburden a country's economic base and lead to long-term decline. He suggests that the United States and other major powers are experiencing the same historical dynamics that previously affected Spain, France, Great Britain, and Germany, and that the United States must come to grips with its own what he calls "imperial overstretch."[18]

Kennedy argues that the critical factor determining the rise and fall of the great powers is that the dominant world powers/empires "steadily overextend themselves in the course of repeated conflicts and become militarily top-heavy for their weakening economic base."[19]

As a result, such military over-extension, which drains productive resources of a nation, a Great Power increasingly runs the risk of being replaced by rival states which do not have such a military burden and are thus in a better economic position to overtake and surpass a declining empire. Moreover, the burden of military spending to maintain a global empire becomes more serious and the decline and fall of a state from empire status that much more likely if the state in question is also experiencing a relative economic decline. While without a sufficiently large economic base an empire cannot for long be able to sustain political-military power and remain a dominant force on the world scene, it is ultimately the over-extended projection of strategic military force with all the economic costs it entails and with it a corresponding decline in the economy itself that finally brings about the decline and fall of a world empire, according to Kennedy.[20]

American political scientist Calmers Johnson, a self-defined longtime cold-warrior and a consultant to the Central Intelligence Agency (CIA) during the Cold War years, who later came to the realization of the consequences of American power around the world and became a critic of the American Empire, warned about the impending catastrophe looming over the republic. In a series of books that he wrote between 2000 and 2010, he highlighted the urgency of the problem posed by the rise of the American Empire. In *Blowback: The Costs and Consequences of American Empire* (2000), he exposed the growth of America's military presence around the globe (now, in 2021, through a network of more than 800 U.S. military bases in some 80 countries throughout the world), in effect imposing its imperial presence across the planet as well as the costs and consequences of this for America and the American people.[21] In a follow-up book *The Sorrows of Empire: Militarism, Secrecy, and the End of the Republic* (2004) and subsequently in *Nemesis: The Last Days of the American Republic* (2007), and in his final book *Dismantling the Empire: America's Last Best Hope* (2010), published just prior to his death later that year, Johnson warned that if we do not learn from the lessons of past empires, our decline and fall are certain.[22] Delivering an urgent call for the dismantling of the American Empire, he argued that this is the only real chance for America to survive and prosper as a nation.

While both Kennedy and Johnson are correct that the immense military expenditures required by foreign entanglements, wars, and the policing of the empire would translate into enormous costs for the American Empire, they nevertheless overemphasized and misplaced the role of the military as the sole power in expanding the American Empire to global supremacy through conquest and domination of the world. They overlooked the fact that it is in reality the ruling U.S. capitalist class through its trillions of dollars in foreign investments around the world and its control of the U.S. state (including the military) that uses the public purse for private gain is what has led to the growth and expansion of the American Empire at the service of the giant American corporations owned by the wealthy to expand their power across the globe.

Echoing the concerns raised by both Kennedy and Johnson on the present and future predicament of the American Empire, the distinguished historian Alfred W. McCoy, in a series of books on the rise and fall of the American Empire, lays out the impending decline and demise of U.S. global supremacy in the late 20th and early 21st century in great detail. In his book *Policing America's Empire* (2009) and his subsequent book *In the Shadows of the American Century: The Rise and Decline of U.S. Global Power* (2017), McCoy expands his analysis of the approaching collapse of U.S. global power within the broader context of the political economy of U.S. imperialism and its impact at home and abroad.[23] Going a step further in his latest book, *To Govern the Globe: World Orders and Catastrophic Change* (2021), McCoy, after examining several hundred years of the history of past empires, highlights the coming shift in global economic, political, and military power from the American Empire to China as the chief contender to govern the globe by 2030 when the Chinese economy will have become at least 50 percent larger than the U.S. economy, which will translate into major changes regarding China's economic *and* political/military position in the world.[24]

The American Empire is the outcome of capitalist *economic* interests that control the U.S. state, using the U.S. military to advance their financial gains around the world—a century and a half of capitalist development that has led to the predicament that the United States is in today.[25] Thus, to dismantle the Empire through limits placed on the power of the military while ignoring the economic roots of the problem, as Kennedy and

Johnson have done, would not be a successful strategy to save America from itself. The only viable solution to preventing the impending crisis that McCoy predicts will soon be upon us, would be one that engages the working people of America in fighting against the capitalist class and its stranglehold on the capitalist state, which includes its supportive arm—the military—in the service of *capitalism*, which is the *root cause* of the problem that workers face in America under the dictates of the American Empire.

A New Imperative for the American Empire

A new imperative for the American Empire would be the dismantling of its empire, that is, the dissolution of America's vast global reach (as a world superpower) that has provided for its capitalist ruling class the reign over not only its people at home, but also those in much of the rest of the world on whom it has imposed its rule. While the American Empire has secured for itself and for its capitalist class great fortunes across the planet over the course of the past century, hence attaining and imposing its might over its rivals and all others that have come under its sway, the limits to the arrogance of power that all past empires have exercised throughout history have been the chief determinant of an empire's ultimate predicament—one that will cast the final verdict on its very existence. But this verdict to dismantle the American Empire will not come from the capitalists or the capitalist state. It will of necessity come from the working people of America and of the world by not only dismantling the exploitative and oppressive empire under which they all have suffered for so long, but by building a new America after empire that serves the interests of all working people at home and abroad—a new America with a vision that promotes the interests of workers everywhere in the 21st century.

The future prosperity of the American people as a whole would not be a reflection of the wealth of its millionaires and billionaires whose vast accumulated capital has come from the exploitation of working people of America and the world (from the surplus value or value added that the workers have created across the world over several generations). It is the private accumulation of capital from the collective labor of working people who have nothing but debt to show that the Empire has amassed riches at one pole and poverty and destitution at the other across the globe, with a few in the middle enjoying the crumbs that they have been given in return for their loyalty to the powers that be. And all along it has been the working people of America and of the world who have come to shoulder the enormous burdens of the empire, policing the world on behalf of U.S. and global capital and incurring vast expenditures on a global scale that will shake it at its foundations and eventually bankrupt the empire out of existence.[26]

With the awakening of not only the American working class, but also of workers of the world around the globe, the masses of working people are not only increasingly able to understand the dynamics of the global economy and the global capitalist system, but also are able to mobilize and struggle against the capitalist-imperialist system on a global scale. The international solidarity of the working class will thus be an important component of the struggles of the American workers in their efforts to disown and dismantle the American Empire to achieve their liberation, and in this way to realize the new imperative in doing away with the American Empire, which is the only way for them to transition from the old to the new America to fulfill the vision for its rebirth in the 21st century—an America that we Americans will come to embrace and rejoice, *after the end of the empire.*

Notes

1 Stanley Aronowitz, *False Promises: The Shaping of American Working Class Consciousness* (New York: McGraw Hill, 1973). See also, Berch Berberoglu (ed.), *Labor and Capital in the Age of Globalization* (Lanham, MD: Rowman and Littlefield Publishers, 2002).
2 See the series of articles in Michael Zweig (ed.), *What's Class Got to Do with It? American Society in the Twenty-first Century* (Cornell, NY: ILR Press, an imprint of Cornel University Press, 2004). See also the video documentary "Requiem for the American Dream," featuring Noam Chomsky. https://www.amazon.com/Requiem-American-Dream-Noam-Chomsky/dp/B01DL350MA/ref=sr_1_13?dchild=1&keywords=american+dream&qid=1629001615&sr=8-13. (accessed August 15, 2021) and the documentary film "The American Dream and Other Fairy Tales" co-produced by Abigail Disney (granddaughter of Disneyland co-founder Roy Disney) and Kathleen Hughes, featured at the Sundance Film Festival. https://americandreamdoc.com (accessed June 16, 2022).
3 See Robert Reich, *Inequality for All* (Anchor Bay Entertainment, 2013). See also Michael Moore, *Capitalism: A Love Story* (Overture Films, 2009).
4 See Noam Chomsky, *Propaganda and the Public Mind* (Audible Studios, 2015).
5 Richard O. Boyer and Herbert M. Morais, *Labor's Untold Story* (New York: United Electrical, Radio & Machine Workers of America, 1980).
6 Albert J. Szymanski, *The Capitalist State and the Politics of Class* (Cambridge, MA: Winthrop, 1978).
7 Richard D. Wolff, *Capitalism's Crisis Deepens* (Chicago, IL: Haymarket Books, 2016).
8 Alejandro Reuss, *Labor and the Global Economy* (Boston, MA: Dollars & Sense, 2013), Ch. 15.
9 Alan Spector, "Class Polarization and Class Struggle under Advanced Capitalism," in Berch Berberoglu (ed.), *Globalization and Change: The Transformation of Global Capitalism* (Lanham, MD: Lexington Books, 2005), Ch. 3.
10 Albert J. Szymanski, *The Logic of Imperialism* (New York: Praeger, 1981). See also the various essays in Jeff Maskovsky and Ida Susser (eds.), *Rethinking America: The Imperial Homeland in the 21st Century* (Boulder, CO: Paradigm, 2009).
11 John Bellamy Foster, *Naked Imperialism: The U.S. Pursuit of Global Dominance* (New York: Monthly Review Press, 2006). See also David Harvey, *The New Imperialism* (New York: Oxford University Press, 2003), and Noam Chomsky, *Hegemony or Survival: America's Quest for Global Dominance* (New York: Macmillan, 2004).

12 Michael D. Yates, *The Great Inequality* (New York: Routledge, 2016) and Howard J. Sherman and Paul D. Sherman, *Inequality, Boom and Bust: From Billionaire Capitalism to Equality and Full Employment* (New York: Routledge, 2018).
13 R. Jeffrey Lustig, "The Tangled Knot of Race and Class in America," in Michael Zweig (ed.), *What's Class Got to Do with It?* (Ithaca, NY: ILR Press, 2004).
14 Francois Polet (ed), *The State of Resistance: Popular Struggles in the Global South* (London: Zed Books, 2007).
15 James Petras, *Rulers and Ruled in the U.S. Empire* (Atlanta, GA: Clarity Press, 2007).
16 V.I. Lenin reached this conclusion after his careful analysis of the contradictions of modern imperialism as the highest stage of capitalism in the early 20th century. See V.I. Lenin, *Imperialism, the Highest Stage of Capitalism* (New York: International Publishers, 1978).
17 Paul M. Kennedy, *The Rise and Fall of the Great Powers* (New York: Random House, 1987).
18 Kennedy, *The Rise and Fall of the Great Powers.*
19 Kennedy, *The Rise and Fall of the Great Powers*, p. xxiii.
20 Kennedy, *The Rise and Fall of the Great Powers.*
21 Chalmers Johnson, *Blowback: The Costs and Consequences of American Empire* (New York: Metropolitan Books, 2000). See also the second edition of this book published in 2004 in the aftermath of 9/11 to the U.S. war against Iraq.
22 See Chalmers Johnson, *The Sorrows of Empire: Militarism, Secrecy, and the End of the Republic* (New York: Metropolitan Books, 2004); *Nemesis: The Last Days of the American Republic* (New York: Metropolitan Books, 2007); and *Dismantling the Empire: America's Last Best Hope* (New York: Metropolitan Books, 2010).
23 See Alfred W. McCoy, *Policing America's Empire: The United States, the Philippines, and the Rise of the Surveillance State* (Madison: University of Wisconsin Press 2009) and Alfred McCoy, *In the Shadows of the American Century: The Rise and Decline of U.S. Global Power* (Chicago, IL: Haymarket Books, 2017).
24 Alfred McCoy, *To Govern the Globe: World Orders and Catastrophic Change* (Chicago, IL: Haymarket Books, 2021). See also Martin Jacques, *When China Rules the World: The End of the Western World and the Birth of a New Global Order*, 2nd ed. (New York: Penguin, 2012).
25 Petras, *Rulers and Ruled in the U.S. Empire.*
26 Felix Greene, *The Enemy: What Every American Should Know about Imperialism* (New York: Vintage, 1970). See also Szymanski, *The Logic of Imperialism*; Berch Berberoglu, *The Internationalization of Capital: Imperialism and Capitalist Development on a World Scale* (New York: Praeger, 1987); Berch Berberoglu, *Globalization of Capital and the Nation State: Imperialism, Class Struggle, and the State in the Age of Global Capitalism* (Lanham, MD: Rowman and Littlefield Publishers, 2003); James Petras and Henry Veltmeyer, *Globalization Unmasked: Imperialism in the 21st Century* (Halifax, Canada: Fernwood Publications, 2001); and James Petras, *U.S. Imperialism: The Changing Dynamics of Global Power* (New York: Routledge, 2020).

9 A New Beginning for America

After Empire and Imperialism

A new beginning for America can come only after America gives up its Empire. It is only *after Empire* that America will be able to come to terms with its tormented past and its uncertain future. America has failed to deliver the "American Dream" to a great majority of its people because of its myriad entanglements across much of the world during its "glorious" days cast as the "American Century"—one that lasted merely a few decades in the postwar period in the latter half of the 20th century.[1] Thus, the burden of imperial overreach in maintaining its once mighty power around the world finally rang true, when the Empire began to crack and started to crumble toward an impending collapse in the aftermath of another failed dream that turned into an epic nightmare.[2]

The trauma that America went through for over four long years under the pseudo-populist and pseudo-nationalist Trump Presidency by twice-impeached 45th President of the United States, Donald J. Trump, who by promoting and presiding over a racist, authoritarian regime that he created was destined to fail against his promise of "Making America Great Again" when he took the country to the gates of a right-wing dictatorship. In this he may indeed have prevailed had the "insurrection" that he incited through his "storm troopers" succeeded on January 6, 2021, thus potentially triggering a second American Civil War. While his defeat in the 2020 presidential elections put a damper on such an eventuality for the time being, the predicament of America in its political crisis seems far from over, as the American Empire comes to terms with its other discontents who, from another (and this time legitimate) vantage point, must *and will* come forward with their own grievances for the Empire's past and present crimes committed in the name of "liberty and justice for all," while all along violating the most basic human rights of its working people (natives, slaves, and immigrants alike) on the bottom rungs of American society.

Settling of Old Accounts before a New Beginning

Taking stock of past crimes of the American Empire is the first step in the healing process that also requires recognition and reconciliation based on

DOI: 10.4324/9781003282105-9

the truths of the crimes committed in the name of the American people and the American nation long before America had embarked on the road to empire and imperialism.[3] The genocide committed against native peoples of the first nations of North America, the enslavement of the people of Africa and their transport to the "new" world through the Transatlantic slave trade in human flesh were just the beginning of other crimes that were yet to be committed against those trapped on the home front of the emerging American Empire. And these crimes of empire continued across the world after America began to embark on the road to imperialism some years later, outdoing its colonial and imperial masters from whom it learned the practice of subordination, oppression, and exploitation of people around the globe on a grand scale.[4]

The conquest and genocide perpetrated against the native peoples of this land were the most egregious acts of inhumanity visited upon a people who suffered in the hands of so-called civilized nations that colonized, enslaved, and massacred millions of victims whose only fault was to live in peace in their own home territories.[5] Land, raw materials and resources, and human labor in chains became the battle cry of the invading armies of the first undocumented illegal immigrants (European landowners and capitalists) who arrived in these shores without the permission of the original inhabitants of these lands. Without passports, visas, or permits to claim residency, the hordes of invading European colonists (the British, the French, the Dutch, and the Spanish) and later their descendants pillaged the lands of the indigenous peoples in search of gold and silver, land, human labor, and other treasures that they mercilessly plundered and exploited in the name of "God and Glory," destroying everything on their path for money, power, and fame in pursuit of "a more perfect union"—one in which only the white wealthy landowners, slave-owners, merchants, financiers, and capitalists reigned supreme, while all others were seen as less than humans, despite the fact that all the atrocities and crimes committed against humanity were done by these "civilized" people.[6]

The original local inhabitants of these lands (the indigenous Native Americans), the imported slaves who were dragged onto mighty ships in chains and brought to these shores (the first Africans who were bought and sold on this soil in human flesh), and later poor immigrant laborers who flocked across the oceans from the East and the West in search of work in hard manual labor in the mills and mines ushered in the second industrial revolution. They formed the basis of the exploitation of "free" (wage-) and unfree (slave) labor that built the foundations of American society, whose blood, sweat, and tears became the driving force of the struggles and rebellions that they waged throughout American history.[7]

And here we are, nearly two and a half centuries later, when we are still immersed into the depths of racism, bigotry, and inequality affecting the lives of the masses of men and women (the workers, the poor, the powerless, and the ruled of all shades) crying out that their lives matter, now as they did then, when they were first exploited and oppressed while their labor was stolen from them and their humanity was stripped and in dire straits. And all these were magnified a thousandfold across the oceans and lands of others far and near, when a rising Empire mercilessly sacrificed those who came under its reign and globalized the oppression and exploitation of the masses on a grand scale across the world.[8] These are all part of our history that made America what it is today—the concentration and centralization of wealth created by native-, slave-, and wage-labor that ended up in a few hands (of the wealthy slave-owners, capitalists, and their retainers in the bureaucratic institutions of the imperial state).

Now we must come to terms with these realities that resulted in wealth and income inequality, racism, sexism, and imperialism from which people have been suffering at home and abroad. Given these predicaments, how can we move forward toward a new America without settling these old (and new) accounts of inhumane treatment of the people from whose labor some became very rich while others struggled to stay alive by securing the minimal necessities of life that they were able to gather from one day to the next, hand-to-mouth, and now barely paycheck to paycheck?

The time has come for the Empire to respond—first through reconciliation and then with reparations—for all the crimes committed in the name of this great nation of working people. It must now come to terms with the old accounts of unpaid and partly paid labor at home and abroad. America cannot move forward with its vision for a new nation until these accounts are settled. This can be done through a radical redistribution of wealth and income through a wealth tax and the nationalization of the major means of production owned by monopolies and oligopolies when the wealth and profits of the few big capitalists are redistributed to the many, so that the accumulated capital/wealth/profits of the few are returned back to the many—to those who broke their backs through their labor for more than two centuries, first as slaves, pure and simple, and then as wage-slaves in factories, mines, and mills to make their bosses rich while they remained poor.[9]

America will have to pay its native peoples for the wealth taken from them, the descendants of its slaves for their endurance of back-breaking labor without pay, and for the humiliation of being bought and sold when entire families (husbands, wives, and children) were auctioned off to the highest bidder! And what about all those wage-laborers who have worked in the factories and mills in the Empire's heartland and many more workers in the sweatshops of the global economy in distant lands, where U.S. transnational corporations have been exploiting the cheap labor of adults and children alike?[10] They too will need to be compensated for their tormented lives, morning till night, day after day, for endless months and years over the course of the Empire's existence through extraction of the surplus value created by labor and expropriated by industrial and finance capital that rules the Empire.

And what about all those who were killed and maimed in the Empire's endless wars—from the Mexican-American War through World War I and World War II to Vietnam, Iraq, and Afghanistan as well as dozens of undeclared wars, military coups, and the installation of right-wing fascist dictatorships in Central and South America, East Asia, Africa, and the Middle East, where hundreds of thousands of innocent people were killed or maimed by the American Empire.[11] They and their families too must be compensated for these crimes of empire for the violation of their most basic human rights—the right to live!

The Empire will also need to pay billions of dollars to countries whose raw materials and resources were extracted from the ground and turned into cash in furthering the imperialist accumulation process while many of these countries remained underdeveloped and poor, subjected to the dictates of the empire that collaborated with corrupt local cronies that sold out their countries and their people to the imperialists in the name of wealth and power that they were able to gain as junior partners of the Empire and becoming accomplices of the Empire's misdeeds and crimes across the world. New democratic regimes in these countries around the globe will also need to be compensated for the loss of their wealth that could have been used for their own social and economic development. They, too, will need to be paid billions of dollars to rebuild their economies and nations free of domination, exploitation, and oppression.

The Vision for a New America in the 21st Century

America will be on the road to recovery after it gives up its empire, and the best way for it to recover from its exploitation and oppression of people and nations on a global scale is for it to give up imperialism. But this is not going to be an easy task because entrenched capitalist interests will not easily give up their acquired wealth that they accumulated through the exploitation of labor at home and abroad. Thus, it will be incumbent upon working people of America and the world to decide what is to be done to recover their lost wealth that they created through their own hard labor. America cannot embark on the path to recovery with a vision for a new nation in the 21st century until it comes to terms with itself as an Empire. Recognition and realization of its misdeeds would be the first step in the reconciliation process—with its own people and with others across the world—when it embarks on a new path, *after empire and imperialism*.

Giving up the Empire will require the mobilization of working people who will demand the dismantling of the Empire so that the vast expenditures wasted on the maintenance of power around the world would now be used to elevate its people, which will at the same time elevate all others in the world to achieve well-being for all when funds would be expanded to improve the condition of people in America and the world through better healthcare, better nutrition, better education, and better living. There will be resistance to such change, to be sure, by the powers that be (by the vested interests in maintaining wealth and power in their own hands). However, once the power of labor is unleashed in an organized way through the various organizations of workers against those vested interests currently in power (the capitalists) who want to maintain that power to perpetuate inequalities in society, there is nothing that can stop labor from accomplishing its goals in making America a really great nation. It is only then, when its wealth is evenly distributed among its people, that the working people of America will be able to control and utilize the wealth that they have created in an equitable way to make their society and government that is "of the people, by the people, and for the people" as promised long ago.[12]

The releasing of trillions of dollars spent for the protection of the American Empire to defend and advance the interests of the capitalist class and the capitalist state around the world would instead make available funds to pay for people's necessities and provide a high standard of living for everyone. These would all be decided and planned by workers themselves and their own grassroots, class-conscious organizations and leadership that would control and run the state on behalf of all workers.

In a new, democratic America of the future run by working people and for working people, when all the wealth created by the workers over the past two centuries (now redistributed back to them) and without foreign entanglements in wars and policing of the world, one can imagine what can be done by the trillions of dollars that would be available to spend on the American people. This would provide them with an abundance of food, shelter, healthcare, and higher education when the sons and daughters of all working people could go to college tuition-free, have a good early retirement at age 60 that provides full coverage of living expenses with an annual guaranteed minimum income equivalent to a middle-income lifestyle, and free environmentally sustainable transportation through public and private means. Subsidized housing of one's choosing (private free-standing homes of one's own, purchased by funds provided by the workers' state, or shared public housing of the highest quality), vacations with full pay for at least two months a year, and other benefits for people to enhance their well-being and happiness—all of these would be possible when working people collectively own, control, and manage the wealth of society, control and govern the state, its laws, and its budget, by becoming the supreme authority in the land and governing society on behalf of all working people.[13]

These and other necessities of life in a new America led by working people can be provided from the profits generated by large monopoly corporations that would be nationalized and managed by the workers themselves from the bottom up by their rank and file, and small businesses based on family labor would provide goods and services for the people in their local communities, maintaining their independence, while being fully subsidized by the workers' state to keep mom-and-pop operations viable without the fear of failure and bankruptcy. The Federal budget would be devoted to the provision of goods and services as well as other benefits to the American people from the savings attained by the absence of empire and imperialist expenditures in policing the world through military bases that span the globe, waging wars, and supporting corrupt authoritarian puppet dictatorships. All these point to a people's government and society in which all public funds would come from the profits of corporations that are now owned and operated by the workers' state which is democratically controlled and run by working people.

America has never been better positioned to put to good use the enormous wealth (surplus value or value added) created by labor and expropriated by capital as profits by large capitalist corporations that have become giant conglomerates through the super exploitation of workers at home and abroad.[14] Thus, the time has come to expropriate the expropriators to return this wealth created by labor to its true creators—to all those who have labored throughout their lives and received only a fraction of the value they have produced, much of which has gone to the owners of the means of production—to the mighty corporations that have enriched their owners at the expense of their workers and the public in general. All that wealth that the capitalists have accumulated will now have to be returned to its rightful owners—working people—who are the sole creators of the value generated under the capitalist mode of production based on wage-labor.

This has been clearly articulated by critical, classical, social theorists like Karl Marx, but also by prominent advocates of the capitalist system like Adam Smith, David Ricardo, and many others.[15] It is a well-known fact, and the capitalists know and admit, that without human labor nothing can be produced in the world, and without the surplus labor time (hence the surplus value) produced by labor and expropriated by the capitalists, the capitalists would not be able to accumulate the vast amounts of wealth that they now possess. And they know that the time is fast approaching when the true creators of wealth will come to claim that wealth, and they will one day be obliged to transfer all wealth to the coffers of society for the collective sustenance and well-being of the people—working people! It is only after working people become fully class-conscious of their own class interests and decide to wage a determined struggle and succeed in taking state power will they be able to establish a workers' state and begin the reconstitution of society and social life in a new way in America and the rest of the world without capitalism and capitalist empires. It is only then will the vision for a new America be fulfilled—in a new America after empire, after capitalist imperialism, and after working people establish a democratic workers' state (i.e., socialism).

Beyond the material benefits that such a popular socialist system can bring to its hard-working citizens, America would also need to offer to everyone, young and old, abled and disabled, male and female, gay and straight, Black, red, brown, and White, a principled and compassionate social system that upholds the highest standards of humanity: freedom of thought and speech, mobility, wellness, and caring for each other in a collective way; socializing future generations of citizens in a cooperative spirit against individualism and selfishness; embracing all that is good with humanity and rejecting all the wrong things that previous socialization has taught us. This would, indeed, move us in a new direction: from the private sphere wrapped up in the self with addiction to consumerism toward the social sphere in embracing others beyond our personal needs and those of our immediate families; developing social skills to accept others as we would our own family and neighbors, so that we all live in peace, without selfish and individualistic competition that is often *destructive* and toward cooperation with others that is always *constructive.* All these are noble ideals to promote the well-being of all. Such a high social and moral standard would cherish peace, not war (except in self-defense), promote equality and comradery (as against inequality, oppression, and exploitation), inculcate love of humanity (as against hate of others, at home and abroad), and develop respect toward people and the social and natural environment (as opposed to their degradation and destruction). These are all honorable and desirable societal goals for all of us to achieve so we can live in peace and prosperity in a new and just America that we all can feel proud of now and for the foreseeable future; a high societal standard indeed that one hopes others would emulate in a world in which we all live together—today, tomorrow, and in the future.

What defines us as human beings is *not* (and ought *not* be) our class, race, ethnicity, nationality, gender, religion, culture, language, or other characteristics—all of which are socially constructed. But, above and beyond all our apparent differences, it is our *humanity* that is unique to our species as *human beings*; that is what binds us to each other, that gives meaning to us as a people—American or otherwise. It is this unique character as humans that allows us to embrace each other to fight for what is right and what is just. This is what a grassroots working people's society would look like and this is what ordinary working people are demanding and will continue to struggle to achieve. And this is the moment that we all have been waiting for, and we will all be there to celebrate—the vision that we all have for *a new America after empire* in the 21st century.

Notes

1 See the documentary on the "American Dream" featuring Noam Chomsky, "Requiem for the American Dream" (2016) https://www.amazon.com/Requiem-American-Dream-Noam-Chomsky/dp/B01DL350MA/

ref=sr_1_13?dchild=1&keywords=american+dream&qid=1629001615&sr=8-13 (accessed August 15, 2021).

2 We are, of course, referring here to the fake hype and "dream" promoted by Donald J. Trump during his presidency (2016–2020), when the slogan "Make America Great Again" became the rallying point in mobilizing his "base" for his own personal political advancement.

3 Carl Boggs, *The Crimes of Empire* (London: Pluto Press, 2010).

4 On the crimes committed against Native Americans, see Ward Churchill, *A Little Matter of Genocide: Holocaust and Denial in the Americas 1492 to the Present* (San Francisco, CA: City Lights, 2001). See also Ward Churchill, *Struggle for the Land: Native North American Resistance to Genocide, Ecocide, and Colonization*, 2nd ed. (San Francisco, CA: City Lights Publishers, 2002). On the Transatlantic slave trade and the crimes committed against slaves in the Americas, see Eric Williams, *Capitalism and Slavery* (New York: Capricorn, 1966), and on the crimes committed against imported African slaves in the U.S. South, see Eugene Genovese, *The Political Economy of Slavery: Studies in the Economy and Society of the Slave South,* 2nd ed. (Middletown, CT: Wesleyan University Press, 1988).

5 Churchill, *A Little Matter of Genocide: Holocaust and Denial in the Americas 1492 to the Present.* See also Roxanne Dunbar-Ortiz, *An Indigenous Peoples' History of the United States* (Boston, MA: Beacon Press, 2015).

6 Dunbar-Ortiz, *An Indigenous Peoples' History of the United States.* See also James W. Russell, *Class and Race Formation in North America* (Toronto: University of Toronto Press, 2008).

7 Richard O. Boyer and Herbert M. Morais, *Labor's Untold Story* (New York: United Electrical, Radio & Machine Workers of America, 1984).

8 Ernesto Screpanti, *Global Imperialism and the Great Crisis: The Uncertain Future of Capitalism* (New York: Monthly Review Press, 2014), Chapters 2 and 3.

9 The wealth created by labor and expropriated by capital is the basis of the maldistribution of wealth resulting from the exploitation of labor that has led to wealth and income inequality in America and the world, which is a product of the development of capitalism on a global scale. See Berch Berberoglu, *The Internationalization of Capital: Imperialism and Capitalist Development on a World Scale* (New York: Praeger, 1987), Chapter 2.

10 On the sweatshops of the global capitalist economy, see Naomi Klein, *No Logo* (New York: Random House, 1999) and Ashok Kumar, *Monopoly Capitalism: Power and Production in the Twilight of the Sweatshop Age* (Cambridge: Cambridge University Press, 2020), especially pp. 1–16 and 52–88.

11 According to the Watson Institute for International and Public Affairs "Costs of War" Project at Brown University, "At least 801,000 people have been killed by direct war violence in Iraq, Afghanistan, Syria, Yemen, and Pakistan. The number of people who have been wounded or have fallen ill as a result of the conflicts is far higher" and that:

> Thousands of United States service members have died in combat, as have thousands of civilian contractors. Many have died later on from injuries and illnesses sustained in the war zones. Hundreds of thousands of soldiers and contractors have been wounded and are living with disabilities and war-related illnesses"

The Report goes on to point out:

> However, the vast majority of people killed are civilians. More than 335,000 civilians have been killed in the fighting since 2001. Millions of people living in the war zones have also been displaced by war. The U.S.

> post-9/11 wars have forcibly displaced at least 38 million people in and from Afghanistan, Iraq, Pakistan, Yemen, Somalia, the Philippines, Libya, and Syria. This number exceeds the total displaced by every war since 1900, except World War II.

See Watson Institute for International and Public Affairs "Costs of War: Human Costs" https://watson.brown.edu/costsofwar/costs/human (accessed August 28, 2021). In a subsequent report, the Watson Institute researchers provide an update to their earlier 2019 estimates by indicating that as of August 2021, at least 929,000 people have been killed in U.S.'s post-9/11 wars in Afghanistan, Iraq, and elsewhere during the 20-year period 2001–2021. See Neta C. Crawford and Catherine Lutz, "Human Cost of Post-9/11 Wars" (September 1, 2021) https://watson.brown.edu/costsofwar/files/cow/imce/papers/2021/Costs%20of%20War_Direct%20War%20Deaths_9.1.21.pdf (accessed September 11, 2021).

12 The statement was made by President Abraham Lincoln in the middle of the Civil War, during his Gettysburg Address on November 19, 1863, on the battlefield near Gettysburg, Pennsylvania, where he stated:

> Four score and seven years ago our fathers brought forth, upon this continent, a new nation, conceived in liberty, and dedicated to the proposition that 'all men are created equal.' Now we are engaged in a great civil war, testing whether that nation, or any nation so conceived, and so dedicated, can long endure. . . That the nation shall have a new birth of freedom, and that *government of the people by the people for the people shall not perish from the earth.*

Abraham Lincoln, Draft of the Gettysburg Address: Nicolay Copy. Transcribed and annotated by the Lincoln Studies Center, Knox College, Galesburg, Illinois. Available at Abraham Lincoln Papers at the Library of Congress, Manuscript Division (Washington, DC: American Memory Project, [2000–2002]), http://memory.loc.gov/ammem/alhtml/malhome.html (accessed July 4, 2022)

13 In effect, a socialist society in which the working class becomes the ruling class and governs society, that is, a socialist state of workers, by workers, for workers, and all other laboring people in society.

14 See Berch Berberoglu, *Globalization of Capital and the Nation State: Imperialism, Class Struggle, and the State in the Age of Global Capitalism* (Lanham, MD: Rowman and Littlefield, 2003), Chapters 4 and 6.

15 Adam Smith, *The Wealth of Nations: An Inquiry into the Nature and Causes of the Wealth of Nations* (London: W. Strahan and T. Cadell, 1776); David Ricardo, *The Principles of Political Economy and Taxation* (London: John Murray, 1817); Karl Marx, *Capital: Critique of Political Economy* (Berlin: Verlag von Otto Meisner, 1867).

10 Conclusion

Toward a New America in the 21st Century

We have in this book engaged in a careful and candid examination of our past, taken stock of our present, and re-imagined a bright future for us and for generations yet to come. In the process, we have met the enemy and he is us! But we have also become reassured that the American people—above all, the honest, decent, working people of America—are good people and represent the shining future of a new and glorious nation in the decades ahead. We have come to find that the *American Empire*, as an outgrowth of more than a century of capitalist development during which it has turned into capitalist imperialism, is the *root cause* of much of the problems we have been facing and continue to face at home and abroad throughout the 20th and early 21st centuries.

Before any progress can be made for a new and equitable society on the home front and in the rest of the world, the American Empire, as Chalmers Johnson, a long-time consultant to the Central Intelligence Agency (CIA) has insisted "must be dismantled." Ringing the alarm bells of catastrophe that we will be facing in the years ahead, Johnson must have foreseen the tragic defeat and collapse of the American Empire and the last minute mass evacuation of Americans and allied Afghans from Kabul, Afghanistan, when in August 2021 the previously overthrown Taliban regime 20 years earlier took over the country and returned to power. Ordering the empire to leave immediately, the Taliban terrorists caused havoc among both Americans and Afghans alike who faced an urgent evacuation amidst ISIS-K suicide bombings that took the lives of 13 American soldiers and military personnel and 170 Afghan civilians in the mass exodus of Americans and Afghan allies of the United States trying to leave the country. Johnson's foresight must have been based on his own experience as an ex-CIA operative who witnessed a similar episode several decades earlier—the empire's humiliating defeat and expulsion from Vietnam with the fall of Saigon in April 1975—which must have troubled him enough to warn us against the American Empire becoming entangled into "another Vietnam." But to no avail, as the United States again became engaged in such imperial wars, this time against Iraq and Afghanistan for 20 long years. Johnson warned us that if we do not learn from the lessons of past empires and from our own misdeeds (saying "we are the new Rome"), our

DOI: 10.4324/9781003282105-10

decline and fall are certain. Making an urgent call for the "dismantling of the American Empire," he argued that this is the only real chance (perhaps the last chance) for America to survive and prosper as a nation.

There is to be sure going to be a new America in the 21st century, and this will come about through a working-class *socialist* revolution. But it will not be broadcast through another episode of "The Next Revolution" hosted by Steve Hilton of Fox TV! That one caters to the uninformed and falsely conscious segments of the working class and small business, wrapped in ultra-right-wing pseudo-populist/nationalist and pro-capitalist propaganda that this channel spreads through the airwaves on a daily basis. It does so to confuse the working class and to distract and disorient it from its historic mission to rise up against the capitalist state and establish a democratic political rule of working people through a complete transformation and restructuring of the state, economy, and society in America in the 21st century.

The new America that the exploited and class-conscious working class will usher in is an egalitarian, just, and a democratic society based on the interests of the great majority of the people of America—wage-labor working class—that has been suffering exploitation and oppression under the yoke of capital for over two centuries. It will be an America that is anti-capitalist, anti-imperialist, anti-racist, anti-sexist, pro-labor, and pro-socialist, and destined to build an advanced socialist society based on the ideals of all oppressed and exploited peoples across the nation and the world.

With a multi-cultural, multi-racial working class at the helm of the state and society, America would be well positioned to win the class struggle in favor of labor against capital after confronting the powers-that-be in both private and public life. It is through this process of empowerment that labor will become the leading force and take center stage to guide American society in a new direction to safeguard and advance the class interests of the working class through political action along socialist lines. Thus, the new America of the 21st century will definitely be a socialist America that caters to the needs of its working people, while transforming the monopoly capitalist system to serve the workers' state in transition from capitalism to socialism. Thus, through this process, it will render capitalism to become extinct when the exploitation of wage-labor by capital is finally abolished much as the abolition of slavery that ended the exploitation of slaves by their masters under the slave system in the U.S. South following Northern victory in the U.S. Civil War.

The abolition of capitalism and capitalist imperialism, in effect the abolition of the capitalist American Empire, is the first step toward the rebuilding of a new America *after empire*. And this new America must be a reflection of the interests of the working class, which is multi-racial, multi-ethnic, multi-cultural, and revolutionary with a high level of class consciousness that it needs in order to attain political power and take control of the state. But beyond the political changes that we anticipate will take place in America in the years ahead, it is also important to highlight America's global obligations in building the basis of cooperation through labor internationalism to assist workers in other countries who are organizing and fighting against their own corrupt states to abolish capitalism and establish socialism throughout the world. It is through this process of international working-class solidarity that labor can build bridges between workers in power in America and workers who are in the process of taking power in other countries across the globe.

The central issue that remains to be articulated to further bring awareness of these changes to the working people of America is a clear political ideology that would serve to consolidate the rule of the working class in a new *socialist* America. This would mean not only the end of the American Empire, but also the abolition of capitalist imperialism when there won't be an empire to meddle in the internal affairs of other states that would freely collaborate with a growing number of new socialist states across the world through international labor solidarity.

A new socialist America, as the wealthiest, most powerful, and leading nation in the world, would be a great inspiration and a shining example to millions of people throughout the world—a model to follow to liberate humanity from the shackles of capitalist imperialism. Declaring peace, not war, friendship with and respect for others, not the arrogance, xenophobia, hatred, and racism of empire, ready to invade, occupy, and dominate based on misplaced notions of superiority. Nay, the new America will not engage in such crimes against humanity; on the contrary, it will become an agent of change for the better, not only for its own people but for all of humanity—a shining example of what humanity can be "with [*real*] liberty and justice for all" across the earth, gaining the love and respect of others as it respects the sovereignty of others, when others, in turn, emulate its example in a peaceful and cooperative world order in which all would co-exist with the racial, ethnic, and cultural diversity under a united sisterhood and brotherhood of nations working together as one human family.

These are not idle utopian dreams, but very real eventualities that can be achieved under conditions of social harmony, social cooperation, and social justice—in a word, under global socialism. And world history, since the days of colonialism, slavery, empire, and imperialism, points us in the direction of further human progress and development until we achieve "a more perfect union" of our species here on earth together with all others which includes our most precious natural environment that we must collectively protect and preserve for us and for future generations yet to come in *America after empire and imperialism*.

Bibliography

Ackerman, Frank, et al. (eds.). 2000. *The Political Economy of Inequality*. Washington, DC: Island Press.

Adler, Lee H., Maite Tapia, and Lowell Turner (eds.). 2014. *Mobilizing Against Inequality: Unions, Immigrant Workers, and the Crisis of Capitalism*. Ithaca, NY: ILR Press.

Amaladoss, Michael (ed.). 1999. *Globalization and Its Victims as Seen by Its Victims*. Delhi, India: Vidyajyoti Education and Welfare Society.

Amin, Samir. 2003. *Obsolescent Capitalism: Contemporary Politics and Global Disorder*. New York: Zed Books.

Amoroso, Bruno. 2001. *On Globalization: Capitalism in the 21st Century*. New York: St. Martin's.

Appadurai, Arjun. 2001. *Globalization*. Durham, NC: Duke University Press.

Aptheker, Herbert. 1976. *The American Revolution, 1763-1783*. New York: International Publishers.

Aptheker, Herbert. 1976. *Early Years of the Republic*. New York: International Publishers.

Aptheker, Herbert. 1978. *The Unfolding Drama: Studies in U.S. History*. New York: International Publishers.

Aronowitz, Stanley. 1973. *False Promises: The Shaping of American Working-Class Consciousness*. New York: McGraw-Hill Co.

Aronowitz, Stanley. 1983. *Working Class Hero: A New Strategy for Labor*. New York: Adama Books.

Atkinson, Anthony B. 2015. *Inequality: What Can Be Done?* Cambridge, MA: Harvard University Press.

Ayala, Cesar J. 1989. "Theories of Big Business in American Society." *Critical Sociology* 16, no. 2–3 (Summer-Fall): 92–120.

Azoulay, Ariella. 2019. *Potential History: Unlearning Imperialism*. London: Verso.

Bacevic, Andrew. 2006. *The New American Militarism: How Americans Are Seduced by War*. New York: Oxford University Press.

Bacevic, Andrew. 2010. *Washington Rules: America's Path to Permanent War*. New York: Metropolitan Books.

Baker, Dean. 2009. *Plunder and Blunder: The Rise and Fall of the Bubble Economy*. New York: Berrett-Koehler Publishers.

Baker, Yousef K. 2014. "Global Capitalism and Iraq: The Making of a Neoliberal State." *International Review of Modern Sociology* 40, no. 2 (Autumn): 121–148.

Baran, Paul and Paul M. Sweezy. 1966. *Monopoly Capital*. New York: Monthly Review Press.

Beams, Nick. 1998. *The Significance and Implications of Globalization: A Marxist Assessment*. Southfield: Mehring Books.

Beard, Charles. 1962. *An Economic Interpretation of the Constitution of the United States*. New York: Macmillan.

Beard, Charles and Mary Beard. 1930. *The Rise of American Civilization*. New York: Macmillan.

Bello, Walden. 2005. *Deglobalization: Ideas for a New World Economy*. Revised ed. London: Zed Books.

Bello, Walden. 2009. "The Global Collapse: A Non-orthodox View." *MRZine*, February 20. http://www.monthlyreview.org/mrzine/</ds> bello200209.html

Berberoglu, Berch. 1987. *The Internationalization of Capital: Imperialism and Capitalist Development on a World Scale*. New York: Praeger.

Berberoglu, Berch. 1992. *The Legacy of Empire: Economic Decline and Class Polarization in the United States*. New York: Praeger Publishers.

Berberoglu, Berch. 1996. "Imperialism and Class Struggle in the Late 20th Century." *Humanity and Society* 20, no. 2 (May): 72–80.

Berberoglu, Berch. 1999. *Turmoil in the Middle East: Imperialism, War, and Political Instability*. Albany: State University of New York Press.

Berberoglu, Berch (ed.). 2002. *Labor and Capital in the Age of Globalization: The Labor Process and the Changing Nature of Work in the Global Economy*. Boulder, CO: Rowman and Littlefield.

Berberoglu, Berch. 2003. *Globalization of Capital and the Nation-State: Imperialism, Class Struggle, and the State in the Age of Global Capitalism*. Boulder, CO: Rowman and Littlefield.

Berberoglu, Berch (ed.). 2005. *Globalization and Change: The Transformation of Global Capitalism*. Lanham, MD: Lexington Books.

Berberoglu, Berch. 2009. *Class and Class Conflict in the Age of Globalization*. Lanham, MD: Lexington.

Berberoglu, Berch (ed.). 2010. *Globalization in the 21st Century: Labor, Capital, and the State in the 21st Century*. New York: Palgrave Macmillan.

Berberoglu, Berch. 2012. *Beyond the Global Capitalist Crisis: The World Economy in Transition*. New York: Routledge.

Berberoglu, Berch. 2014. *The Global Capitalist Crisis and Its Aftermath: The Causes and Consequences of the Great Recession of 2008-2009*. New York: Routledge.

Berberoglu, Berch. 2017. "The Nature, Extent, and Sources of Wealth and Income Inequality in the United States." *International Review of Modern Sociology* 43, no. 2: 193–216.

Berberoglu, Berch (ed.). 2019. *The Palgrave Handbook of Social Movements, Revolution, and Social Transformation*. New York: Palgrave Macmillan.

Berberoglu, Berch. (ed.). 2020. *The Global Rise of Authoritarianism in the 21st Century: Crisis of Neoliberalism and the Nationalist Response*. New York: Routledge.

Bergman, Gregory. 1986. "The 1920s and the 1980s: A Comparison." *Monthly Review* 38, no. 5 (October): 29–36.

Bina, Cyrus and Behzad Yaghmaian. 1991. "Post-War Global Accumulation and the Transnationalization of Capital." *Capital & Class* 15, no. 1: 107–130.

Bina, Cyrus and Chuck Davis. 2002. "Dynamics of Globalization: Transnational Capital and the International Labor Movement" in Berch Berberoglu (ed.), *Labor and Capital in the Age of Globalization*. Boulder, CO: Rowman and Littlefield Publishers.

Bivens, Josh. 2011. *Failure by Design: The Story behind America's Broken Economy*. Ithaca, NY: ILR Press.

Block, Fred L. 2018. *Capitalism: The Future of an Illusion*. Oakland, CA: University of California Press.

Bluestone, Barry. 1984. *The Deindustrialization of America: Plant Closings, Community Abandonment, and the Dismantling of Basic Industry*. New York: Basic.

Blum, William. 2000. *Rogue State: A Guide to the World's Only Superpower*. Monroe: Common Courage Press.

Boggs, Carl. 2010. *The Crimes of Empire*. London: Pluto Press.

Bonosky, Phillip. 2001. *Afghanistan: Washington's Secret War*, 2nd ed. New York: International Publishers.

Bornschier, Volker and Christopher Chase-Dunn. 1999. *The Future of Global Conflict*. Thousand Oaks, CA: Sage Publications.

Bowles, Samuel and Richard Edwards. 1985. *Understanding Capitalism*. New York: Harper & Row, Publishers.

Boyer, Richard and Herbert Morais. 1984. *Labor's Untold Story*, 3rd ed. New York: United Electrical, Radio, and Machine Workers of America.

Braby, Don. 2008. *The Greatest Depression of All Time*. North Charleston, SC: CreateSpace.

Braun, Denny. 1991. *The Rich Get Richer: The Rise of Income Inequality in the United States and the World*. Chicago, IL: Nelson Hall.

Braverman, Harry. 1974. *Labor and Monopoly Capital: The Degradation of Work in the Twentieth Century*. New York: Monthly Review Press.

Brecher, Jeremy. 1972. *Strike!* Greenwich: Fawcet.

Brenner, Robert. 1991. "Why Is the United States at War with Iraq?" *New Left Review*, no. 185: 122–137.

Brenner, Robert. 2000. *The Economics of Global Turbulence*. London: Verso.

Brenner, Robert. 2003. *The Boom and the Bubble: The U.S. in the World Economy*. London: Verso.

Brenner, Robert. 2006. "What Is, and What Is Not, Imperialism?" *Historical Materialism* 14, no. 4: 79–105.

Bresheeth, Haim and Nira Yuval-Davis (eds.). 1991. *The Gulf War and the New World Order*. London: Zed.

Brewer, Anthony. 1990. *Marxist Theories of Imperialism: A Critical Survey*, 2nd ed. London: Routledge.

Bromley, Simon. 2003. "Reflections on Empire, Imperialism and United States Hegemony." *Historical Materialism* 11, no. 3: 17–68.

Budria, Santiago et al. 2002. "Updated Facts on the U.S. Distribution of Earnings, Income, and Wealth." *Federal Reserve Bank of Minneapolis Quarterly Review* 26, no. 3: 2–34.

Burbach, Roger and Ben Clarke (eds.). 2002. *September 11 and the U.S. War: Beyond the Curtain of Smoke*. San Francisco, CA: City Lights.

Burris, Val. 1999. "Class Structure and Political Ideology." *Critical Sociology* 25, no. 2–3 (Summer): 5–46.

Bustillo, Inés and Helvia Helloso. 2009. *The Global Financial Crisis: What Happened and What's Next*. Washington, DC: ECLAC, Washington Office, February.

Butler, Smedley. 1935. *War is a Racket*. New York: Round Table Press.

Cagetti, Marco and Mariactristina De Nardi. 2005. *Wealth Inequality: Data and Models*. Chicago, IL: Federal Reserve Bank of Chicago.

Calhoun, Craig and Georgi Derluguian (eds.). 2011. *The Deepening Crisis: Governance Challenges after Neoliberalism*. New York: NYU Press.

Caliendo, Stephen M. 2015. *Inequality in America*. Boulder, CO: Westview Press.

Callari, Antonio. 2010. "2008: A New Chapter for U.S. Imperialism." *Rethinking Marxism: A Journal of Economics, Culture & Society* 22, no. 2: 210–218.

Callinicos, Alex. 2009. *Imperialism and Global Political Economy*. Cambridge: Polity.

Calvert, Peter. 1982. *The Concept of Class*. New York: St. Martin's Press.

Cameron, Kenneth Neill. 1977. *Humanity and Society: A World History*. New York: Monthly Review Press.

Cappo, Joe. 1977. "A Little Closer Look at Free Enterprise." *Chicago Daily News* (17 May).

Carroll, William K. 2010. *The Making of a Transnational Capitalist Class: Corporate Power in the 21st Century*. London: Zed.

Chase-Dunn, Christopher and Bruce Lerro. 2013. *Social Change: Globalization from the Stone Age to the Present*. Boulder, CO: Paradigm Publishers.

Chase-Dunn, Christopher and Paul Almeida. 2020. *Global Struggles and Social Change: From Prehistory to World Revolution in the Twenty-first Century*. Baltimore, MD: Johns Hopkins University Press.

Chomsky, Noam. 2004. *Hegemony or Survival: America's Quest for Global Dominance*. New York: Macmillan.

Chomsky, Noam. 2015. *Propaganda and the Public Mind*. Audible Studios.

Chossudovsky, Michel and Andrew Gavin Marshall (eds.). 2010. *The Global Economic Crisis: The Great Depression of XXI Century*. Stockton, CA: Global Research Publishers.

Churchill, Ward. 2001. *A Little Matter of Genocide: Holocaust and Denial in the Americas 1492 to the Present*. San Francisco, CA: City Lights Publishers.

Churchill, Ward. 2002. *Struggle for the Land: Native North American Resistance to Genocide, Ecocide, and Colonization*. San Francisco, CA: City Lights Publishers.

Churchill, Ward. 2003. *On the Justice of Roosting Chickens: Reflections on the Consequences of U.S. Imperial Arrogance and Criminality*. Chico, CA: AK Press.

Clawson, Dan. 2003. *The Next Upsurge: Labor and the New Social Movements*. Ithaca, NY: Cornell University Press.

Clawson, Patrick. 1977. "The Internationalization of Capital and Capital Accumulation in Iran and Iraq." *Insurgent Sociologist* 7, no. 2 (Spring): 64–73.

Collier, Paul. 2018. *The Future of Capitalism: Facing the New Anxieties*. New York: Harper.

Collins, Chuck and Felice Yeskel. 2005. *Economic Apartheid in America*. New York: The New Press.

Cope, Zak. 2015. *Divided World Divided Class: Global Political Economy and the Stratification of Labor under Capitalism*. Montreal: Kersplebedeb Publishing.

Crawford, Neta C. 2018. "Human Cost of the Post-9/11 Wars: Lethality and the Need for Transparency." Costs of War Project, Watson Institute for International and Public Affairs, Brown University, Providence, Rhode Island (November). https://watson.brown.edu/costsofwar/files/cow/imce/papers/2018/Human%20Costs%2C%20Nov%208%202018%20CoW.pdf

Crawford, Neta C. 2019. "United States Budgetary Costs and Obligations of Post-9/11 Wars through FY2020: $6.4 Trillion." *20 Years of War: A Cost of War Research Series*, Watson Institute for International and Public Affairs, Brown University, Providence, RI and The Frederick S. Pardee Center for the Study of the Longer-Range Future, Boston University, Boston, MA (November 13).

https://watson.brown.edu/costsofwar/files/cow/imce/papers/2019/US%20Budgetary%20Costs%20of%20Wars%20November%202019.pdf?utm_source=-Daily%20on%20Defense%20(2019%20TEMPLATE)_11/15/2019&utm_medium=email&utm_campaign=WEX_Daily%20on%20Defense&rid=84648

Cypher, James M. 2012. "Nearly $2 Trillion Purloined from U.S. Workers in 2009" in Linda Pinkow and Sam Pizzigati (eds.), *The Wealth Inequality Reader.* Boston, MA: Dollars & Sense – Economic Affairs Bureau.

Davis, Mike. 1984. "The Political Economy of Late Imperial America." *New Left Review*, no. 143 (January–February): 6–38.

Davis, Mike. 1986. *Prisoners of the American Dream: Politics and Economy in the History of the U.S. Working Class.* London: Verso.

Devine, Jim. 1982. "The Structural Crisis of U.S. Capitalism." *Southwest Economy and Society* 6, no. 1 (Fall): 49–64.

Diamond, Jared. 2005. *Collapse: How Societies Choose to Fail or Succeed.* New York: Penguin.

Diaz-Gimenez, Javier et al. 1997. "Dimensions of Inequality: Facts on the U.S. Distributions of Earnings, Income, and Wealth." *Federal Reserve Bank of Minneapolis Quarterly Review* 21, no. 2 (Spring): 3–21.

Domhoff, G. William. 1967. *Who Rules America?* Englewood Cliffs, NJ: Prentice-Hall.

Domhoff, G. William. 1971. *The Higher Circles: The Governing Class in America.* New York: Vintage.

Domhoff, G. William. 1978. *The Powers That Be: Processes of Ruling Class Domination in America.* New York: Vintage.

Domhoff, G. William. 2010. *Who Rules America? Challenges to Corporate and Class Dominance,* 6th ed. New York: McGraw Hill.

Dowd, Douglas F. 1974. *The Twisted Dream: Capitalist Development in the United States since 1776.* Cambridge, MA: Winthrop Publishers.

Duboff, Richard B. 1989. *Accumulation and Power: An Economic History of the United States.* Armonk: M.E. Sharpe.

Du Bois, W.E.B. 2003. "Negroes and the Crisis of Capitalism in the United States." *Monthly Review* 54, no. 11: 34–41.

Du Bois, W.E.B. 1970. "The Social Effects of Emancipation" and "The Class Struggle" in Meyer Weinberg (ed.), *W.E.B. Du Bois: A Reader.* New York: Harper & Row.

Duménil, Gérard and Dominique Lévy. 2011. *The Crisis of Neoliberalism.* Cambridge, MA: Harvard University Press.

Dunbar-Ortiz, Roxanne. 2015. *An Indigenous People's History of the United States.* Boston, MA: Beacon Press.

Duncan R. 2012. *The New Depression.* Singapore: John Wiley & Sons.

Dunne, John G. 1967. *Delano, the Story of the California Grape Strike.* New York: Farrar, Straus & Giroux.

Eichengreen, Barry. 2008. *Globalizing Capital: A History of the International Monetary System*, 2nd ed. Princeton, NJ: Princeton University Press.

Eichengreen, Barry. 2011. *Exorbitant Privilege: The Rise and Fall of the Dollar and the Future of the International Monetary System.* New York: Oxford University Press.

Elliott, Michael. 2002. "Special Report: The Secret History—They Had a Plan." *Time* (12 August).

Enfu, Cheng and Lu Baolin. 2021. "Five Characteristics of Neoimperialism: Building on Lenin's Theory of Imperialism in the Twenty-First Century." *Monthly Review* 73, no. 1 (May): 22–58.

Engdahl, F. William. 2004. *A Century of War: Anglo-American Oil Politics and the New World Order.* London: Pluto Press.

Erickson, Gerald and Harold L. Schwartz (eds.). 1977. *Social Class in the Contemporary United States.* Minneapolis, MN: Marxist Educational Press.

Fahnbulleh, Miatta. 2020. "The Neoliberal Collapse: Markets Are Not the Answer." *Foreign Affairs*, 99, no. 1 (January-February): 38–43.

Falk, Richard. 1999. *Predatory Globalization: A Critique.* Malden, MA: Blackwell.

Fantasia, Rick. 1988. *Cultures of Solidarity: Consciousness, Action, and Contemporary American Workers.* Berkeley: University of California Press.

Faux, Geoffrey P. 2006. *The Global Class War.* Hoboken, NJ: Wiley.

Ferguson, Niall. 2005. *Colossus: The Rise and Fall of the American Empire.* New York: Penguin Books.

Filger, Sheldon. 2009. *Global Economic Forecast 2010-2015: Recession into Depression.* www.GlobalEconomicCrisis.com

Fletcher Jr., Bill. 2004. "How Race Enters Class in the United States". In Michael Zweig (ed.), *What's Class Got to Do with It? American Society in the Twenty-first Century*, pp. 35–44. Ithaca, NY: ILR Press.

Foran, John (ed.). 2002. *The Future of Revolutions: Rethinking Political and Social Change in the Age of Globalization.* London: Zed Books.

Foster, John Bellamy. 1986. *The Theory of Monopoly Capitalism.* New York: Monthly Review Press.

Foster, John Bellamy. 2006. "Aspects of Class in the United States: An Introduction." *Monthly Review* 58, no. 3 (July-August): 1–5.

Foster, John Bellamy. 2006. *Naked Imperialism: The U.S. Pursuit of Global Dominance.* New York: Monthly Review Press.

Foster, John Bellamy. 2010. "The Age of Monopoly-Finance Capital." *Monthly Review* (February). http://monthlyreview.org/2010/02/01/the-age-of-monopoly-finance-capital

Foster, John Bellamy and Henryk Szlajfer (eds.). 1984. *The Faltering Economy: The Problem of Accumulation under Monopoly Capitalism.* New York: Monthly Review Press.

Friedman, Gerald, Fred Moseley and Chris Sturr (eds). 2009. *The Economic Crisis Reader.* Boston, MA: Dollars and Sense.

Friedman, Jonathan (ed.). 2002. *Globalization, the State, and Violence.* Lanham, MD: Rowman and Littlefield.

Fuentes, Annette and Barbara Ehrenreich. 1983. *Women in the Global Factory.* Boston, MA: South End Press.

Galbraith, John Kenneth. 1988. *The Great Crash, 1929.* New York: Houghton-Mifflin.

Gardner, Matthew et al. 2019. "Corporate Tax Avoidance in the First Year of the Trump Tax Law" (Institute on Taxation and Economic Policy (December 16). https://itep.org/corporate-tax-avoidance-in-the-first-year-of-the-trump-tax-law/

Gardner, Matthew et al. 2019. "Corporate Tax Avoidance Remains Rampant Under New Tax Law" Institute on Taxation and Economic Policy (April 11). https://itep.org/notadime/

Garson, Barbara. 2013. *Down the Up Escalator: How the 99 Percent Live in the Great Recession*. New York: Doubleday.

Gartman, David. 1986. *Auto Slavery: The Labor Process in the American Automobile Industry*. New Brunswick, NJ: Rutgers University Press.

Genovese, Eugene. 1976. *Roll Jordan Roll: The World the Slaves Made*. New York: Vintage.

Genovese, Eugene. 1988. *The Political Economy of Slavery: Studies in the Economy and Society of the Slave South*, 2nd ed. Middletown, CT: Wesleyan University Press.

Geschwender, James. 1977. *Class, Race, and Worker Insurgency*. Cambridge: Cambridge University Press.

Ghotge, Sanjeev. 2009. "Financial Meltdown: An Intriguing Silence at the Core." *Capitalism, Nature, Socialism* (December) 20 (4): 85–88.

Gills, Barry (ed.). 2011. *Globalization in Crisis*. New York: Routledge.

Gimenez, Martha. 1987. "The Feminization of Poverty: Myth or Reality." *Critical Sociology* 25, no. 2–3: 336–351.

Gindin, Sam and Leo Panitch. 2012. *The Making of Global Capitalism: The Political Economy of American Empire*. London: Verso.

Gitlin, Todd. 2012. *Occupy Nation: The Roots, the Spirit, and the Promise of Occupy Wall Street*. New York: It Books, Harper Collins Publishers.

Glenn, Evelyn Nakano and Roslyn L. Feldberg. 1977. "Degraded and Deskilled: The Prolatarianization of Clerical Work." *Social Problems* 25 (1): 52–64.

Gohari, M.J. 2001. *The Taliban: Ascent to Power*. New York: Oxford University Press.

Gowan, Peter. 1999. *The Global Gamble: Washington's Faustian Bid for World Dominance*. New York: Verso.

Gowan, Peter. 2010. *A Calculus of Power: Grand Strategy in the Twenty-first Century*. London: Verso.

Gramsci, Antonio. 1971. *Prison Notebooks*. New York: International Publishers.

Green, Gil. 1976. *What's Happening to Labor*. New York: International Publishers.

Green, J. 1980. *The World of the Worker: Labor in Twentieth Century America*. New York: Hill and Wang.

Greene, Felix. 1970. *The Enemy: What Every American Should Know about Imperialism*. New York: Vintage.

Greer, Edward. 1991."The Hidden History of the Iraq War." *Monthly Review* 43, no. 1: 1–14.

Griffen, Sarah. 1991. "The War Bill: Adding Up the Domestic Costs of War." *Dollars & Sense*, no. 165 (April).

Guthrie, Doug. 2006. *China and Globalization: The Social, Economic, and Political Transformation of Chinese Society*. New York: Routledge.

Hall, Burton (ed.). 1972. *Autocracy and Insurgency in Organized Labor*. New Brunswick, NJ: Transaction Books.

Halliday, Fred. 1979. *Iran: Dictatorship and Development*. New York: Penguin.

Halliday, Fred. 2001. *The World at 2000*. New York: St. Martin's Press.

Halliday, John and Gavan McCormack. 1973. *Japanese Imperialism Today*. New York: Monthly Review Press.

Hamilton, Alexander, James Madison and John Jay, 1961. *The Federalist*. Edited by Jacob E. Cooke. Middletown, CT: Wesleyan University Press.

Hamilton, Richard. 1972. *Class and Politics in the United States*. New York: Wiley.

Hardt, Michael and Antonio Negri. 2000. *Empire*. Cambridge, MA: Harvard University Press.

Harman, Chris. 2010. *Zombie Capitalism: Global Crisis and the Relevance of Marx*, Reprint ed. Chicago, IL: Haymarket Books.

Harris, Jerry. 2003. "Transnational Competition and the End of U.S. Hegemony." *Science and Society* 67, no. 1: 68–80.

Harrison, Bennett and Barry Bluestone. 1988. *The Great U-Turn: Corporate Restructuring and the Polarizing of America*. New York: Basic Books.

Hart, Jeffrey A. 1992. *Rival Capitalists: International Competitiveness in the United States, Japan, and Western Europe*. Ithaca, NY: Cornell University Press.

Hart-Landsberg, Martin. 2013. *Capitalist Globalization: Consequences, Resistance, and Alternatives*. New York: Monthly Review Press.

Harvey, David. 2003. *The New Imperialism*. New York: Oxford University Press.

Harvey, David. 2006. *A Brief History of Neoliberalism*. New York: Oxford University Press.

Harvey, David. 2007. "Neoliberalism as Creative Destruction." *The Annals of the American Academy of Political and Social Science* 160, no. 1: 21–44.

Harvey, David. 2011. *The Enigma of Capital and the Crises of Capitalism*. New York: Oxford University Press.

Harvey, David. 2014. *Seventeen Contradictions and the End of Capitalism*. New York: Oxford University Press.

Headley, Bernard. 1991. "The 'New World Order' and the Persian Gulf War." *Humanity and Society* 15, no. 3 (August): 317–324.

Herold, Marc. 2002. "Who Will Count the Dead? Civilian Casualties in Afghanistan." in Roger Burbach and Ben Clarke (eds.), *September 11 and the U.S. War: Beyond the Curtain of Smoke*. San Francisco, CA: City Lights.

Hertz, Noreena. 2002. *Silent Takeover: Global Capitalism and the Death of Democracy*. New York: Free Press.

Hobson, John A. [1905] 1972. *Imperialism: A Study*, Rev. ed. Ann Arbor: University of Michigan Press.

Holloway, John and Sol Picciotto. 1977. "Capital, Crisis and the State." *Capital and Class* 1, no. 2: 76–101.

Houtart, Francois and Francois Polet (eds.). 2001. *The Other Davos Summit: The Globalization of Resistance to the World Economic System*. London: Zed Books.

Howard, Andrew. 2005. "Global Capital and Labor Internationalism: Workers' Response to Global Capitalism" in Berch Berberoglu (ed.), *Globalization and Change: The Transformation of Global Capitalism*. Lanham, MD: Lexington Books.

Howe, Irving (ed.). 1972. *The World of the Blue Collar Worker*. New York: Quadrangle Books.

Hudson, Michael. 2003. *Super Imperialism: The Origin and Fundamentals of U.S. World Dominance*, Rev. ed. Herndon, VA.: Pluto.

Hunnius, Gerry et al. (eds.). 1973. *Workers' Control: A Reader on Labor and Social Change*. New York: Vintage Books.

Hurrell, Andrew (ed.). 1999. *Inequality, Globalization, and World Politics*. New York: Oxford University Press.

Hutton, Will and Anthony Giddens (eds.). 2000. *Global Capitalism*. New York: New Press.

Hytrek, Gary and Kristine M. Zentgraf. 2008. *America Transformed: Globalization, Inequality, and Power.* New York: Oxford University Press.

Immerwahr, Daniel. 2020. *How to Hide an Empire: A History of the Greater United States.* New York: Picador.

Institute for Labor Education and Research. 1982. *What's Wrong with the U.S. Economy?* Boston, MA: South End Press.

Institute for Women's Policy Research. 2017. "Women's Median Earnings as a Percentage of Men's, 1984-2017 (Full-time, Year-Round Workers) with Projections for Pay Equity, by Race/Ethnicity," IWPR Quick Figures #Q075 (November). https://iwpr.org/publications/womens-median-earnings-1984-2017/ (accessed March 2019).

Institute for Women's Policy Research. 2019. *Fact Sheet,* no. C478 (March).

International Monetary Fund. Various Years. *Direction of Trade Statistics, Yearbook.* Washington, DC: IMF.

Jacques, Martin. 2012. *When China Rules the World: The End of the Western World and the Birth of a New Global Order,* 2nd ed. New York: Penguin.

Jalée, Pierre. 1968. *The Pillage of the Third World.* New York: Monthly Review Press.

James, Harold. 2002. *The End of Globalization: Lessons from the Great Depression.* Cambridge, MA: Harvard University Press.

Jenkins, Rhys. 1987. *Transnational Corporations and Uneven Development.* New York: Methuen.

Jessop, Bob. 1982. *The Capitalist State.* New York: New York University Press.

Johnson, Chalmers. 2000. *Blowback: The Costs and Consequences of American Empire.* New York: Holt.

Johnson, Chalmers. 2004. *The Sorrows of Empire.* New York: Holt.

Johnson, Chalmers. 2010. *Dismantling the Empire: America's Last Best Hope.* New York: Holt.

Johnson, Simon. 2011. "A Second Great Depression, or Worse?" *The New York Times* (August 18).

Kagarlitsky, Boris. 2000. *The Twilight of Globalization: Property, State, and Capitalism.* Herndon, VA: Pluto.

Kapstein, Ethan B. 1999. *Sharing the Wealth: Workers and the World Economy.* New York: W.W. Norton.

Katz, Jonathan M. 2022. *Gangsters of Capitalism: Smedley Butler, the Marines, and the Breaking of America's Empire.* New York: St. Martin's Press.

Katz-Fishman, Walda, Jerome Scott and Ife Modupe. 2005. "Global Capitalism, Class Struggle, and Social Transformation" in Berch Berberoglu (ed.), *Globalization and Change: The Transformation of Global Capitalism.* Lanham, MD: Lexington Books.

Katznelson, Ira and Al Zolberg (eds.). 1986. *Working Class Formation: Nineteenth Century Patterns in Western Europe and the United States.* Princeton, NJ: Princeton University Press.

Keeran, Roger. 1980. *The Communist Party and the Auto Workers' Unions.* Bloomington: Indiana University Press.

Keister, Lisa A. 2000. *Wealth in America: Trends in Wealth Inequality.* Cambridge: Cambridge University Press.

Kennedy, Paul. 1987. *The Rise and Fall of the Great Powers.* New York: Random House.

Kidron, Michael. 1970. *Western Capitalism since the War.* Harmondsworth, England: Penguin Books.

Kimeldorf, Howard. 1988. *Reds or Rackets? The Making of Radical and Conservative Unions on the Waterfront.* Berkeley: University of California Press.

Klak, Thomas (ed.). 1997. *Globalization and Neoliberalism.* Boulder, CO: Rowman and Littlefield.

Klare, Michael T. 2001. *Resource Wars: The New Landscape of Global Conflict.* New York: Henry Holt and Company.

Klein, Matthew C. and Michael Pettis. 2020. *Trade Wars Are Class Wars: How Rising Inequality Distorts the Global Economy and Threatens International Peace.* New Haven, CT: Yale University Press.

Klein, Naomi. 1999. *No Logo.* New York: Random House.

Klein, Naomi. 2008. *Shock Doctrine: The Rise of Disaster Capitalism.* New York: Metropolitan Books.

Kliman, Andrew. 2012. *The Failure of Capitalist Production: Underlying Causes of the Great Recession.* New York: Pluto Press.

Kloby, Jerry. 1987. "The Growing Divide: Class Polarization in the United States in the 1980s." *Monthly Review* 39, no. 4 (September): 1–8.

Kloby, Jerry. 1993. "Increasing Class Polarization in the United States: The Growth of Wealth and Income Inequality" in Berch Berberoglu (ed.), *Critical Perspectives in Sociology: A Reader,* 2nd ed. Dubuque, Iowa: Kendall/Hunt Publishing Company.

Knowlton, Christopher and Carla Rapaport. 1991. "Germany and Japan: Missing in Action." *Fortune* (March 11).

Kohli, Atul. 2020. *Imperialism and the Developing World: How Britain and the United States Shaped the Global Periphery.* New York: Oxford University Press.

Konings, Martijn (ed.). 2010. *Beyond the Subprime Headlines: Critical Perspectives on the Financial Crisis.* London: Verso.

Kotz, David M. 2009. "The Financial and Economic Crisis of 2008: A Systemic Crisis of Neoliberal Capitalism." *Review of Radical Political Economy* 41, no. 3: 305–317.

Kotz, David M. 2014. *The Rise and Fall of Free Market Capitalism.* Cambridge, MA: Harvard University Press.

Kozul-Wright, Richard and Robert Rowthorn (eds.). 1998. *Transnational Corporations and the Global Economy.* New York: St. Martin's.

Kranhold, Kathryn. 2019. "Twice as Many Companies Paying Zero Taxes under Trump Tax Plan," The Center for Public Integrity, Washington, DC (April 11).

Kreitner, Richard. 2020. *Break It Up: Secession, Division, and the Secret History of America's Imperfect Union.* New York: Little, Brown, and Company.

Krippner, Greta R. 2011. *Capitalizing on Crisis: The Political Origins of the Rise of Finance.* Cambridge, MA: Harvard University Press.

Krugman, Paul. 2009. *The Return of Depression Economics and the Crisis of 2008.* New York: W.W. Norton and Company.

Kumar, Ashok. 2020. *Monopoly Capitalism: Power and Production in the Twilight of the Sweatshop Age.* Cambridge: Cambridge University Press.

Lembcke, Jerry. 1988. *Capitalist Development and Class Capacities: Marxist Theory and Union Organization.* Westport, CT: Greenwood Press.

Lenin, V.I. 1978. *Imperialism, the Highest Stage of Capitalism.* New York: International Publishers.

Levenstein, Harvey. 1981. *Communism, Anticommunism, and the CIO.* Westport, CT: Greenwood Press.

Levine, Rhonda. 1988. *Class Struggle and the New Deal: Industrial Labor, Industrial Capital, and the State.* Lawrence: University Press of Kansas.

Lewis, Cleona. 1938. *America's Stake in International Investments.* Washington, DC: Brookings Institution.

Loren, Charles. 1977. *Classes in the United States.* Davis, CA: Cardinal Publishers.

Lotta, Raymond. 1984. *America in Decline,* vol. 1. Chicago, IL: Banner Press.

Lucarelli, B. 2011. *The Economics of Financial Turbulence.* Cheltenham: Edward Elgar.

Luger, Stan. 2000. *Corporate Power, American Democracy, and the Automobile Industry.* Cambridge: Cambridge University Press.

Lustig, R. Jeffrey. 2004. "The Tangled Knot of Race and Class in America" in Michael Zweig (ed.), *What's Class Got to Do with It?* Ithaca, NY: ILR Press.

Lutz, Catherine. 2009. *The Bases of Empire.* New York: New York University Press.

MacEwan, Arthur. 1999. *Neo-liberalism or Democracy?* London: Zed Books.

Macias, Amanda. 2019. "America has Spent $6.4 Trillion on Wars in the Middle East and Asia Since 2001, A New Study Says" (November 20). https://www.cnbc.com/2019/11/20/us-spent-6point4-trillion-on-middle-east-wars-since-2001-study.html

Magdoff, Harry. 1969. *The Age of Imperialism.* New York: Monthly Review.

Magdoff, Harry. 1978. *Imperialism: From the Colonial Age to the Present.* New York: Monthly Review Press.

Magdoff, Harry. 1992. *Globalization: To What End?* New York: Monthly Review Press.

Magdoff, Harry and Paul M. Sweezy. 1977. *The End of Prosperity: The American Economy in the 1970s.* New York: Monthly Review Press.

Magdoff, Harry and Paul M. Sweezy. 1981. *The Deepening Crisis of U.S. Capitalism.* New York: Monthly Review Press.

Magdoff, Harry and Paul M. Sweezy. 1987. *Stagnation and the Financial Explosion.* New York: Monthly Review Press.

Magdoff, Fred and Michael Yates. 2009. *The ABCs of the Economic Crisis: What Working People Need to Know.* New York: Monthly Review Press.

Maitra, Priyatosh. 1996. *The Globalization of Capitalism in Third World Countries.* Westport, CT: Praeger Publishers.

Mandel, Ernest. 1975. *Late Capitalism.* London: New Left Books.

Mandel, Ernest. 1978. *The Second Slump: A Marxist Analysis of Recession in the Seventies.* London: Verso.

Mandel, Ernest. 1979. *From Class Society to Communism.* London: Ink Links.

Marazzi, Christian. 2010. *The Violence of Financial Capitalism.* Los Angeles, CA: Semiotics(e).

Martin, Linda Grant. 1975. "The 500: A Report on Two Decades." *Fortune* (May).

Marx, Karl. 1867. *Capital: Critique of Political Economy.* Berlin: Verlag von Otto Meisner.

Maskovsky, Jeff and Ida Susser (eds.). 2009. *Rethinking America: The Imperial Homeland in the 21st Century.* Boulder, CO: Paradigm.

Mason, David S. 2009. *The End of the American Century.* Lanham, MD: Rowman and Littlefield.

Mayer, Tom. 1991. "Imperialism and the Gulf War." *Monthly Review* 42, no. 11: 1–11.

McBride, Stephen and John Richard Wiseman (eds.). 2000. *Globalization and Its Discontents.* New York: Palgrave Macmillan.

McCoy, Alfred W. 2009. *Policing America's Empire: The United States, the Philippines, and the Rise of the Surveillance State.* Madison: University of Wisconsin Press.

McCoy, Alfred W. 2017. *In the Shadows of the American Century: The Rise and Decline of U.S. Global Power.* Chicago, IL: Haymarket Books.

McCoy, Alfred W. 2021. *To Govern the Globe: World Orders and Catastrophic Change.* Chicago, IL: Haymarket Books.

McCoy, Alfred W. and Francisco A. Scarano (eds.). 2009. *Colonial Crucible: Empire in the Making of the Modern American State.* Madison: University of Wisconsin Press.

McCoy, Alfred W., Joseph M. Fradera and Stephen Jacobson (eds.). 2012. *Endless Empire: Spain's Retreat, Europe's Eclipse, America's Decline.* Madison: University of Wisconsin Press.

McDonough, Terrence, Michael Reich and David M. Kotz (eds.). 2010. *Contemporary Capitalism and Its Crises.* New York: Cambridge University Press.

McMichael, Philip, et al. 1974. "Imperialism and the Contradictions of Development." *New Left Review*, no. 85 (May-June): 83–102.

McNally, David. 2010. *Global Slump: The Economics and Politics of Crisis and Resistance.* Oakland, CA: P.M. Press.

Medlen, Craig. 1984. "Corporate Taxes and the Federal Deficit." *Monthly Review* 36, no. 6 (November): 10–26.

Meiksins Wood, Ellen et al. (eds.). 1998. *Rising from the Ashes?: Labor in the Age of "Global" Capitalism.* New York: Monthly Review Press.

Melman, Seymour. 1965. *Our Depleted Society.* New York: Holt, Rinehart and Winston.

Melman, Seymour. 1970. *Pentagon Capitalism: The Political Economy of War.* New York: McGraw-Hill Book Co.

Meszaros, Istvan and John Bellamy Foster. 2011. *The Structural Crisis of Capital.* New York: Monthly Review Press.

Milanovich, Branko. 2018. *Global Inequality: A New Approach for the Age of Globalization.* Cambridge, MA: Belknap Press.

Milanovic, Branko. 2019. *Capitalism, Alone: The Future of the System That Rules the World.* Cambridge, MA: Belknap Press.

Mills, C. Wright. 1951. *White Collar: The American Middle Classes.* New York: Oxford University Press.

Mills, C. Wright. 1956. *The Power Elite.* New York: Oxford University Press.

Mittleman, James H. (ed.). 1996. *Globalization: Critical Reflections.* Boulder, CO: Lynne Rienner.

Mittleman, James H. 2000. *The Globalization Syndrome: Transformation and Resistance.* Princeton, NJ: Princeton University Press.

Moody, Kim. 1988. *An Injury to All: The Decline of American Unionism.* London: Verso.

Moody, Kim. 1997. *Workers in a Lean World: Unions in the International Economy.* London: Verso.

Morais, Herbert M. 1944. *The Struggle for American Freedom*. New York: International Publishers.

Morris, George. 1971. *Rebellion in the Unions*. New York: New Outlook.

Munck, Ronaldo. 2002. *Globalization and Labor: The New Great Transformation*. London: Zed.

Nabudere, Dan. 1977. *The Political Economy of Imperialism*. London: Zed Press.

Nathanson, Charles E. 1969. "The Militarization of the American Economy" in David Horowitz (ed.), *Corporations and the Cold War*. New York: Monthly Review Press.

Negri, Antonio. 2008. *Empire and Beyond*. Cambridge: Polity Press.

Nissen, Bruce. 1981. "U.S. Workers and the U.S. Labor Movement." *Monthly Review* 33, no. 1 (May): 17–31.

Nissen, Bruce. (ed.). 2002. *Unions in a Globalized Environment: Changing Borders, Organizational Boundaries, and Social Roles*. Armonk, NY: Sharpe.

O'Connor, James. 1973. *The Fiscal Crisis of the State*. New York: St. Martin's Press.

O'Connor, James. 1974. *The Corporations and the State*. New York: Harper & Row.

O'Connor, James. 1984. *Accumulation Crisis*. New York: Basil Blackwell.

Odekon, Mehmet (ed.). 2010. *Booms and Busts: An Encyclopedia of Economic History from the First Stock Market Crash of 1792 to the Current Global Economic Crisis*. Armonk, NY: ME Sharpe Reference.

Ollman, Bertell. 1987. "How to Study Class Consciousness and Why We Should." *Critical Sociology* 14, no. 1 (Winter): 57–96.

O'Meara, Patrick et al. (eds.). 2000. *Globalization and the Challenges of the New Century: A Reader*. Indianapolis: Indiana University Press.

Orr, Martin. 2005. "The Struggle against Capitalist Globalization: The Worldwide Protests against the WTO" in Berch Berberoglu (ed.), *Globalization and Change: The Transformation of Global Capitalism*. Lanham, MD: Lexington Books.

Palast, Greg. 2002. *The Best Democracy Money Can Buy: An Investigative Reporter Exposes the Truth about Globalization, Corporate Cons, and High Finance Fraudsters*. London: Pluto.

Panitch, Leo and Colin Leys (eds.). 2003. *The New Imperial Challenge*. New York: Monthly Review Press.

Panitch, Leo and Sam Gindin. 2013. *The Making of Global Capitalism: The Political Economy of American Empire*. New York: Verso.

Panitch, Leo and Sam Gindin with Stephen Maher. 2020. *The Socialist Challenge Today: Syriza, Corbyn, Sanders*. Chicago, IL: Haymarket Books.

Parenti, Michael. 1989. *The Sword and the Dollar: Imperialism, Revolution, and the Arms Race*. New York: St. Martin's Press.

Parenti, Michael. 1995. *Against Empire*. San Francisco, CA: City Lights.

Parenti, Michael. 2002. *The Terrorism Trap: September 11 and Beyond*. San Francisco, CA: City Lights.

Parenti, Michael. 2011. *Democracy for the Few*, 9th ed. Boston, MA: Wadsworth.

Parenti, Michael. 2011. *The Face of Imperialism*. New York: Routledge.

Patnaik, Utsa and Prabhat Patnaik. 2017. *A Theory of Imperialism*. New York: Columbia University Press.

Perelman, Michael. 2008. "The Corrosive Qualities of Inequality: The Roots of the Current Meltdown." *Challenge* 51, no. 5: 40–64.

Perlo, Victor. 1951. *American Imperialism*. New York: International Publishers.

Perlo, Victor. 1957. *The Empire of High Finance*. New York: International Publishers.

Perlo, Victor. 1973. *The Unstable Economy: Booms and Recessions in the United States since 1945*, Rev. ed. New York: Lawrence and Wishart.

Perlo, Victor. 1988. *Super Profits and Crises: Modern U.S. Capitalism*. New York: International Publishers.

Perrucci, Carolyn C. et al. 1988. *Plant Closings: International Context and Social Costs*. New York: Aldine de Gruyter.

Perrucci, Robert and Earl Wysong. 2003. *The New Class Society*. Boulder, CO: Rowman and Littlefield.

Petras, James. 1978. *Critical Perspectives on Imperialism and Social Class in the Third World*. New York: Monthly Review Press.

Petras, James. 1995. *Empire or Republic, Global Power, Domestic Decay: The U.S. in the 1990s*. Abingdon: Routledge.

Petras, James. 2007. *Rulers and Ruled in the U.S. Empire*. Atlanta, GA: Clarity Press.

Petras, James. 2009. *Global Depression and Regional Wars*. Atlanta, GA: Clarity Press.

Petras, James. 2020. *U.S. Imperialism*. New York: Routledge.

Petras, James and Christian Davenport. 1990. "The Changing Wealth of the U.S. Ruling Class." *Monthly Review* 42, no. 7 (December): 33–38.

Petras, James and Henry Veltmeyer. 2001. *Globalization Unmasked: Imperialism in the 21st Century*. London: Zed Books.

Petras, James and Henry Veltmeyer. 2003. *System in Crisis: The Dynamics of Free Market Capitalism*. London: Zed Books.

Petras, James and Henry Veltmeyer. 2005. *Empire with Imperialism: Dynamics of Globalizing Capitalism*. Halifax: Fernwood Publications.

Petras, James and Henry Veltmeyer. 2015. *Power and Resistance: U.S. Imperialism in Latin America*. Leiden: Brill Publishers.

Phillips, Andrew and J.C. Sharman. 2020. *Outsourcing Empire: How Company-States Made the Modern World*. Princeton, NJ: Princeton University Press.

Phillips, Brian. 1998. *Global Production and Domestic Decay: Plant Closings in the U.S.* New York: Garland.

Phillips, Peter. 2018. *Giants: The Global Power Elite*. New York: Seven Stories Press.

Pieterse, Jan Nederveen. 2007. *Globalization or Empire?* London: Taylor and Francis.

Piketty, Thomas. 2015. *The Economics of Inequality*. Cambridge, MA: Belknap Press.

Piketty, Thomas. 2017. *Capital in the Twenty-first Century*. Cambridge, MA: Belknap Press.

Piketty, Thomas. 2020. *Capital and Ideology*. Cambridge, MA: Belknap Press.

Pinkow, Linda and Sam Pizzigati (eds.). 2012. *The Wealth Inequality Reader*, 4th ed. Boston, MA: Dollars and Sense.

Piven, Frances Fox and Richard Cloward. 1982. *The New Class War*. New York: Pantheon Books.

Polet, Francois (ed.). 2007. *The State of Resistance: Popular Struggles in the Global South*. London: Zed Books.

Prechel, Harland. 2000. *Big Business and the State: Historical Transitions and Corporate Transformation, 1880s-1990s*. Albany: State University of New York Press.

ProQuest. Various Years. *Statistical Abstract of the United States*. ProQuest.

Rajan, Raghuram G. 2010. “Let Them Eat Credit: How Inequality Is at the Root of the Great Recession.” *The New Republic* (August 27).

Rajan, Raghuram G. 2010. *Fault Lines: How Hidden Fractures Still Threaten the World Economy*. Princeton, NJ: Princeton University Press.

Rall, Ted. 2002. “The New Great Game: Oil Politics in Central Asia” in Roger Burbach and Ben Clarke (eds.), *September 11 and the U.S. War: Beyond the Curtain of Smoke*. San Francisco, CA: City Lights Publishers.

Reich, Robert B. 2013. *Aftershock: The Next Economy and America’s Future*. New York: Vintage Books.

Reuss, Alejandro. 2013. *Labor and the Global Economy*. Boston, MA: Dollars & Sense.

Ricardo, David. 1817. *The Principles of Political Economy and Taxation*. London: John Murray.

Ritholtz, Barry and Aaron Task. 2009. *Bailout Nation: How Greed and Easy Money Corrupted Wall Street and Shook the World Economy*. Hoboken, NJ: John Wiley & Sons, Inc.

Roberts, Michael. 2009. *The Great Recession: Profit Cycles Economic Crisis*. London: lulu.com.

Robinson, William I. 1996. *Promoting Polyarchy: Globalization, U.S. Intervention and Hegemony*. Cambridge: Cambridge University Press.

Robinson, William I. 2004. *A Theory of Global Capitalism: Production, Class, and State in a Transnational World*. Baltimore, MD: The Johns Hopkins University Press.

Robinson, William I. 2014. *Global Capitalism and the Crisis of Humanity*. Cambridge: Cambridge University Press.

Robinson, William I. 2019. *Into the Tempest: Essays on the New Global Capitalism*. Chicago, IL: Haymarket Books.

Robinson, William I. 2020. *The Global Police State*. London: Pluto Press.

Rose, Stephen J. and Heidi I. Hartmann. 2019. *Still a Man’s Labor Market: The Slowly Narrowing Gender Wage Gap*. Washington, DC: Institute for Women’s Policy Research. https://iwpr.org/publications/still-mans-labor-market/ (accessed March 2019).

Ross, Robert J. S. and Kent C. Trachte. 1990. *Global Capitalism: The New Leviathan*. Albany: SUNY Press.

Roubini, Nouriel and Stephen Mihm. 2010. *Crisis Economics: A Crash Course in the Future of Finance*. New York: Penguin.

Roy, Arundhati. 2002. “War Is Peace” in Roger Burbach and Ben Clarke (eds.), *September 11 and the U.S. War*. San Francisco, CA: City Lights.

Russell, James W. 2009. *Class and Race Formation in North America*. Toronto: University of Toronto Press.

Saez, Emmanuel and Thomas Piketty. 2003. “Income Inequality in the United States, 1913-1998.” *Quarterly Journal of Economics* 118, no. 1: 1–39.

Saez, Emmanuel and Gabriel Zucman. 2014. “Wealth Inequality in the United States Since 1913: Evidence from Capitalized Income Tax Data,” *Working Paper 20625*. Cambridge, MA: National Bureau of Economic Research. http://www.nber.org/papers/w20625

Sassen, Saskia. 2009. "Too Big to Save: The End of Financial Capitalism." *Open Democracy News Analysis,* April 2.

Satgar, Vishwas (ed.). 2020. *BRICS and the New American Imperialism: Global Rivalry and Resistance.* Johannesburg, South Africa: Wits University Press.

Screpanti, Ernesto. 2014. *Global Imperialism and the Great Crisis: The Uncertain Future of Capitalism.* New York: Monthly Review Press.

Servan-Schreiber, J.J. 1968. *The American Challenge.* New York: Atheneum.

Shaiken, Harley. 1986. *Work Transformed: Automation and Labor in the Computer Age.* Lexington, MA: Lexington Books.

Sherman, Howard J. 1987. *Foundations of Radical Political Economy.* New York: M.E. Sharpe.

Sherman, Howard. 1991. *The Business Cycle: Growth and Crisis under Capitalism.* Princeton, NJ: Princeton University Press.

Sherman, Howard J. 2006. *How Society Makes Itself: The Evolution of Political and Economic Institutions.* Armonk, NY: M.E. Sharpe.

Sherman, Howard J. 2010. *The Roller Coaster Economy: Financial Crisis, Great Recession, and the Public Option.* Armonk, NY: M.E. Sharpe.

Sherman, Howard J. and Paul D. Sherman. 2018. *Inequality, Boom and Bust: From Billionaire Capitalism to Equality and Full Employment.* New York: Routledge.

Sklair, Leslie. 2001. *The Transnational Capitalist Class.* Malden, MA: Blackwell Publishers.

Sklair, Leslie. 2002. *Globalization: Capitalism and Its Alternatives.* New York: Oxford University Press.

Slaughter, Jane. 1990. "Is the Labor Movement Reaching a Turning Point?" *Labor Notes,* no. 130 (January).

Smith, Adam. 1776. *The Wealth of Nations: An Inquiry into the Nature and Causes of the Wealth of Nations.* London: W. Strahan and T. Cadell.

Smith, Jackie and H. Johnston (eds.). 2002. *Globalizing Resistance: Transnational Dimensions of Social Movements.* Lanham, MD: Rowman and Littlefield.

Smith, John. 2016. *Imperialism in the Twenty-first Century: Globalization, Super Exploitation, and Capitalism's Final Crisis.* New York: Monthly Review Press.

So, Alvin Y. 1990. "How to Conduct Class Analysis in the World Economy?" *Sociological Perspectives,* 33, no. 3: 423–427.

Spector, Alan. 2005. "Class Polarization and Class Struggle under Advanced Capitalism" in Berch Berberoglu (ed.), *Globalization and Change: The Transformation of Global Capitalism.* Lanham, MD: Lexington Books.

Spector, C. 1981. "U. E. Convention Call: New Political Party Needed." *Peoples World* (September 26).

Stepan-Norris, Judith and Maurice Zeitlin. 1989. "'Who Gets the Bird?. or, How the Communists Won Power in America's Unions." *American Sociological Review* 54, no. 4 (August 1989), 503–523.

Stephens, Philip. 2009. "A Summit Success That Reflects a Different Global Landscape." *Financial Times* (April 3).

Steven, Rob. 1994. "New World Order: A New Imperialism." *Journal of Contemporary Asia,* 24, no. 3: 271–296.

Stiglitz, Joseph E. 2011. *Freefall: America, Free Markets, and the Sinking of the World Economy.* New York: W.W. Norton.

Stiglitz, Joseph E. 2013. *The Price of Inequality: How Today's Divided Society Endangers Our Future.* Boston, MA: W. W. Norton.

Sugihara, Kaoru. 1993. "Japan, the Middle East, and the World Economy" in K. Sugihara and J.A. Allan (eds.), *Japan in the Contemporary Middle East*. London: Routledge.

Sweezy, Paul M. and Harry Magdoff. 1972. *The Dynamics of U.S. Capitalism*. New York: Monthly Review Press.

Sweezy, Paul M. and Harry Magdoff. 1988. "The Stock Market Crash and Its Aftermath." *Monthly Review* 39, no. 10 (March): 1–13.

Szymanski, Albert. 1978. *The Capitalist State and the Politics of Class*. Cambridge, MA: Winthrop.

Szymanski, Albert. 1981. *The Logic of Imperialism*. New York: Praeger.

Szymanski, Albert. 1983. *Class Structure: A Critical Perspective*. New York: Praeger.

Tabb, William K. 1989. "Capital Mobility, the Restructuring of Production, and the Politics of Labor" in Arthur MacEwan and William K. Tabb (eds.), *Instability and Change in the World Economy*. New York: Monthly Review Press.

Tabb, William K. 2004. "Neoliberalism and Anticorporate Globalization as Class Struggle" in Michael Zweig (ed.), *What's Class Got to Do with It? American Society in the Twenty-first Century*. Ithaca, NY: ILR Press.

Tabb, William. 2012. *The Restructuring of Capitalism in Our Time*. New York: Columbia University Press.

Tanzer, Michael. 1974. *The Energy Crisis: World Struggle for Power and Wealth*. New York: Monthly Review Press.

Tanzer, Michael. 1991. "Oil and the Gulf Crisis." *Monthly Review* 42, no. 11: 12–16.

Taylor, Keeanga-Yamahtta. 2021. *From #BlackLivesMatter to Black Liberation*, Expanded 2nd ed. Chicago, IL: Haymarket Books.

Thomas, Cal. 2020. *America's Expiration Date: The Fall of Empires and Superpowers and the Future of the United States*. Grand Rapids, MI: Zondervan.

Union for Radical Political Economics. 1978. *U.S. Capitalism in Crisis*. New York: Union for Radical Political Economics.

U.S. Bureau of the Census, Various Years. *Statistical Abstract of the United States*. Washington, DC: Government Printing Office.

U.S. Council of Economic Advisers. Various Years. *Economic Report of the President*. Washington, DC: Government Printing Office.

U.S. Department of Commerce. Various Issues. *Survey of Current Business*. Washington, DC: Government Printing Office.

Valvano, Vince. 1988. "No Longer #1? Assessing U.S. Economic Decline." *Dollars & Sense*, no. 142 (December).

Veltmeyer, Henry (ed.). 2008. *New Perspectives on Globalization and Antiglobalization: Prospects for a New World Order?* Burlington, VT: Ashgate.

Veltmeyer, Henry (ed.). 2010. *Imperialism, Crisis, and Class Struggle: The Verities of Capitalism*. Leiden: Brill Publishers.

Vine, David. 2015. *Base Nation: How U.S. Military Bases Abroad Harm America and the World*. New York: Metropolitan Books.

Vine, David. 2020. *The United States of War: A Global History of America's Endless Conflicts, from Columbus to the Islamic State*. Berkeley: University of California Press.

Wagner, Helmut (ed.). 2000. *Globalization and Unemployment*. New York: Springer.

Wallerstein, Immanuel. 1974. "The Rise and Future Demise of the World Capitalist System." *Comparative Studies in Society and History* 16, no. 4 (September): 387–415.

Wallerstein, Immanuel. 2002. "The United States in Decline?" in Thomas E. Reifer (ed.), *Hegemony, Globalization, and Anti-Systemic Movements*. Westport, CT: Greenwood.

Wallerstein, Immanuel. 2003. *The Decline of American Power: The United States in a Chaotic World*. New York: New Press.

Warren, Bill. 1980. *Imperialism, Pioneer of Capitalism*. London: Verso.

Watson Institute for International and Public Affairs. 2021. "Costs of War: Human Costs." Providence, RI: Brown University. https://watson.brown.edu/costsofwar/costs/human

Weber, Steven (ed.). 2001. *Globalization and the European Political Economy*. New York: Columbia University Press.

Weeks, John. 1981. *Capital and Exploitation*. Princeton, NJ: Princeton University Press.

Welch, Levin. 2014. "The Global Capitalist Crisis and the 2008 Financial Meltdown in the United States" in Berch Berberoglu (ed.), *The Global Capitalist Crisis and Its Aftermath*. New York: Routledge.

Williams, Eric. 1966. *Capitalism and Slavery*. New York: Capricorn.

Wiseman, Paul. 2011. "A Boom in Corporate Profits, A Bust in Jobs, Wages." *Associated Press* (July 22).

Wolff, Edward N. 1995. *Top Heavy: A Study of the Increasing Inequality of Wealth in America*. New York: The Twentieth Century Fund Press.

Wolff, Edward N. 2004. "Changes in Household Wealth in the 1980s and 1990s in the United States," *Working Paper No. 407* (May).

Wolff, Edward N. 2010. "Recent Trends in Household Wealth in the United States: Rising Debt and the Middle Class Squeeze," *Working Paper No. 589* (March).

Wolff, Edward N. 2017. *A Century of Wealth in America*. Cambridge, MA: Harvard University Press.

Wolff, Richard. 2009. "Capitalism Hits the Fan" in Gerald Friedman et al., (eds.), *The Economic Crisis Reader*. Boston, MA: Dollars & Sense.

Wolff, Richard. 2016. *Capitalism's Crisis Deepens*. Chicago, IL: Haymarket Books.

Wood, Ellen Meiksins. 2005. *Empire of Capital*. London: Verso.

Wood, Stephen (ed.). 1982. *The Degradation of Work? Skill, Deskilling, and the Labor Process*. London: Hutchinson and Company.

Wood, Stephen. 1989. *The Transformation of Work?* London: Unwin Hyman.

Wright, Erik Olin. 1976. "Class Boundaries in Advanced Capitalist Societies." *New Left Review*, no. 98: 3–41.

Wright, Erik Olin. 1978. *Class, Crisis and the State*. London: New Left Books.

Wright, Erik Olin. 1985. *Classes*. London: Verso.

Wright, Erik Olin. 1989. *The Debate on Classes*. London: Verso.

Wright, Erik Olin. 2005. *Approaches to Class Analysis*. Cambridge: Cambridge University Press.

Yannopoulos, Dimitris. 2002. "Checkerboard of Oil, Minefields" in Roger Burbach and Ben Clarke (eds.), *September 11 and the U.S. War: Beyond the Curtain of Smoke*. San Francisco, CA: City Lights.

Yates, Michael D. 2003. *Naming the System: Inequality and Work in the Global Economy*. New York: Monthly Review.

Yates, Michael D. 2016. *The Great Inequality*. New York: Routledge.

Zeitlin, Maurice. 1980. *Classes, Class Conflict, and the State.* Cambridge, MA: Winthrop.

Zinn, Howard. 1999. *A People's History of the United States.* New York: Harper Collins.

Zupnick, Elliot. 1999. *Visions and Revisions: The United States in the Global Economy.* Boulder, CO: Westview.

Zweig, Michael (ed.). 2004. *What's Class Got to Do with It? American Society in the Twenty-first Century.* Ithaca, NY: ILR Press.

Index

Note: **Bold** page numbers refer to tables; *italic* page numbers refer to figures and page numbers followed by "n" denote endnotes.

For Product Safety Concerns and Information please contact our EU representative GPSR@taylorandfrancis.com
Taylor & Francis Verlag GmbH, Kaufingerstraße 24, 80331 München, Germany

www.ingramcontent.com/pod-product-compliance
Ingram Content Group UK Ltd.
Pitfield, Milton Keynes, MK11 3LW, UK
UKHW022018180926
475701UK00005B/902
9781032222837